EYEWITNESSES OF SHAKESPEARE

EYEWITNESSES OF SHAKESPEARE

First Hand Accounts of
Performances 1590–1890

❀

GĀMINI SALGĀDO

BOOKS
10 East 53d St. New York 10022
(a division of Harper & Row Publishers, Inc.)

Published in the U.S.A. 1975 by
HARPER & ROW PUBLISHERS, INC.
BARNES & NOBLE IMPORT DIVISION

ISBN: 0-06-496071-4

© Gāmini Salgādo 1975

Published in the U.S.A. 1975 by
HARPER & ROW PUBLISHERS, INC.
BARNES & NOBLE IMPORT DIVISION

Printed in Great Britain by
Cox & Wyman Ltd
London, Fakenham and Reading

FOR
PROFESSOR ARTHUR COLBY SPRAGUE

A small return for the pleasure and profit I have derived from his many studies of Shakespeare in the theatre.

It is a very good office one man does another, when he tells him the manner of his being pleased.

RICHARD STEELE

CONTENTS

ILLUSTRATIONS

Acknowledgements

A full bibliography of all works consulted would add several pages to this volume. On the first mention of a work I have given enough information to identify it. The work of compiling Part I has been made immeasurably easier because of *The Shakespeare Allusion Book* edited by John Munro, *More Seventeenth Century Allusions to Shakespeare* by G. Thorn Drury and the invaluable volumes on Shakespeare and on the Elizabethan stage by E. K. Chambers. Where I have been unable to verify an allusion directly I have included after the source the initials S.A.B. (Shakespeare Allusion Book) or T.D. (Thorn Drury). Though spelling and punctuation have been generally modernised, I have occasionally retained older forms where they may reveal a reading or emphasis of interest.

I am indebted to the Leverhulme Trust for a Fellowship which enabled me to prepare this book for publication. The staff of the Birmingham Shakespeare Library and Sussex University Library were unfailingly helpful; I would like especially to thank Bet Inglis of the latter library for energetic and efficient pursuit of many elusive quarries on my behalf. The staff of the Enthoven Collection at the Victoria and Albert Museum, particularly Mr. Anthony Latham and Miss Gillian Walkling, helped me to track down most of the illustrations courteously and efficiently at very short notice. Grateful thanks too, to Brenda Magurran, Jacky Smith and Sally Swain for help in preparing a typescript that presented many problems, not all of them typographical.

The extracts from the *Dramatic Opinions and Essays* of Bernard Shaw are reproduced by permission of the Society of Authors on behalf of the Bernard Shaw Estate. The extracts from the *Diaries of Lewis Carroll* edited by R. L. Green are reproduced by permission of Oxford University Press, New York © 1954. The passage from George Lichtenberg's *Visits to England* edited by M. L. Mare and W. H. Quarrell is reproduced by permission of The Clarendon Press, Oxford. The extract from Gordon Crosse's *Shakespearian Play-Going 1890–1952* is reproduced by permission of Mowbray and Co. Ltd.

The illustrations are reproduced by permission of the Enthoven Collection, The Victoria and Albert Museum, with the exception of those on pages 19, 73, 97, 129, 146, 183, 190, 237, 283, 299 which are reproduced by permission of the Raymond Mander and Joe Mitchenson Theatre Collection, and that on page 17 which is by permission of the Marquess of Bath and the Courtauld Institute.

The illustrations of Garrick are from originals in the possession of The Garrick Club and are reproduced with their permission. The original of that on page 97 is in the possession of the National Theatre and reproduced by permission.

G.S.

Preface

In 1809 or thereabouts, at the Royal Circus in London a performance of *Hamlet* was given by a troupe of dogs; history does not, alas, record whether or not the leading role was taken by a great Dane.

Nor does this volume contain any further details concerning this fascinating production. I have confined myself to accounts of human performers; more precisely, most of the extracts in this anthology are devoted to English players and London performances, though there are a few distinguished exceptions.

Neither the notion of an eye-witness account nor that of a Shakespearean performance has proved as trouble-free and unambiguous as I at first blithely assumed. Ideally one thinks of someone like the admirable Professor Bell of Edinburgh who seems to have gone straight home from seeing Mrs. Siddons as Lady Macbeth and annotated his copy of the play with detailed notes of her performance. But such scrupulous records are very scanty indeed, especially in the first hundred years or so of Shakespearean representation. For the period up to 1700 I have therefore interpreted the term 'eyewitness' rather generously and have included everything that can be reasonably called a record, a memory or even an allusion to a Shakespearean performance. These range from surprisingly detailed accounts such as Sir Henry Wotton's letter on the burning of the Globe to the merest mention of a performance, such as those in the Revels Accounts, but I have drawn the line at Henslowe's crabbed book-keeping entries. I have arranged the entries in this section in chronological order of writing, as far as this can be ascertained.

For the later end of the period, the problem is one of superabundance rather than scarcity. I have represented the professional critics—Hazlitt, Shaw, G. H. Lewes, Archer, Leigh Hunt, Morley and others—fairly substantially because they do in many cases give the most vivid and readable accounts of Shakespearean performances in their time. But lesser known writers and sometimes anonymous ones are also included because my intention has been not only to provide critiques of performers and productions but also to give some sense of a theatrical occasion, even when, as sometimes happened, the occasion swamped the performance. In this section the entries are arranged chronologically within individual plays, which are given in the order suggested in Professor Peter Alexander's one-volume edition of Shakespeare.

13

As for the idea of a Shakespearean performance, this has a beguiling and totally deceptive simplicity. It is probably true to say that no Shakespearean play has ever been performed anywhere in the *exact* form in which it is printed, whether Quarto or Folio. After the Restoration however, even the *intention* of performing Shakespeare's plays as he wrote them was submerged under the desire to 'improve' him. The problem therefore, is where to draw the line between legitimate and generally conservative adaptation and wholesale demolition or conversion. It is impossible to lay down a rigid rule in the matter, but, for example, while I include an account of Garrick's *Katharine and Petruchio*, which, though it was a travesty, preserved a good deal of Shakespeare's text, I have not given house-room to John Lacy's tasteless *Sauny the Scott* which has little of Shakespeare's *Shrew* but the plot. In general I have avoided adaptations which merely share the story with Shakespeare but have often included versions in which Shakespeare's play is suffocated, though still breathing, under mountains of pageant, song-and-dance and assorted extraneous rubble.

I have compiled this collection for the ordinary reader who is interested in any or all the topics it deals with—Shakespeare, the changing face of the English theatre, styles of acting and styles of criticism. The second half of it is of course almost infinitely expandable and the decision to exclude an item on grounds of space has often been painful. If the reader gets half the enjoyment in reading through it as I did in putting it together he is in for a very good time.

Gāmini Salgādo

PART I 1590–1700

Tears in the Theatre

Poet, playwright, pamphleteer and contemporary of Shakespeare, Thomas Nashe is probably alluding here to the first part of Shakespeare's Henry VI.

How would it have joyed brave Talbot (the terror of the French) to think that after he had lain two hundred years in his tomb, he should triumph again on the stage, and have his bones new embalmed with the tears of ten thousand spectators at least, (at several times) who, in the tragedian that represents his person, imagine they behold him fresh bleeding!

Thomas Nashe,
Pierce Penilesse his supplication to the Devil, 1592

A Night of Errors

Shakespeare may well have been in the company at this performance of one of his earliest plays at Gray's Inn Hall on December 28, 1594.

In regard whereof . . . it was thought good not to offer anything of account, saving dancing and revelling with gentlewomen; and after such sports, a Comedy of Errors (like to Plautus his *Menechmus*) was played by the players. So that night was begun, and continued to the end, in nothing but confusion and errors; whereupon, it was ever afterwards called The Night of Errors. . . . We preferred judgments . . . against a sorcerer or conjuror that was supposed to be the cause of that confused inconvenience . . . And lastly, that he had foisted a company of base and common fellows to make up our disorders with a play of Errors and Confusions; and that the night had gained to us discredit, and itself a nickname of Errors.

Henry Helmes, *Gesta Grayorum*, ed. W. W. Greg

A Performance in the Country[1]

On New Year's day (1596) there was evidence of the liberality of these good people, and especially of the Countess Russell,

---

[1] Jacques Petit, French tutor to Anthony Bacon, brother of Sir Francis, describes a performance at the home of Lord Harington in Rutland, probably in 1596. The original letter is in French.

The earliest drawing of a scene from Shakespeare—*Titus Andronicus* from an Elizabethan MS. 1594 or 1595.

for she gave sign thereof to everyone, from the greatest to the smallest, as I too can bear witness.

The actors of London came here to get their share, and were required to act on the evening of their arrival. The following day they were despatched.

A masquerade devised by Sir Edward Wingfield was performed here; and there was also a performance of the tragedy of Titus Andronicus, but the staging was better than the subject.

Shakespeare Survey 14, 1961

An Unwilling Spectator

Loves Labour Lost, I once did see a play
Y-cleped so, so called to my pain.
Which I to hear to my small joy did stay,
Giving attendance on my forward dame:
    My misgiving mind presaging to me ill,
    Yet was I drawn to see it 'gainst my will.

       *   *   *

Each actor played in cunning wise his part,
But chiefly those entrapt in Cupid's snare;
Yet all was feigned, 'twas not from the heart,
They seemed to grieve, but yet they felt no care:
    'Twas I that grief (indeed) did bear in breast,
    The others did but make a show in jest.

Robert Tofte—
The Months Minde of a Melancholy Lover, 1598

Shakespeare the Actor?

A hall, a hall,
Room for the spheres, the orbs celestial
We'll dance Kemp's Jig. They'll revel with neat jumps
A worthy poet hath put on their pumps.

*   *   *

Luscus, what's played today? faith now I know
I set thy lips abroach, from whence doth flow
Naught but pure Juliet and Romeo.
Say, who acts best? Drusus or Roscio?[1]
Now I have him, that ne'er of ought did speak
But when of plays or players he did treat.
H'ath made a commonplace book out of plays,
And speaks in print: at least what e'er he says
Is warranted by curtain plaudities.

John Marston—*The Scourge of Villainy,*
1598. Satire 10. (Humours)

A Swiss Traveller

Thomas Platter, a Swiss traveller in England, describes a performance of Julius Caesar *in 1599 though it may not have been Shakespeare's play.*

'On September 21, after dinner, at about two o'clock, I went over the water with my companions and saw in the strewn roof-house the tragedy of the first emperor Julius Caesar, with about fifteen characters very well acted; at the end of the comedy[2], they danced as was their custom, very elegantly; two people in men's clothes and two in women's, combining wonderfully with each other, gave this performance.'

from G. Binz, (*Anglia* xxii, 456)

[1] Roscius—possibly Burbage; Drusus has been improbably identified as Shakespeare himself.
[2] i.e., play.

The SWAN THEATRE, 1595 (by Avend van Buchell, based on observations by Johannes de Witt).

Politics and the Theatre

On the eve of the Essex rebellion, the supporters of the earl arranged a special performance of Richard II, *which got them into trouble. Three glimpses of the event are given below.*

Sir Gelly Meyrick 17th Feb. 1600

The examination of Sir Gelly Meyrick, knight, taken the 17th of February, 1600. He sayeth that upon Saturday last was sennight he dined at Gunter's in the company of the Lord Monteagle, Sir Christopher Blount, Sir Charles Percy, Ellis Jones, and Edward Bushell, and who else he remembreth not and after dinner that day and at the motion of Sir Charles Percy and the rest they went all together to the Globe over the water where the Lord Chamberlain's men use to play and were there somewhat before the play began, Sir Charles telling them that the play would be of Harry the viii. Whether Sir John Davies were there or not this examinate cannot tell, but he said he would be there if he could. He cannot tell who procured that play to be played at that time except it were Sir Charles Percy, but as he thinketh it was Sir Charles Percy. Then he was at the same play and came in somewhat after it was begun, and the play was of King Harry the viii, and of the killing of King Richard the Second played by the Lord Chamberlain's Players.

Ex. per   Gelly Meyrick
J. Popham
Edward Fenner

MS in the Public Record Office, Domestic
State Papers, Elizabeth

Augustine Phillips 18 Feb., 1600

The Examination of Augustine Phillips (*an actor in Shakespeare's company*), servant unto the Lord Chamberlain and one of his players taken the 18th of February 1600 upon his oath:

He sayeth that on Friday last was sennight or Thursday Sir Charles Percy Sir Joslyn Percy and the Lord Monteagle with some three more spake to some of the players in the presence of this examinate to have the play of the deposing and killing of King Richard the Second to be played the Saturday next promising to get them 40 shillings more than their ordinary to play it. Where this Examinate and his fellows were determined to have played some other play, holding that play of King Richard to be so old and so long out of use as that they should have small or no company at it. But at their request this Examinate and his fellows were content to play it the Saturday and had their 40 shillings more than their ordinary for it and so played it accordingly.

Augustine Phillips

Ex. per
J. Popham
Edward Fenner

Domestic State Papers, Elizabeth

Lord Bacon, 1601[1]

And further to prove him [Sir Gelly Meyrick] privy to the plot, it was given in Evidence, that some few days before the Rebellion, with great heat and violence he had displaced certain gentlemen lodged in an house fast by Essex house, and there planted divers of my lord's followers and complices, all such as went forth with him in the action of rebellion.

The afternoon before the rebellion, Meyrick, with a great company of others, that afterwards were all in the action, had procured to be played before them, the play of deposing King Richard the Second.

Neither was it casual, but a play bespoken by Meyrick.

And not so only, but when it was told him by one of the players, that the play was old, and they should have loss in playing it, because few would come to it: there was forty shillings extraordinary given to play it, and so thereupon played it was.

So earnest he was to satisfy his eyes with the sight of that tragedy, which he thought soon after his lord should bring from the stage to the state, but that God turned it upon their own heads.

A Declaration of the practices and
Treasons attempted and committed by
Robert late Earl of Essex. 1601

Ancient Pistol

Master Wildgoos, it is not your hustie-tustie can make me afraid of your big looks: for I saw the play of Ancient Pistol,[2] where a cracking coward was well cudgelled for his knavery: your railing is so near the rascal, that I am almost ashamed to bestow so good a name as the rogue on you.

Nicholas Breton—
A Post with a Packet of Mad Letters (Part I. 1603)

---

[1] When the Essex rebellion failed, the chief prosecuting counsel at the trial was Essex's erstwhile follower, Francis Bacon.
[2] In *Henry IV* and *Henry V*.

The Queen and the Player King

In 1601, William Lambarde, a Kentish antiquary, had an audience with Queen Elizabeth I.

[That which passed from the Excellent Majesty of Queen Elizabeth, in her Privy Chamber at East Greenwich, 4th August 1601, towards William Lambarde.]

He presented her Majesty with his Pandecta of all her rolls, bundles, membranes, and parcels that he reposed in Her Majesty's Tower at London; whereof she had given to him the charge 21st January last past.

*   *   *

She proceeded to further pages, and asked where she found cause of stay * * he expounded these all according to their original diversities * * so her Majesty fell upon the reign of King Richard II saying, 'I am Richard II, know ye not that?'
W. L.: 'Such a wicked imagination was determined and attempted by a most unkind gent. the most adorned creature that ever your Majesty made.'
Her Majesty: 'He that will forget God, will also forget his benefactors; this tragedy was played forty times in open streets and houses.'

> Printed in John Nichols' *Progresses and Processions of Queen Elizabeth, 1823,* Vol. III. p. 552

Roman eloquence

The many-headed multitude were drawn
By Brutus' speech, that Caesar was ambitious,
When eloquent Mark Antony had shown
His virtues, who but Brutus then was vicious?
    Man's memory, with new, forgets the old,
    One tale is good, until another's told.

> John Weever—*The Mirror of Martyrs, 1601*

Public Revels—

At our feast we had a play called *Twelfth Night, or What You Will*, much like the *Comedy of Errors*, or *Menachmi* in Plautus, but most like and near to that in Italian called *Inganni*.[1] A good practice in it to make the steward believe his lady widow was in love with him, by counterfeiting a letter as from his lady, in general terms, telling him what she liked best in him, and prescribing his gesture in smiling, his apparel, etc., and then when he came to practise making him believe they took him to be mad.

—and Private

Upon a time when Burbage played Richard III there was a citizen grew so far in liking with him, that before she went from the play she appointed him to come that night unto her by the name of Richard III. Shakespeare overhearing their conclusion went before, was entertained, and at his game ere Burbage came. Then message being brought that Richard III was at the door, Shakespeare caused return to be made that William the Conqueror was before Richard III. Shakespeare's name William.

Diary of John Manningham, 1602–3. Edited by John Bruce, 1868

Presented at Court[2]
1604–5

The Players		*The poets which made the plays*
By the King's Majesty's Players	Hallowmas Day, being the 1st. of November, a play in the banqueting house at Whitehall, called *The Moor of Venice*.	
By His Majesty's Players	The Sunday following, a play of *The Merry Wives of Windsor*.	

[1] There were two Italian plays with this title, but a third called Gl'Ingannati, 1581, is closest to Shakespeare.

[2] The Revels Accounts are records of expenditure in connection with the presentation of plays at court. Two accounts exist for the reign of James I (those for Elizabeth's reign unfortunately precede Shakespeare's dramatic career), one for 1604–5 and one for 1611–12. The entries relating to Shakespeare's plays are given above. 'Shaxberd' is of course none other than.

23

By His Majesty's Players	On St. Stephen's night (Dec. 26) in the Hall, a play called *Measure for Measure*.	*Shaxberd*
By His Majesty's Players	On Innocents' Night (Dec. 28), the play of *Errors*.	*Shaxberd*
By His Majesty's Players	Between New Year's and Twelfth Day, a play of *Love's Labours Lost*.	
By His Majesty's Players	On the 7th. of January was played the play of *Henry V*.	
By His Majesty's Players	On Shrove Sunday (Feb. 8, 1605) a play of *The Merchant of Venice*.	*Shaxberd*
By His Majesty's Players	On Shrove Tuesday, a play called *The Merchant of Venice*, again commanded by the King's Majesty.	

Revels Accounts (Public Record Office)

Play within play

Parodies and anthologies excepted, the following extract from an anonymous play may well be the earliest quotation from Shakespeare.

Kempe : Few of the University pen plays well, they smell too much of that writer Ovid, and that writer Metamorphoses, and talk too much of Prosperina and Jupiter. Why, here's our fellow Shakespeare puts them all down, ay, and Ben Jonson too. O that Ben Jonson is a pestilent fellow, he brought up Horace giving the poets a pill, but our fellow Shakespeare hath given him a purge that made him bewray his credit :
Burbage : It's a shrewd fellow indeed : I wonder these scholars stay so long, they appointed to be here presently that we might try them : oh, here they come.

*   *   *

Burbage : I like your face, and the proportion of your body for Richard III. I pray, Master Philomusus let me see you act a little of it.
Philomusus : 'Now is the winter of our discontent,
Made glorious summer by the son of York.'

The Return from Parnassus, 1606

24

Hamlet on Stage?

[Diaphantus in love] To quench his thirst:
Runs to his ink-pot, drinks, then stops the hole,
And thus grows madder, than he was at first.
    Tasso, he finds, by that of Hamlet, thinks
    Terms him a mad-man then of his inkhorn drinks.
Calls players fools, the fool he judgeth wisest,

          *   *   *

Puts off his clothes; his shirt he only wear,
Much like mad-Hamlet; thus as passion tears.

Anthony Scoloker—*Diaphantus, or the*
Passions of Love, 1604

Advance Notice

Sir,
    I have sent and been all this morning hunting for players
jugglers and such kind of creatures, but find them hard to find,
wherefore leaving notes for them to seek me, Burbage is come,
and says there is no new play that the Queen[1] hath not seen, but
they have revived an old one, called *Loves Labour Lost*, which for
wit and mirth he says will please her exceedingly. And this is
appointed to be played tomorrow night at my Lord of Southampton's, unless you send a writ to remove the Corpus Cum
Causa to your house in Strand. Burbage is my messenger ready
attending your pleasure.

Yours most humbly,
Walter Cope

Letter dated 'From your Library,' written by Sir Walter Cope, addressed
'To the right honorable the Lorde Viscount Cranborne at the Court.'
Endorsed: 1604, Sir Walter Cope to my Lord. Hatfield House MSS.

Hamlet again

The anonymous writer of this tract seems to have Shakespeare ('some
that have gone to London') and Burbage ('if one man were dead') in
mind.

Get thee to London, for if one man were dead, they will have

---

[1] Anne of Denmark, James I's wife.

much need of such a one as thou art. There would be none in my opinion fitter than thyself to play his parts: my conceit is such of thee, that I durst venture all the money in my purse on thy head, to play Hamlet with him for a wager. There thou shalt learn to be frugal (for players were never so thrifty as they are now about London) and to feed upon all men, to let none feed upon thee; to make thy hand a stranger to thy pocket, thy heart flow to perform thy tongue's promise: and when thou feelest thy purse well lined, buy thee some place or Lordship in the country, that growing weary of playing, thy money may there bring thee to dignity and reputation. * * * Sir, I thank you (quoth the Player) for this good counsel, I promise you I will make use of it, for, I have heard indeed, of some that have gone to London very meanly, and have come in time to be exceeding wealthy.

Ratsey's Ghost, or the second part of
his mad pranks and robberies. c. 1605

History as theatre

The author seems to be thinking rather of Shakespeare's play on the stage than of historical record in his summary.

I will not omit that which is yet fresh in our late Chronicles; and hath been many times represented unto the vulgar upon our English theatres of Richard Plantagenet, third son to Richard Duke of York, who (being eldest brother next surviving to King Edward the fourth), after he had unnaturally made away his elder brother, George Duke of Clarence (whom he thought a grievous eye-sore betwixt him and the mark at which he levelled), did upon death of the King his brother, take upon him protection of this realm, under his two nephews left in his butcherly tuition: both which he caused at once to be smothered together, within a keep of his Majesty's Tower, at London: which ominous bad lodging in memorial thereof, is to this day known, and called by name of the Bloodly Tower. Hereupon, this odious uncle usurped the crown; but within little more than two years was deposed, and confounded in the battle at Bosworth in Leicestershire, 1485, by King Henry the Seventh, sent by God to make restitution of the people's liberties; and after so long and horrible a shower of civil blood, to send a golden sunshine of peace, closed up in the princely leaves of that sweet, and modest Rose of Lancaster; which being worn in

26

the beautiful bosom of Lady Elizabeth the daughter of King Edward, (late mentioned of the Family of York) dispersed those seditious clouds of war which had a long time obscured our firmament of peace, banishing that sulphurous smoke of the newly devised cannon, with the divine odour of that blessed inoculation of roses: yielding by their sacred union the Lady Margaret, the first flower of that conjunction; and great grandmother (as I declared) to our Sovereign's Majesty, in these happy bodies reigning over us: whose blessed reign, I beseech God to lengthen as the days of heaven.

Barnaby Barnes—*Four Books of Offices: 1606*

The Death of Antony[1]

... Which when his love,
His royal Cleopatra understood,
She sends with speed his body to remove,
The body of her love imbru'd with blood.
Which brought unto her tomb, (lest that the press
Which came with him, might violate her vow)
She draws him up in rolls of taffaty
T'a window at the top, which did allow
A little light unto her monument.
    There Charmian, and poor Iras, two weak maids
Foretir'd with watching, and their mistress' care,
Tug'd at the pulley, having n'other aids,
And up they hoist the swounding body there
Of pale Antonius, show'ring out his blood

---

[1] This passage, which occurs in the 1607 version of Daniel's play but not in the earlier one of 1594 may, according to Miss Joan Rees (*Shakespeare Survey 6*), be based on the poet's recollection of an actual performance. The detailed account certainly suggests something seen and remembered. If Miss Rees' notion is true, this is the only account of Shakespeare's play before the Restoration. Drayton's lines refer to the following scene in Shakespeare:

Cleopatra: Help me, my women—we must draw thee up:
    Assist, good friends.
Antony: O, quick, or I am gone.
Cleopatra: Here's sport indeed! How heavy weighs my lord!
    Our strength is all gone into heaviness,
    That makes the weight: had I great Juno's power,
    The strong-wing'd Mercury should fetch thee up,
    And set thee by Jove's side. Yet come a little—
    Wishers were ever fools—O, come, come, come. (IV, XV, 30–7)

On th'under lookers, which there gazing stood.
And when they had now wrought him up half way
(Their feeble powers unable more to do)
The frame stood still, the body at a stay,
When Cleopatra all her strength thereto
Puts, with what vigour love, and care could use,
So that it moves again, and then again
It comes to stay. When she afresh renews
Her hold, and with reinforced power doth strain,
And all the weight of her weak body lays,
Whose surcharg'd heart more then her body weighs.
At length she wrought him up, and takes him in,
Lays his yet breathing body on her bed. . . .

Samuel Daniel, Cleopatra, 1607

Shipboard Performances

These extracts are from the journal of William Keeling, commander of the East India Company's ship Dragon *on a voyage to the East Indies. The* Hector *was under the command of Captain William Hawkins. The two earlier performances took place while the* Dragon *was anchored off Sierra Leone. The original journal is no longer extant, but the entries are generally regarded as genuine.*[1]

[*1607 September 5*]
I sent the interpreter, according to his desire, aboard the *Hector* where he broke fast, and after came aboard me, where we gave the tragedy of *Hamlet*.

[*September*] *30:*
Captain Hawkins dined with me, where my companions acted *King Richard II*.

[*1608 March 31*]
I invited Captain Hawkins to a fish dinner, and had *Hamlet* acted aboard me; which I permit to keep my people from idleness and unlawful games, or sleep.

from T. Rundall, Narratives of Voyages
towards the North-West, 1849

[1] A slightly different version appears in *The European Magazine* (August 1825–January 1826) where the interpreter is identified as Portuguese and we are told that after *Hamlet* the company went ashore 'to see if we could shoot an elephant'. An article in *Notes and Queries* (21 July, 1951) suggests that this might be the work of the nineteenth-century Shakespearean scholar and forger John Payne Collier.

Banquo remembered?

and in stead of a Jester, we'll ha' the ghost i' th' white sheet
sit at upper end o' th' table

The Puritan, 1607

When you are at thy table with thy friends,
Merry in heart and filled with swelling wine,
I'll come in midst of all thy pride and mirth,
Invisible to all men but thyself,
And whisper such a sad tale in thine ear
Shall make thee let the cup fall from thy hand,
And stand as mute and pale as Death itself.

Beaumont & Fletcher, *Knight of the
Burning Pestle (acted 1607)*

The popularity of Pericles

Amazed I stood, to see a crowd
Of civil throats stretched out so lowd;
(As at a new play) all the rooms
Did swarm with gentles mix'd with grooms,
So that I truly thought all these
Came to see Shore[1] or Pericles.

Anon.—*Pimlico or Run Red-Cap. Tis
a mad world at Hogsdon, 1609.* (S.A.B.)

Distinguished Visitors

*In 1610, Prince Lewis Frederick of Wirtemberg visited England. His
secretary records a performance of* Othello *at the Globe.*

Lundi, 30. S. E[minence]. alla au Globe, lieu ordinaire ou
l'on Joue les Commedies, y fut representé l'histoire du More de
Venise.

H. J. Wurmsser von Vendenheym—*Journal of Prince Lewis
Frederick of Wirtemberg, Representative of the United German
Princes to France and England, in 1610. Written by his
Secretary Wurmsser. Printed in W. Brenchley
Rye's England as seen by Foreigners. 1865*

[1] Possibly *Shore's Wife* by Chettle and Day (*c.* 1599).

29

Othello at Oxford

Henry Jackson, a member of Corpus Christi College, Oxford, writes briefly of a visit to Oxford by the King's Men and pays a striking tribute to the skill of the boy actor who played Desdemona. The original letter, which is in Latin, is dated September 1610 and extracts from it were transcribed 50 years later by another Corpus Christi man, William Fulman.

—Postremis his diebus adfuerunt Regis Actores Scenici. Egerunt cum applausu maximo, pleno theatro. . . . Habuerunt et Tragœdias, quas decorè, et aptè agebant. In quibus non solum dicendo, sedetiam faciendo quaedam lachrymas movebant.—

—At verò Desdemona illa apud nos a marito occisa, quanquam optimè semper causam egit, interfecta tamen magis movebat; cum in lecto decumbens spectantium misericordiam ipso vultu imploraret.—

Sept. 1610

—In the last few days the King's players have been here. They acted with enormous applause to full houses. . . . They had tragedies (too) which they acted with skill and decorum and in which some things, both speech and action, brought forth tears.—

—Moreover, that famous Desdemona killed before us by her husband, although she always acted her whole part supremely well, yet when she was killed she was even more moving, for when she fell back upon the bed she implored the pity of the spectators by her very face.

from a *letter in Corpus Christi College Library*
(Ms ccc 304ff 83v and 84r

Shakespeare as Actor

To our English Terence, Mr. Will. Shakespeare

Some say (good Will) which I, in sport, do sing,
Had'st thou not played some kingly parts in sport,
Thou hadst been a companion for a king;
And, been a king among the meaner sort.
Some others rail; but, rail as they think fit,
Thou hast no railing, but, a reigning wit:
    And honesty thou sow'st, which they do reap,
    So, to increase their stock which they do keep.

John Davies of Hereford—*The Scourge of Folly. c. 1611*

Dr. Forman at the Globe

*Simon Forman was in turn schoolmaster, astrologer (he correctly pre-
dicted the day of his death and may have committed suicide just to be
right) and physician. But lovers of Shakespeare are grateful to him for
recording in his 'Book of Plays' three visits to The Globe to see Shakespeare's plays in 1611. While the entries are largely plot summaries,
they do give hints of stage business, especially in the case of the* Macbeth
entry.

(a) In Macbeth at the Globe, 1610 [1611], the 20 of April
[Saturday],[1] there was to be observed, first, how Macbeth and
Banquo, two noble men of Scotland, riding through a wood,
there stood before them three women fairies or nymphs, and
saluted Macbeth, saying, three times unto him, hail Macbeth,
king of Codon; for thou shalt be a king, but shalt beget no kings,
etc. Then said Banquo, What all to Macbeth and nothing to
me? Yes, said the nymphs, hail to thee Banquo, thou shalt beget
kings, yet be no king. And so they departed and came to the
court of Scotland to Duncan king of Scots, and it was in the days
of Edward the Confessor. And Duncan bade them both kindly
welcome, and made Macbeth forthwith Prince of Northumber-
land, and sent him home to his own castle, and appointed
Macbeth to provide for him, for he would sup with him the next
day at night, and did so. And Macbeth contrived to kill
Duncan, and thoro' the persuasion of his wife did that night
murder the king in his own castle, being his guest. And there
were many prodigies seen that night and the day before. And
when Macbeth had murdered the king, the blood on his hands
could not be washed off by any means, nor from his wife's
hands, which handled the bloody daggers in hiding them, by
which means they became both much amazed and affronted.
The murder being known, Duncan's two sons fled, the one to
England, the [other to] Wales, to save themselves; they being
fled, they were supposed guilty of the murder of their father,
which was nothing so. Then was Macbeth crowned king, and
then he for fear of Banquo, his old companion, that he should
beget kings but be no king himself, he contrived the death of
Banquo, and caused him to be murdered on the way as he rode.
The next night, being at supper with his noblemen whom he
had bid to a feast to the which also Banquo should have come,
he began to speak of noble Banquo, and to wish that he were

[1] April 20 was a Saturday in 1611, not 1610.

there. And as he thus did, standing up to drink a carouse to him, the ghost of Banquo came and sat down in his chair behind him. And he turning about to sit down again saw the ghost of Banquo, which fronted him so, that he fell into a great passion of fear and fury, uttering many words about his murder, by which, when they heard that Banquo was murdered they suspected Macbeth.

Then Macduff fled to England to the king's son, and so they raised an army, and came into Scotland, and at Dunston Anyse overthrew Macbeth. In the meantime while Macduff was in England, Macbeth slew Macduff's wife and children, and after in the battle Macduff slew Macbeth.

Observe also how Macbeth's queen did rise in the night in her sleep, and walked and talked and confessed all, and the doctor noted her words.

(b)   *Of Cymbeline king of England*

Remember also the story of Cymbeline king of England, in Lucius' time, how Lucius came from Octavius Caesar for tribute, and being denied, after sent Lucius with a great army of soldiers who landed at Milford Haven, and after were vanquished by Cymbeline, and Lucius taken prisoner, and all by means of three outlaws, of the which two of them were the sons of Cymbeline, stolen from him when they were but two years old by an old man whom Cymbeline banished, and he kept them as his own sons twenty years with him in a cave. And how [one] of them slew Cloten, that was the queen's son, going to Milford Haven to seek the love of Imogen the king's daughter, whom he had banished also for loving his daughter, and how the Italian that came from her love conveyed himself into a chest, and said it was a chest of plate sent from her love and others, to be presented to the king. And in the deepest of the night, she being asleep, he opened the chest, and came forth of it, and viewed her in her bed, and the marks of her body, and took away her bracelet, and after accused her of adultery to her love, etc. And in th'end how he came with the Romans into England and was taken prisoner, and after revealed to Imogen, who had turned herself into man's apparel and fled to meet her love at Milford Haven, and chanced to fall on the cave in the woods where her two brothers were, and how by eating a sleeping dram they thought she had been dead, and laid her in the woods, and the body of Cloten by her, in her love's apparel that he left behind him, and how she was found by Lucius, etc.

Observe there now Leontes the king of Sicilia was overcome with jealousy of his wife with the king of Bohemia his friend that came to see him, and how he contrived his death and would have had his cup-bearer to have poisoned, who gave the king of Bohemia warning thereof and fled with him to Bohemia.

Remember also how he sent to the Oracle of Apollo and the answer of Apollo, that she was guiltless and that the king was jealous etc. and how except the child was found again that was lost the king should die without issue, for the child was carried into Bohemia and there laid in a forest and brought up by a shepherd and the king of Bohemia his son married that wench and how they fled into Sicilia to Leontes, and the shepherd having showed the letter of the nobleman by whom Leontes sent a was [away?] that child and the jewels found about her, she was known to be Leontes' daughter and was then sixteen years old.

Remember also the rogue that came in all tattered like Coll Pixi and how he feigned him sick and to have been robbed of all that he had and how he cozened the poor man of all his money, and after came to the sheep shear[ing] with a pedlar's pack and there cozened them again of all their money, and how he changed apparel with the king of Bohemia's son, and then how he turned courtier etc. Beware of trusting feigned beggars or fawning fellows.

Simon Forman, *Book of Plays, 1611* (Bodleian Library)

Echoes of Hamlet

To come to Rhetoric, it not only emboldens a scholar to speak, but instructs him to speak well, and with judgement, to observe his commas, colons, and full points, his parentheses, his breathing spaces, and distinctions, to keep a decorum in his countenance, neither to frown when he should smile, nor to make unseemly and disguised faces in the delivery of his words, not to stare with his eyes, draw awry his mouth, confound his voice in the hollow of his throat, or tear his words hastily betwixt his teeth, neither to buffet his desk like a mad-man, nor stand in his place like a lifeless image, demurely plodding, and without any smooth and formal motion. It instructs him to fit his phrases to his action, and his action to his phrase, and his pronunciation[1] to them both.

Thomas Heywood—An Apology for Actors, 1612

More Court Performances
1611[12]

The Players

| By the King's Players | Hallowmas Night (Nov. 1st) was presented at Whitehall before the King's Majesty a play called *The Tempest* |
| The King's Players | The 5th. of November, a play called *The Winter's* (Night's) *Tale* |

Revels Accounts (Public Record Office)

Fire at the Globe

In 1613, a performance of Shakespeare's Henry VIII *literally brought the house down.*

London this last of June 1613

(1) No longer since than yesterday, while Burbage his company were acting at the Globe the play of *Henry VIII*: and there shooting of certain chambers[2] in way of triumph; the fire catch'd and fastened upon the thatch of the house and there burned so furiously as it consumed the whole house and all in less than two hours (the people having enough to do to save themselves).

Thomas Lorkins—Letter from Thomas Lorkins
to Sir Thos. Puckering. Harl. MS (S.A.B.)

(2) Now to let matters of state sleep, I will entertain you at the present with what hath happened this week at the Bankside. The King's Players had a new play, called *All is true*, representing some principal pieces of the reign of Henry VIII, which was set forth with many extraordinary circumstances of pomp and majesty, even to the matting of the stage; the Knights of the Order, with their Georges and Garter, the Guards with their embroidered coats, and the like: sufficient in true within a

---

[1] *Pronunciation*—general expressive demeanour.   [2] *chambers*—cannon.

while to make greatness very familiar, if not ridiculous. Now, King Henry making a masque at the Cardinal Wolsey's house, and certain cannons being shot off at his entry, some of the paper, or other stuff, wherewith one of them was stopped, did light on the thatch, where being thought at first but an idle smoke, and their eyes more attentive to the show, it kindled inwardly, and ran round like a train,[1] consuming within less than an hour the whole house to the very ground.

This was the fatal period of that virtuous fabric; wherein yet nothing did perish, but wood and straw, and a few forsaken cloaks; only one man had his breeches set on fire, that would perhaps have broiled him, if he had not by the benefit of a provident wit put it out with bottle-ale.

> *Letter from Sir Henry Wotton* to his
> nephew Sir Edmund Bacon, reprinted in
> *Reliquiae Wottoniae,* 1685

(3)
All you that please to understand,
    Come listen to my story,
To see Death with his raking brand
    'Mongst such an auditory:
Regarding neither cardinal's might,
Nor yet the rugged face of Henry the eight.

> Anon—*c.* 1613 *A Sonnet upon the Pitiful Burning
> of the Globe Play House in London.* Reprinted in
> W. C. Hazlitt's *The English Drama and Stage, 1869*

(4) If I should here set down the several terrors and damages done this year by fire, in very many and sundry places of this kingdom, it would contain many a sheet of paper, as is evident by the incessant collections throughout all churches of this realm for such as have been spoiled by fire. Also upon St. Peter's day last, the play-house or theatre called the Globe, upon the Bankside near London, by negligent discharging of a peal of ordinance, close to the south side thereof, the thatch took fire, and the wind suddenly dispersed the flame round about, and in a very short space the whole building was quite consumed, and no man hurt: the house being filled with people, to behold the play, viz. of *Henry VIII.* And the next spring it was new builded in far fairer manner than before.

> John Stow, *Survey* continued by Edmund Howes, 1615

---

[1] i.e., continuously.

35

Paying the Players

The following dry statement of accounts gives a glimpse of royal patronage of the theatre.

The Account of the right honourable the Lord Stanhope of Harrington, Treasurer of his Majesty's Chamber, for all such sums of money as hath been received and paid by him within his office, from the feast of St. Michael the Archangel, Anno Regni Regis Jacobi Decimo (1612), until the feast of St. Michael, Anno Regni Regis Jacobi undecimo (1613), containing one whole year.

*   *   *

Item paid to John Hemmings upon the Council's warrant dated at Whitehall 20 May 1613, for presenting before the Princess' Highness the Lady Elizabeth and the Prince Palatine Elector fourteen several plays, viz: one play called *Philaster*, one other called the *Knot of Fools*, one other *Much Ado about Nothing*, *The Maid's Tragedy*, *The Merry Devil of Edmonton*, *The Tempest*, *A King and No King*, *The Twins' Tragedy*, *The Winter's Tale*, *Sir John Falstaff*, *The Moor of Venice*, *The Nobleman*, *Caesar's Tragedy*, and one other called *Love Lies a-bleeding*; all which plays were played within the time of this Account, viz: paid the sum of £93 : 6 : 8.

Item paid to the said John Hemmings upon the like warrant, dated at Whitehall 20 May 1613, for presenting six several plays, viz: one play called *A Bad Beginning Makes a Good Ending*, one other called *The Captain*, one other *The Alchemist*, one other *Cardeno*, one other *The Hotspur*[1] and one other called *Benedick and Beatrice*,[2] all played within the time of this Account, viz: paid forty pounds, and by way of His Majesty's reward twenty pounds, in all £60.[3]

1613. Lord Treasurer Stanhope's Account. (S.A.B.)

[1] Probably *1 Henry IV*.
[2] Probably *Much Ado About Nothing*.
[3] These plays were all presented as part of the festivities connected with the betrothal of James I's daughter Elizabeth to the Elector Palatine.

Jonson on Shakespeare

(1) It is also agreed, that every man here, exercise his own judgement, and not censure by contagion, or upon trust, from another's voice, or face. * * * He that will swear Heronimo or Andronicus are the best plays, yet shall pass unexcepted at, here, as a man whose judgement shews it is constant, and hath stood still, these five and twenty, or thirty years.

*   *   *

(2) If there be never a Servant-monster i' the Fair, who can help it? He says; nor a nest of antics? He is loth to make Nature afraid in his plays, like those that beget Tales, Tempests, and such like Drolleries, to mix his head with other men's heels.[1]

Bartholomew Fair. Induction

(3)
> [The author will not]
>   purchase your delight at such a rate
> As, for it, he himself must justly hate:
> To make a child, now swaddled, to proceed
> Man, and then shoot up, in one beard, and weed,
> Past threescore years: or, with three rusty swords,
> And help of some few foot-and-half-foot words,
> Fight over York, and Lancaster's long jars:
> And in the tiring-house bring wounds, to scars.
> He rather prays, you will be pleas'd to see
> One such, to-day as other plays should be;
> Where neither Chorus wafts you ore the seas;
> Nor creaking throne comes down, the boys to please.[2]

Every Man in his Humour. Prologue. 1616

Burbage as Richard

Mine host was full of ale and history;

*   *   *

               Why, he could tell
The inch where Richmond stood, where Richard fell:
Besides what of his knowledge he could say,

---

[1] An obvious reference to a piece of stage business in *The Tempest.*

[2] Here Jonson tilts at several of Shakespeare's plays, among them the Histories, *The Winter's Tale* and *Cymbeline.*

He had authentic notice from the play;
Which I might guess, by's must'ring up the ghosts,
And policies, not incident to hosts;
But chiefly by that one perspicuous thing,
Where he mistook a player for a king.
For when he would have said, King Richard died,
And call'd—A horse! a horse!—he, Burbage cried.

Iter Boreale. c. 1618. Poems of Richard Corbet.
Edited by Octavius Gilchrist, 1807

Lament for Burbage

Two versions of an extract from an elegy on Burbage which deals with the great actor's Shakespearean roles.

(1) *On the Death of the famous Actor R. Burbage.* H.[1]

He's gon' & with him what a world are dead!

Oft have I seen him leap into a grave
Suiting the person, (which he us'd to have)
Of a mad lover, with so true an eye
That there I would have sworn he meant to die
Oft have I seen him play his part in jest,
So lively, that spectators, and the rest
Of his crews, whilst he did but seem to bleed
Amazed, thought he had been dead indeed.

Printed by Joseph Haslewood in the
Gentleman's Magazine, June 1826

(2) *A Funeral Elegy on the Death of the famous Actor Richard Burbage who died on Saturday in Lent the 13th of March 1618.*

He's gone and with him what a world are dead!
Which he reviv'd, to be revived so,
No more young Hamlet, old Hieronymo
Kind Lear, the grieved Moor, and more beside,
That lived in him; have now for ever died,
Oft have I seen him, leap into the grave
Smiting the person which he seem'd to have
Of a sad lover with so true an eye
That there I would have sworn, he meant to die;
Oft have I seen him, play this part in jest,

[1] H—the author?

38

So lively, that spectators, and the rest
Of his sad crew, whilst he but seem'd to bleed,
Amazed, thought even then he died indeed.

Printed by J. P. Collier, Annals of the Stage, 1831, Vol. I

A Dissenting Voice

A Puritan opinion, with a side glance at at least two of Shakespeare's plays.

Or why are women rather grown so mad,
That their immodest feet like planets gad
With such irregular motion to base plays,
Where all the deadly sins keep holidays
There shall they see the vices of the times,
Orestes' incest, Cleopatra's crimes.

*　　*　　*

Sooner may shameless wives hate Braindford feasts,
Albertus Magnus, or the pilfered jests
Of some spruce skipjack citizen from plays,
A coach, the secret bawdy house for ways,
And riotous waste of some new freeman made,
That in one year to pieces breaks his trade,
Than wash the toad-like speckles of defame,
That swell the world with poison of their shame:
What Comedies of Errors swell the stage
With your most public vices, when the age
Dares personate in action, for your eyes
Rank scenes of your lust-sweating qualities.

Robert Anton, The Philosopher's Satires, 1616

Pericles at the Palace

The Marquis Trenell [Tremouille], on Thursday last took leave of the King: that night was feasted at Whitehall, by the Duke of Lennox in the Queen's great chamber, where many great lords were to keep them company but no ladies. The Savoy Ambassador was also there: the English lords, was the Marquis Buckingham my Lord Privy Seal my Lord of Lennox, my Lord of Oxford, my Lord Chamberlain, my Lord Hamilton, my Lord Arundel, my Lord of Leicester: my Lord Cary, my

Lord Digby, Mr. Treasurer, Mr. Secretary Calvert: my Lord
Beaucham, and my Lord General, the rest English gallants, and
all mixed with the French along the table: the Marquis Trenell
sitting alone at the table's end: at the right hand, the Savoy
Ambassador, by him the Marquis Buckingham, then a French
Count, etc. mixed: on his left hand my Lord Privy Seal, the
Earl of Oxford, a French Marquis, my Lord Chamberlain, and
so forth mixed with French and English. The supper was great
and the banquet curious, served in twentyfour great China
work platters or voiders, full of glass scales or bowls of sweetmeats: in the midst of each voider a green tree of either, lemon,
orange, cypress, or other resembling. After supper they were
carried to the Queen's privy chamber, where French singing
was by the Queen's musicians: after in the Queen's bedchamber, they heard the Irish harp, a viol, and Mr. Lanyer,
excellently singing and playing on the lute. In the King's great
chamber they went to see the play of *Pericles, Prince of Tyre*,
which lasted till two o'clock. After two acts, the players ceased
till the French all refreshed them with sweetmeats brought on
China voiders, and wine and ale in bottles; after, the players
began anew. The Ambassador parted next morning for France
at eight o'clock, full well pleased being feasted also at Tiballes
and exceeding graciously used of the king, who at taking leave
gave him a very rich chain of diamonds, with a watch done
about with diamonds and wherein the king's effigy was very
excellently done.

. . . with the remembrance of my service to my Lady Carlton
and your Lordship I take leave always resting:

Your Lordship's assuredly to command,
Gerr: Herbert.

London, Monday 24 May. 1619.

From a Letter 'To the right honorable Sir Dudley Carlton,
knight: Lord Ambassador for his Majesty at the Hague.' State
Papers. Domestic. James I.

[W. D. SELBY. Part printed in
Halliwell's Folio Shakespeare]

From Jacobean to Caroline

*These extracts from the Office Book of Sir Henry Herbert, Master of the
Revels from 1623 to 1642 give, among other things, a glimpse of
Jacobean censorship and theatre organisation. The 'Mr. Hemmings'*

referred to was one of Shakespeare's two first editors and fellow actor.

To the Duchess of Richmond, in the King's absence, was given *The Winter's Tale*, by the King's company, the 18th January 1623. At Whitehall.

At Candlemas, *Malvolio* was acted at Court by the King's Servants (Feb. 2 1623).

Upon New-year's night, the prince only being there, *The First Part of Sir John Falstaff*, by the King's company. At Whitehall, 1624.

For the King's players. An old play called *Winter's Tale*, formerly allowed of by Sir George Buck, and likewise by me on Mr. Hemmings' his word that there was nothing profane added or reformed, though the allowed book was missing; and therefore I returned it without a fee, this 19th of August, 1623.

*   *   *

On Saturday the 17th of November [mistake for 16th] being the Queen's birthday, *Richard the Third* was acted by the King's players at St. James, where the King and Queen were present, it being the first play the Queen saw since her Majesty's delivery of the Duke of York. 1633.

On Tuesday night at Saint James, the 26th of November 1633, was acted before the King and Queen, *The Taming of the Shrew*. Liked.

On Wednesday night the first of January, 1633, *Cymbeline* was acted at Court by the King's players. Well liked by the King.

The Winter's Tale was acted on Thursday night at court, the 16th January 1633, by the King's players, and liked.

Julius Caesar, at St. James, the 31 January 1636.

Sir Henry Herbert's *Office Book*, manuscript quoted in
Malone's *Historical Account of the English Stage, 1821*

Profits from Plays and Players

1629. The benefit of the winter's day from the King's Company being brought me by Blagrave, upon the play of *The Moor of Venice*, comes, this 22nd of November 1629, unto —£9 16s. od.

1631. Received of Mr. Benfield, in the name of the King's Company, for a gratuity for their liberty gained unto them of playing, upon the cessation of the plague, this 10th of June, 1631 — £3 10s. od. — This was taken upon *Pericles* at the Globe.

1631. Received of Mr. Shanke, in the name of the King's Company, for the benefit of their summer day, upon the second day of *Richard the Second*, at the Globe, this 12th of June, 1631 — £5 6s. 6d.

MS. of Sir Henry Herbert, printed by Malone in his
Historical Account of the English Stage, 1821

Plays acted before the King and Queen this present year of the lord, 1636[37]

The 8th of December at Hampton Court — *The Moor of Venice*.

The 24th of January [1637] at Hampton Court — *Hamlet*.

The 31st of January at St. James' — the tragedy of *Caesar*.

ibid

Stage Effects

The Jesuits being or having Actors of such dexterity, I see no reason but that they should set up a company for themselves, which surely will put down The Fortune, Red-bull, Cock-pit, and Globe. Only three exceptions some make against them * * * * The third abatement of the honor and continuance of this scenical company is, that they make their spectators pay too deare for their income. Representations and apparitions from the dead might be seen far cheaper at other Playhouses. As for example, the Ghost in Hamlet, Don Andrea's Ghost in Hieronimo. As for flashes of light, we might see very cheap in the comedy of *Pyramus and Thisbe*, where one comes in with a lanthorn and acts Moonshine.

John Gee, *New Shreds of the old Snare, 1624*

A Mirror of the Age

The commonplace metaphor gets a precise cutting edge in this extract from a letter.

On Tuesday his Grace[1] was present at the acting of King Henry VIII at the Globe, a play bespoken of purpose by himself: whereat he stayed till the Duke of Buckingham was beheaded, then departed. Some say, he should rather have seen the fall of Cardinal Wolsey, who was a more lively type of himself, having governed this kingdom eighteen years, as he has done fourteen.

> Robert Gell—*Letter to Sir Martyn Stuteville*. Printed in the Shakespeare Society's *Papers, 1845*, vol. ii. p. 151
> (Letter dated August 9, 1628)

A Visit to Blackfriars

1635 . . . May . . . 6: Not far from home all day at the Blackfriars and a play this day called the *Moor of Venice*.

> Sir H. Mildmay's *Diary, 1633–51* (S.A.B.)

A Boy Actor

A young witty lad playing the part of Richard the Third at the Red Bull, the author because he was interested in the play, to encourage him, wrote him this prologue and epilogue.

The Boy the Speaker.

If any wonder by what magic charm,
Richard the Third is shrunk up like his arm:
And where in fulness you expected him,
You see me only crawling, like a limb
Or piece of that known fabric, and no more. . . .
Let all such know: . . . .
He's termed a man that shows a dwarfish thing,
. . . . . . have you never read
Large folio sheets which printers overlook,
And cast in small, to make a pocket book:
So Richard is transform'd: . . . .

[1] George Villiers, Duke of Buckingham, a favourite of James I.

43

The Epilogue

Great I confess your patience has now been,
To see a little Richard: who can win,
Or praise, or credit? aye, or think to excel,
By doing after what was done so well?

Thomas Heywood, *Pleasant Dialogues and Dramas,*
Selected out of Lucian, 1637

Two Performances at
the Cockpit[1]

. . . before the King and Queen this year of our Lord, 1638

At the Cockpit the 18th of November, *Caesar*

At the Cockpit the 15th of November, *The Merry Wives of Windsor*

Anon—reproduced in 'Archaeologic and Historic Fragments',
by George R. Wright, F.S.A. London. 1887

A Prince at the Playhouse

Arthur Bownest, a student of Emmanuel College, Cambridge,
describes a performance of Shakespeare's comedy witnessed by Charles
Louis, nominal Elector Palatine and nephew of Charles I, who was
on a visit to England. Bownest is writing to a friend, William (later
Archbishop) Sancroft.

August 1639

The Palsgrave is at Court. The princes of Germany will
make him their general, if the king will aid him. I saw him
upon Tuesday at the Globe, where *The Merry Wives of Windsor*
were acted.

Letter in Bodleian Library,
reprinted in *Notes and Queries, April 1971*

---

[1] Originally designed as a Cock-fighting arena, the Phoenix or Cockpit
Theatre, lay in the parish of St. Giles-in-the-Fields, adjoining Drury Lane.

In Praise of Shakespeare

Leonard Digges (1588–1634), poet, translator and friend of Shakespeare, uses his panegyric on Shakespeare for one or two sly pokes at the latter's great rival Ben Jonson who published his Works *in 1616, the year of Shakespeare's death.*

Upon Master WILLIAM SHAKESPEARE, the Deceased Author, and his Poems

Poets are born not made, when I would prove
This truth, the glad remembrance I must love
Of never dying Shakespeare, who alone,
Is argument enough to make that one.
First, that he was a poet none would doubt,
That heard th' applause of what he sees set out
Imprinted; where thou has (I will not say
Reader his works for to contrive a play
To him 'twas none) the pattern of all wit
Art without Art unparalleled as yet.
Next Nature only helped him, for look thoro'
This whole book, thou shall find he doth not borrow,
One phrase from Greeks, nor Latins imitate,
Nor once from vulgar languages translate,
Nor plagiary like from others glean,
Nor begs he from each witty friend a scene
To piece his acts with, all that he does write,
Is pure his own, plot, language exquisite,
But oh! what praise more powerful can we give
The dead, than that by him the King's Men live,
His players, which should they but have shar'd the fate,
All else expir'd within the short term's date;
How could the Globe have prospered, since through want
Of change, plays and poems had grown scant.
But happy verse thou shall be sung and heard,
When hungry quills shall be such honour barred.
Then vanish upstart writers to each stage,
You needy poetasters of this age,
Where Shakespeare liv'd or spake, vermin forbear,
Lest with your froth you spot them, come not near;
But if you needs must write, if poverty

So pinch, that otherwise you starve and die
On God's name may the Bull or Cockpit have
Your lame blank verse, to keep you from the grave:
Or let new Fortune's younger brethren see,
What they can pick from your lean industry.
I do not wonder when you offer at
Blackfriars, that you suffer: 'tis the fate
Of richer veins, prime judgements that have far'd
The worse, with this deceased man compar'd
So have I seen, when Caesar would appear,
And on the stage at half-sword parley were,
Brutus and Cassius: oh how the audience
Were ravish'd, with what wonder they went thence,
When some new day they would not brook a line
Of tedious (though well laboured) *Catiline*:
Sejanus[1] too was irksome, they priz'd more
Honest Iago, or the jealous Moor.
And though the *Fox* and subtle *Alchemist*[2]
Long intermitted could not quite be missed,
Though these have sham'd all the ancients, and might
    raise,
Their author's merit with a crown of bays.
Yet these sometimes, even at a friend's desire
Acted, have scarce defray'd the seacoal fire
And door-keepers: when let but Falstaff come,
Hal, Poins, the rest you scarce shall have a room
All is so pester'd: let but Beatrice
And Benedick be seen, lo in a trice
The Cockpit galleries, boxes, all are full.
To hear Malvolio, that cross-garter'd gull.
Brief, there is nothing in his wit-fraught book,
Whose sound we would not hear, on whose worth look
Like old coin'd gold, whose lines in every page,
Shall pass true current to succeeding age.
But why do I dead praise recite,
Some second Shakespeare must of Shakespeare write;
For me 'tis needless, since an host of men,
Will pay to clap his praise, to free my pen.

Leonard Digges—Prefixed to Shakespeare's *Poems, 1640*

---

[1] Allusions to Ben Jonson's plays.
[2] Jonson's plays.

Hamlet and Othello Compared

Abraham Wright (1611–1690), Vicar of Okeham, kept a common-place book, probably in the 1640s, in which he made comments on contemporary plays for the benefit of his son James who was later to become a historian of the theatre.

Othello, by Shakespeare.

A very good play both for lines and plot, but especially the plot. Iago for a rogue and Othello for a jealous husband, 2 parts well penned. Act 3, the scene betwixt Iago and Othello, and the 1st scene of the 4th Act between the same shew admirably the villainous humour of Iago when he persuades Othello to his jealousy.

Hamlet, a Tragedy by Shakespeare.

But an indifferent play, the lines but mean: and in nothing like *Othello*. *Hamlet* is an indifferent good part for a madman, and the scene in the beginning of the 5th Act between Hamlet and the grave-digger make a good scene, but since bettered in the *Jealous Lovers*.[1]

Abraham Wright, *Commonplace Book*
(British Museum)

Falstaff

I could praise Heywood now: or tell how long,
Falstaffe from cracking nuts has kept the throng:
But for a Fletcher, I must take an age
And scarce invent the title for one page.

T. Palmer—Prefixed to the first edition of
Beaumont and Fletcher's *Works, 1647*

Music for Falstaff

Dinner being near half done * * in comes an old fellow, * * and played us for a novelty, The Passon-fares Galliard; a tune in great esteem, in Harry the Fourth's days; for when Sir John Falstaff makes his amours to Mistress Doll Tear-sheet,

---

[1] Thomas Randolph's play, 1632.

47

Sneak, and his company, the admired fiddlers of that age play this tune, which put a thought into my head, that if time and tune be the composites of music, what a long time this tune had in sailing from England to this place.[1]

Richard Ligon—
A true and exact History of the Island of Barbados, 1657

Lords and Tinkers

The players have a play, where they bring in a tinker, and make him believe himself a lord, and when they have satisfied their humour, they made him a plain tinker again; gentlemen, but that this was a great while ago, I should have thought this play had been made of me: for if ever two cases were alike, 'tis the tinker's and mine.

Anon—The Lord Henry Cromwel's Speech in the House . . .
Printed, . . . 1659. (S.A.B.)

Red Bull Favourites

We have been so perplext with gun and drum,
Look to your hats and cloaks, the red-coats come,
D'amboys is routed, Hotspur quits the field,
Falstaff's out-filch'd, all in confusion yield,
Even auditor and actor, what before
Did make the Red Bull laugh, now makes him roar.

Thomas Jordan—
A Prologue to the King, August 16, 1660. Poems

The first female Desdemona

A Prologue to introduce the first woman that came to act on the stage in the tragedy, call'd The Moor of Venice.

I come, unknown to any of the rest
To tell you news, I saw the lady drest;
The woman plays to day, mistake me not.

*   *   *

In this reforming age
We have intents to civilise the stage.

---

[1] The island of Santiago. The tune has not been certainly identified.

Our women are defective, and so siz'd
You'd think they were some of the guard disguis'd;
For (to speak truth) men act, that are between
Forty and fifty, wenches of fifteen;
With bone so large, and nerve so incompliant,
When you call Desdemona, enter Giant.

ibid

Mr. Pepys at the Playhouse

*Samuel Pepys (1633–1703) gives in his Diary a fascinating glimpse of
Shakespearean performances in the re-opened Restoration theatre. It must
be borne in mind that in many if not most cases he is writing about
adaptations, more or less disastrous, rather than the original versions.*

1660

October 11 — Here, in the Park, we met with Mr. Salisbury, who
took Mr. Creed and me to the Cockpit to see *The Moor of Venice*,
which was well done. Burt acted the Moor; by the same token,
a very pretty lady that sat by me, called out, to see Desdemona
smothered.

December 5 — After dinner I went to the New Theatre and there
I saw *The Merry Wives of Windsor* acted, the humours of the
country gentleman and the French doctor very well done, but
the rest but very poorly, and Sir J. Falstaff as bad as any.

December 31 — In Paul's Church-yard I bought the play of *Henry
the Fourth*, and so went to the new theatre and saw it acted; but
my expectation being too great, it did not please me, as otherwise I believe it would; and my having a book, I believe did
spoil it a little.

1661

June 4 — From thence [my Lord Crew's] to the theatre and saw
Harry the Fourth, a good play.

August 24 — To the Opera, and there saw *Hamlet, Prince of
Denmark*, done with scenes very well, but above all, Betterton[1]
did the Prince's parts beyond imagination.

September 11 — Walking through Lincoln's Inn Fields observed
at the Opera a new play *Twelfth Night*, was acted there, and the
King there; so I, against my own mind and resolution, could
not forbear to go in, which did make the play seem a burden to
me, and I took no pleasure at all in it.

[1] For a description of Betterton in this role see p. 233.

49

September 25—To the theatre, and saw *The Merry Wives of Windsor*, ill done.

November 28—After an hour or two's talk in divinity with my Lady, Captain Ferrers and Mr. Moore and I to the Theatre, and there saw *Hamlet* very well done.

1661–2

March 1—To the Opera, and there saw *Romeo and Juliet*, the first time it was ever acted, but it is a play of itself the worst that ever I heard in my life, and the worst acted that ever I saw these people do, and I am resolved to go no more to see the first time of acting, for they were all of them out more or less.

1662

September 29—To the King's Theatre, where we saw *Midsummer's Night's Dream*, which I had never seen before, nor shall ever again, for it is the most insipid ridiculous play that ever I saw in my life.

1662–3

January 6—After dinner to the Duke's House, and there saw *Twelfth-Night* acted well, though it be but a silly play, and not related at all to the name or day.

1663

May 28—By water to the Royal Theatre; but that was so full they told us we could have no room. And so to the Duke's house; and there saw *Hamlet* done, giving us fresh reason never to think enough of Betterton.

December 22—After dinner abroad with my wife by coach to Westminster, and I perceive the King and Duke and all the Court was going to the Duke's playhouse to see *Henry VIII* acted, which is said to be an admirable play. * * I did not go.

December 26—By and by comes in Captain Ferrers to see us, and, among other talke, tells us of the goodness of the new play of *Henry VIII*, which makes me think it long till my time is out.

1663–4

January 1—Went to the Duke's house, the first play I have been at these six months, according to my last vow, and here saw the so much cried-up play of *Henry the Eighth*; which, though I went with resolution to like it, is so simple a thing made up of a great

50

many patches, that, besides the shows and processions in it, there is nothing in the world good or well done.

1664

November 5—To the Duke's house to a play, *Macbeth*, a pretty good play, but admirably acted.

1666

December 28—To the Duke's house, and there saw *Macbeth* most excellently acted, and a most excellent play for variety. I had sent for my wife to meet me there, who did come, and after the play was done, I out so soon to meet her at the other door that I left my cloak in the play-house, and while I returned to get it, she was gone out and missed me. I not sorry for it much did go to Whitehall, and got my Lord Bellassis to get me into the playhouse; and there, after all staying above an hour for the players, the King and all waiting, which was absurd, saw *Henry the Fifth* well done by the Duke's people, and in most excellent habits, all new vests, being put on but this night. But I sat so high and far off, that I missed most of the words, and sat with a wind coming into my back and neck, which did much trouble me. The play continued till twelve at night; and then up, and a most horrid cold night it was, and frosty, and moonshine.

1666–7

January 7—To the Duke's house, and saw *Macbeth*, which though I saw it lately, yet appears a most excellent play in all respects, but especially in divertisement, though it be a deep tragedy; which is a strange perfection in a tragedy, it being most proper here, and suitable.

1667

April 9—To the King's house, and there saw *The Taming of a Shrew*, which hath some very good pieces in it, but generally is but a mean play; and the best part 'Sawny',[1] done by Lacy; and hath not half its life, by reason of the words, I suppose, not being understood, at least by me.

April 19—To the play-house, where we saw *Macbeth*, which, though I have seen it often, yet is it one of the best plays for a stage, and variety of dancing and music, that ever I saw.

August 15—Sir W. Pen and I to the Duke's house, where a

---

[1] Sauny the Scot, a travesty of *The Taming of the Shrew* by John Lacy (?).

new play. The King and Court there: the house full, and an act begun. And so went to the King's, and there saw *The Merry Wives of Windsor*: which did not please me at all, in no part of it.

October 16—To the Duke of York's house; * * and I was vexed to see Young who is but a bad actor at best act Macbeth in the room of Betterton, who, poor man! is sick: but Lord! what a prejudice it wrought in me against the whole play, and every body else agreed in disliking this fellow. Thence home, and there find my wife gone home; because of this fellow's acting of the part, she went out of the house again.

November 1—My wife and I to the King's playhouse, and there saw a silly play and an old one, *The Taming of a Shrew*.[1]

November 2—To the King's playhouse, and there saw *Henry the Fourth*; and, contrary to expectation, was pleased in nothing more than in Cartwright's speaking of Falstaffe's speech about 'What is Honour?'

November 6—With my wife to a play, and the girl—*Macbeth*, which we still like mightily, though mighty short of the content we used to have when Betterton acted, who is still sick.

November 7—At noon resolved with Sir W. Pen to go to see *The Tempest*, an old play of Shakespeare's, acted, I hear, the first day. * * The house mighty full; the King and Court there: and the most innocent play that ever I saw; and a curious piece of music in an echo of half sentences, the echo repeating the former half, while the man goes on to the latter; which is mighty pretty. The play has no great wit, but yet good, above ordinary plays.

November 13—To the Duke of York's house, and there saw the *Tempest* again, which is very pleasant, and full of so good variety that I cannot be more pleased almost in a comedy, only the seamen's part a little too tedious.

December 12—After dinner all alone to the Duke of York's house, and saw *The Tempest*, which as often as I have seen it, I do like very well, and the house very full.

1667–8

January 6—Away to the Duke of York's house, in the pit, and so left my wife; * * * Thence, after the play, stayed till Harris was undressed, there being acted *The Tempest*, and so he withal, all by coach, home.

---

[1] This may not have been Shakespeare's play but an earlier one.

February 3—To the Duke of York's house, to the play *The Tempest*, which we have often seen, but yet I was pleased again, and shall be again to see it, it is so full of variety, and particularly this day I took pleasure to learn the tune of the seamen's dance.

1668

August 12—After dinner, I, and wife, and Mercer, and Deb., to the Duke of York's house, and saw *Macbeth*, to our great content, and then home.

August 31—To the Duke of York's playhouse, and saw *Hamlet*, which we have not seen this year before, or more, and mightily pleased with it, but above all with Betterton, the best part, I believe, that ever man acted.

September 18—To the King's house, and saw a piece of *Henry the Fourth*.

December 21—Went into Holborn, and there saw the woman that is to be seen with a beard. . . . Thence to the Duke's playhouse, and saw *Macbeth*.

1668–9

December 30—After dinner, my wife and I to the Duke's playhouse, and there did see *King Harry the Eighth*; and was mightily pleased, better than I ever expected, with the history and shows of it.

January 15—With my wife at my cousin Turner's, where I stayed, and sat a while, and carried The. and my wife to the Duke of York's house, to *Macbeth*.

January 20—To the Duke of York's house, and saw *Twelfth Night*, as it is now revived; but, I think, one of the weakest plays that ever I saw on the stage.

January 21—Home, where I find Madam Turner, Dyke, and The.; and had a good dinner for them, and merry; and so carried them to the Duke of York's house, * * and there saw *The Tempest*; but it is but ill done by Gosnell, in lieu of Moll Davis.

February 6—To the King's playhouse, and there in an upper box * * * did see *The Moor of Venice*: but ill acted in most parts; Mohun which did a little surprize me not acting Iago's part by much so well as Clun used to do: nor another Hart's, which was Cassio's; nor, indeed, Burt doing the Moor's so well as I once thought he did.

Diary and Correspondence of Samuel Pepys

53

A King and no King

A company of little boys were by their schoolmaster not many years since appointed to act the play of *King Henry the Eighth*, and one who had the presence (or the absence rather) as being of a whining voice, puling spirit, consumptive body, was appointed to personate King Henry himself, only because he had the richest clothes, and his parents the best people of the parish, but when he had spoke his speech rather like a mouse than a man, one of his fellow actors told him; if you speak not Hoh! with a better spirit and voice, your Parliament will not grant you a farthing.

T.S. *Fragmenta Aulica, 1662* (S.A.B.)

Amateur Theatricals

Thereupon calling a Court at home, and to the best of my understanding having acted *Pyramus and Thisbe*, the Lion and the Moonshine (with less partiality perhaps one way, than would have appeared the other in the votes on your side the water) I stood clearly acquitted upon the whole matter.

Edmund Gayton—Coll. Henry Marten's *Familiar Letters to His Lady of Delight 1662* (S.A.B.)

Tragic Plumage

. . . only the other day, when *Othello* was play'd the Doge of Venice and all his Senators came upon the Stage with Feathers in their Hats, which was like to have chang'd the Tragedy into a Comedy, but that the Moor and Desdemona acted their Parts well.

Catherine Phillips, *Letters from Orinda to Poliarchus . . . 1705.* (Letter dated December 3, 1662)

Pomp and Circumstance

Bayes. Now here's an odd surprise: all these dead men you shall see rise up presently, at a certain note that I have made, in Effaut flat, and fall a-dancing. Do you hear, dead men?

remember your note in Effaut flat. Play on.

> [*To the Music. The Music play his note, and the dead men rise; but cannot get in order.*]

Now, now, now. O Lord, O Lord! Out, out, out! Did ever men spoil a good thing so? no figure, no ear, no time, nothing? you dance worse than the Angels in *Harry the Eighth*, or the fat Spirits in *The Tempest*, egad.

*   *   *

Bayes. Now, Gentlemen, I will be bold to say, I'll shew you the greatest scene that ever England saw: I mean not for words, for those I do not value; but for state, shew, and magnificence. In fine, I'll justify it to be as grand to the eye every whit, egad, as that great Scene in *Harry the Eighth*, and grander too, egad; for, instead of two Bishops, I have brought in two other Cardinals.

George Villiers, 2nd Duke of Buckingham—
The Rehearsal, 1672 (Act II, Sc. v; Act V, Sc. i)

Country Matters

Though not strictly about a Shakespearean performance, the following passage from a prose pamphlet by the poet Andrew Marvell gives a hint of standards of drama outside London.

He is not so weak but knows too much, and is too well instructed, to speak to so little purpose. That would have been like a set of Elizabethan players, that in the country having worn out and over-acted all the plays they brought with them from London, laid their wits together to make a new one of their own. No less man than Julius Caesar was the argument; and one of the chief parts was Moses, persuading Julius Caesar 'not to make war against his own country, nor pass Rubicon.'

Andrew Marvell, *The Rehearsal Transpros'd, 1672*

A Fatal Exit

Thomas Isham was sixteen when he made the following entry in his diary which he kept in Latin for two years because his father wished him to.

20 [August]. Ad nos perlatum est Harrisimum socium suum histrionem in scena casu occidisse. Tragoedia Macbeth appelata

55

erat; in qua Harrissimus qui Macduffi personam gerebat socium suum Macbethum debebat interficere.

Inter dimicandum autem accidit ut Macduffus Macbetham pugionem in oculum infigeret quo vulnere exanimatus concidit ut ne potuerit pronunciare ultima verba quae debuerat, 'Farewell vain world and what is worse, ambition.'

MS Journal among the Isham papers at
Lamport Hall, Northamptonshire.

It is reported that Harris has killed his associate actor, in a scene on the stage, by accident. It was the tragedy called 'Macbeth', in which Harris performed the part of Macduff, and ought to have slain his fellow-actor, Macbeth; but during the scene it happened that Macduff pierced Macbeth in the eye, by which thrust he fell lifeless, and could not bring out the last words of his part.

The Journal of Thomas Isham, from 1 Nov 1671 to 30 Sept 1673 translated by Rev. Robert Isham with an Introduction etc. by Walter Rye, (S.A.B.)

Shakespeare in Disguise

This extract gives some indication of conditions during the eighteen years from 1642 when the theatres were closed and stage plays officially prohibited.

The most part of these pieces were written by such penmen as were known to be the ablest artists that ever this nation produced, by name, Shakespeare, Fletcher, Jonson, Shirley, and others; and these collections are the very souls of their writings, if the witty part thereof may be so termed: And the other small pieces composed by several other authors are such as have been of great fame in this last age. When the public theatres were shut up, and the actors forbidden to present us with any of their tragedies, because we had enough of that in earnest; and comedies, because the vices of the age were too lively and smartly represented; then all that we could divert ourselves with were these humours and pieces of plays, which passing under the name of a merry conceited fellow called Bottom the Weaver, Simpleton the Smith, John Swabber, or some such title, were only allowed us, and that but by stealth too, and under the pretence of rope-dancing, or the like; and these being all that was permitted us, great was the confluence of the audi-

tors; and these small things were as profitable, and as great
get-pennies to the actors as any of our late famed plays. I have
seen the Red Bull playhouse which was a large one so full, that
as many went back for want of room as had entered; and as
meanly as you may now think of these drolls, they were then
acted by the best comedians then and now in being.

Francis Kirkman—Preface to
The Wits or Sport upon Sport, 1673

Shakespeare versus Jonson

We all well know that the immortal Shakespeare's plays (who
was not guilty of much more of this than often falls to women's
share) have better pleas'd the world than Jonson's works,
though by the way 'tis said that Benjamin was no such Rabbi
neither, for I am inform'd his learning was but grammar high;
... and I have seen a man the most severe of Jonson's sect, sit
with his hat remov'd less than a hair's breadth from one sullen
posture for almost three hours at *The Alchemist*; who at that
excellent play of *Harry the Fourth* (which yet I hope is far enough
from farce) hath very hardly kept his doublet whole.

Aphra Behn—*The Dutch Lover*: 1673
An Epistle to the Reader

Noises off

Such noise, such stink, such smoke there was, you'd swear
The Tempest surely had been acted there.
The cries of 'Star-board, larboard, cheerly boys!'
Is but as demy rattles to this noise.

Anon—*The Country Club*. A Poem
London ... 1679

Shakespeare versus the rest

*Though he begins by referring to reading Shakespeare, it is clear that the
author is thinking mainly of stage performance.*

Whene'r I Hamlet, or Othello read,
My hair starts up, and my nerves shrink with dread:

57

Pity and fear raise my concern still higher,
Till, betwixt both, I'm ready to expire!
When cursed Iago, cruelly, I see
Work up the noble Moor to Jealousy,
How cunningly the villain weaves his sin,
And how the other takes the poison in;
Or when I hear his God-like Roman's rage,
And by what just degrees he does assuage
Their fiery temper, recollect their thoughts,
Make 'em both weep, make 'em both own their fau'ts;
When these and other such-like scenes I scan,
'Tis then, great Soul, I think thee more than man!
Homer was blind, yet cou'd all Nature see;
Thou wer't unlearn'd, yet knew as much as he
In *Timon, Lear, The Tempest*, we may find
Vast images of thy unbounded mind;
These have been alter'd by our poets now,
And with success too, that we must allow;
Third days[1] they get when part of thee is shown,
Which they but seldom do when all's their own.

Robert Gould—*Poems, 1689*

Death in the Stalls

Macbeth, a tragedy, which was reviv'd by the Duke's Company, and re-printed with Alterations, and new Songs, 4to London, 1674. At the acting of this tragedy, on the stage, I saw a real one acted in the pit; I mean the death of Mr. Scroop, who received his death's wound from the late Sir Thomas Armstrong, and died presently after he was remov'd to a House opposite to the Theatre in Dorset-Garden.

Gerard Langbaine—
An Account of the English Dramatic Poets, 1691

A Prompter Remembers

John Downes (c. 1640–c. 1710) began as an actor but gave up after a severe attack of stagefright. His Roscius Anglicanus, or an Historical

---

[1] The third performance was usually the author's benefit.

Review of the Stage from 1660 to 1706 *is an old man's memories (published in 1708) based on his long experience as a book-keeper (prompter) in Sir William Davenant's company; they make up in interest for what they lack in reliability.*

TO THE READER

The Editor of the ensuing relation, being long conversant with the plays and actors of the original company, under the patent of Sir William Davenant, at his Theatre in Lincolns-Inn-Fields, open'd there 1662. And as book-keeper and prompter, continued so, till October 1706, he writing out all the parts in each play; and attending every morning the actors' rehearsals, and their performances in afternoons; emboldens him to affirm, he is not very erroneous in his relation. But as to the actors of Drury-Lane Company, under Mr. Thomas Killigrew, he having the account from Mr. Charles Booth, sometimes book-keeper there; if he a little deviates as to the successive order, and exact time of their plays' performances, he begs pardon of the reader, and subscribes himself.

His very humble servant,
John Downes.

I must not omit to mention the parts in several plays of some of the actors; wherein they excell'd in the performance of them. First, Mr. Hart, in the part of . . . Othello, Rollo, Brutus, in Julius Caesar . . . if he acted in any one of these but once in a fortnight, the house was fill'd as at a new play, especially Alexander, he acting that with such grandeur and agreeable majesty . . . in all the comedies and tragedies, he was concerned, he perform'd with that exactness and perfection, that not any of his successors have equalled him.

Major Mohun, he was eminent for . . . Cassius in *Julius Caesar* . . .

The plays there[1] acted were . . . *Pericles Prince of Tyre.* Mr. Betterton, being then but twenty-two years old, was highly applauded for his acting in all these plays, but especially, for . . . Pericles . . . his voice being then as audibly strong, full and articulate, as in the prime of his acting.

Mr. Kynaston . . . being then very young made a complete

[1] Lisle's Tennis Court.

59

female stage beauty, performing his parts so well . . . that it has since been disputable among the judicious, whether any woman that succeeded him so sensibly touch'd the audience as he . . .

EDWARD KYNASTON (*c.* 1640–1706) continued for a while the tradition of boys playing women's roles. He was much admired by Pepys (R. B. Parkes, after R. Cooper).

In this interim, Sir William Davenant gain'd a patent from the King, and created Mr. Betterton and all the rest of Rhodes's Company, the King's Servants, who were sworn by my Lord Manchester then Lord Chamberlain, to serve his Royal Highness the Duke of York, at the Theatre in Lincolns-Inn-Fields.

The tragedy of *Hamlet*; Hamlet being perform'd by Mr. Betterton, Sir William (having seen Mr. Taylor of the Black-Friars Company act it, who being instructed by the author Mr. Shakespeare[1]) taught Mr. Betterton in every particle of it; which by his exact performance of it, gain'd him esteem and reputation, superlative to all other plays. Horatio by Mr. Harris; The King by Mr. Lilliston; The Ghost by Mr. Richards (after by Mr. Medburn), Polonius by Mr. Lovel; Rosencrantz by Mr. Dixon; Guildernstern by Mr. Price; First Grave-maker, by Mr. Underhill: The Second by Mr. Dacres; the Queen by Mrs. Davenport; Ophelia by Mrs. Sanderson: No succeeding tragedy for several years got more reputation, or money to the Company than this.

* * *

Romeo and Juliet, wrote by Mr. Shakespeare: Romeo was acted by Mr. Harris; Mercutio by Mr. Betterton, Count Paris by Mr. Price; The Friar by Mr. Richards; Sampson by Mr. Sandford; Gregory by Mr. Underhill; Juliet by Mrs. Saunderson; Count Paris's [? Montague's] Wife by Mrs. Holden.

Note. There being a fight and scuffle in this play between the House of Capulet and House of Paris [? Montague]; Mrs. Holden acting his wife, enter'd in a hurry, crying 'O my dear Count!' She inadvertently left 'o' out in the pronunciation of the word 'Count!' giving it a vehement accent, put the house into such a laughter, that London Bridge at low water was silence to it.

This tragedy of *Romeo and Juliet*, was made some time after into a tragi-comedy, by Mr. James Howard, he preserving Romeo and Juliet alive; so that when the tragedy was reviv'd again, 'twas play'd alternately, tragical one day, and tragi-comical another for several days together. . . .

Twelfth Night, Or What You Will; wrote by Mr. Shakespeare had mighty success by its well performance: Sir Toby Belch, by Mr. Betterton; Sir Andrew Aguecheek by Mr. Harris, Fool by Mr. Underhill; Malvolio the Steward by Mr. Lovel; Olivia by Mrs. Ann Gibbs; all the parts being justly acted crown'd the play. Note, it was got up on purpose to be acted on Twelfth Night. . . .

King Henry the 8th. This play by order of Sir William Davenant, was all newly clothed in proper habits: the king's was new, all

[1] As Taylor apparently did not join the King's Men till three years after Shakespeare's death, this interesting statement must be regretfully labelled improbable.

61

the lords, the cardinals, the bishops, the doctors, proctors, lawyers, tip-staves, new scenes: the part of the king was so right and justly done by Mr. Betterton, he being instructed in it by Sir William, who had it from old Mr. Lowen, that had his instructions from Mr. Shakespeare himself, that I dare and will aver, none can, or will come near him in this age, in the performance of that part: Mr. Harris's performance of Cardinal Wolsey, was little inferior to that, he doing it with such just state, port and mien that I dare affirm, none hitherto has equall'd him: the Duke of Buckingham, by Mr. Smith; Norfolk by Mr. Nokes; Suffolk by Mr. Lilliston; Cardinal Campeius and Cranmer by Mr. Medburn; Bishop Gardiner by Mr. Underhill; Earl of Surrey by Mr. Young; Lord Sands by Mr. Price; Mrs. Betterton, Queen Catherine: every part by the great care of Sir William, being exactly perform'd; it being all new clothed and new scenes; it continu'd acting fifteen days together with general applause. . . .

These being all the principal, which we call'd stock-plays, that were acted from the time they open'd the theatre in 1662, to the beginning of May, 1665, at which time the plague began to rage: the Company ceas'd acting; till the Christmas after the fire in 1666. Yet there were several other plays acted, from 1662 to 1665, both old and modern: as . . . The tragedy of *King Lear*, as Mr. Shakespeare wrote it; before it was alter'd by Mr. Tate.[1]

The new Theatre in Dorset Garden being finish'd and our Company after Sir William's death, being under the rule and dominion of his widow the Lady Davenant, Mr. Betterton, and Mr. Harris (Mr. Charles Davenant) her son, acting for her they remov'd from Lincoln's-Inn-Fields thither. And on the ninth day of November 1671, they open'd their new Theatre [. . . among the plays acted, were]:

The tragedy of *Macbeth*, alter'd by Sir William Davenant; being dressed in all its finery, as new clothes, new scenes, machines, as flytings for the witches; with all the singing and dancing in it: the first compos'd by Mr. Lock, the other by Mr. Channell and Mr. Joseph Preist; it being all excellently perform'd, being in the nature of an opera, it recompens'd double the expense; it proves still [1708] a lasting play.

Note, that this tragedy, *King Lear* and the *Tempest*, were acted in Lincolns-Inn-Fields; *Lear*, being acted exactly as Mr. Shakespeare wrote' it; as likewise the *Tempest* alter'd by Sir William Davenant and Mr. Dryden, before 'twas made into an opera.

[1] Tate's version of *Lear* which held the stage for well over a hundred years featured a happy ending with Edgar marrying Cordelia.

[1672] *The Jealous Bridegroom*[1] wrote by Mrs. Behn [Aphra Behn] a good play and lasted six days; but this made its exit too, to give room for a greater, the *Tempest*.

Note, in this play, Mr. Otway the poet having an inclination to turn actor; Mrs. Behn gave him the king in the play, for a probation part, but he being not used to the stage, the full house put him to such a sweat and tremendous agony, being dashed spoilt him for an actor. Mr. Nat. Lee,[2] had the same fate in acting Duncan in *Macbeth*, ruin'd him for an actor too.

The year after in 1673, the *Tempest*, or the *Enchanted Island* made into an opera by Mr. Shadwell, having all new in it; as scenes, machines; particularly one scene painted with myriads of aerial spirits; and another flying away, with a table furnished out with fruits, sweet meats, and all sorts of viands, just when Duke Trinculo and his companions, were going to dinner: all was things perform'd in it so admirably well, that not any succeeding opera got more money.

*   *   *

All the preceding plays, being the chief that were acted in Dorset Garden, from November 1671, to the year 1682; at which time the patentees of each Company united patents; and by so incorporating the Duke's Company were made the King's Company, and immediately remov'd to the Theatre Royal in Drury-Lane.

The mixed Company then reviv'd the several old and modern plays, that were the propriety of Mr. Killigrew as, . . . *The Moor of Venice*.

*   *   *

About this time, there were several other new plays acted. As . . . *Troilus and Cressida*.[3]

The Fairy Queen, made into an opera, from a comedy of Mr. Shakespeare's: This in ornaments was superior to the other two; especially in clothes, for all the singers and dancers, scenes, machines and decorations, all most profusely set off; and excellently performed chiefly the instrumental and vocal part composed by the said Mr. Purcel, and dance by Mr. Priest. The Court and Town were wonderfully satisfied with it; but

[1] *The Forc'd Marriage*, or *The Jealous Bridegroom*, Aphra Behn's first play (1671).

[2] Thomas Otway (1652–85) and Nathaniel Lee (1653–92) were both popular dramatists in their own day, and the former's *Venice Preserved* is still revived.

[3] Probably Dryden's alteration of Shakespeare (1679).

63

the expenses in setting it out being so great, the Company got very little by it.

Note, between these operas there were several other plays acted, both old and modern. As, . . . *The Taming of a Shrew* . . .

Note, from Candlemas 1704, to the 23rd of April 1706. There were plays commanded to be acted at Court at St. James's, by the actors of both houses.

The next was, *The Merry Wives of Windsor*, acted the 23rd of April, the Queen's Coronation Day: Mr. Betterton, acting Sir John Falstaff; Sir Hugh by Mr. Dogget; Mr. Page by Mr. Vanbruggen; Mr. Ford by Mr. Powel; Dr. Caius, Mr. Pinkethman; the Host, Mr. Bullock; Mrs. Page, Mrs. Barry; Mrs. Ford, Mrs. Bracegirdle; Mrs. Anne Page, Mrs. Bradshaw.

Next follows the account of the present young company (which united with the old, in October 1706) now acting at Drury Lane; Her Majesty's Company of comedians, under the government of Colonel Breet.

Mr. Dogget. On the stage, he's very aspectabund, wearing a farce in his face; his thoughts deliberately framing his utterance congruous to his looks: He is the only comic original now extant: witness, Ben Salon, Nikin, *The Jew of Venice*,[1] etc.

I must not omit praises due to Mr. Betterton, the first and now [1708] only remain of the old stock, of the Company of Sir William Davenant in Lincolns-Inn-Fields; he like an old stately spreading oak now stands fixed, environ'd round with brave young growing, flourishing plants: there needs nothing to speak of his fame, more than the following [16] parts.

Pericles, Prince of Tyre	Macbeth
. . . .	Timon of Athens
Richard the Third	Othello
King Lear	. . . .
Hamlet	King Henry the Eighth
. . . .	Sir John Falstaff

John Downes, *Roscius Anglicanus, 1708*

Foreign Visitors

February 1. The Morocco Ambassador was at the Duke's Theatre, being entertained at the play called the *Tempest*.

The Monthly Recorder, Feb–Mar 1682

[1] Altered from Shakespeare by Lord Lansdowne, 1701.

An Early Flying Ballet Artiste

L. Brain. A player, ha ha ha, why now you have, Madam, —
Darewell. Thou canst witness the contrary of that; thou toldst me her breeding was such, that she had been familiar with kings and queens.

Darewell. Ay my lord in the play-house, I told you she was a high flyer too, that is, I have seen her upon a machine in the *Tempest*.

L. Brain. In the *Tempest*! Why then I suppose I may seek her fortune in the enchanted island.

Thomas Durfey — The Marriage-Hater Match'd, 1692

A Glimpse of Apemantus[1]

In my opinion he ought to be sat, like Apemantus in the play, at a side-board by himself.

Anon — Pendragon:
Or, The Carpet Knight His Kalendar, 1698 (T.D.)

Art and Life

'Tis true life is more supportable this morning, then yesterday: For, if Hamlet had not been murder'd at the play-house last night, I had been worse then dead today.

Anon — *Familiar Letters*: Vol. II. Containing Thirty Six Letters, By the Right Honourable John, late Earl of Rochester, *1699*

Falstaff Redivivus

The wits of all qualities have lately entertained themselves with a revived humour of Sir John Falstaff in *Henry the Fourth*, which has drawn all the town, more than any new play that has been produced of late; which shows that Shakespeare's wit will always last: and the critics allow that Mr. Betterton has hit the humour of Falstaff better than any that have aimed at it before.

Villiers Bathurst to Dr. Arthur Charlett, Master of University
College, dated Bond St. Jan. 28, 1699–1700.
Printed in Malone's Dryden I. i. 329

---

[1] In *Timon of Athens*.

PART II—to 1890

The Comedy of Errors

THIS play has held the stage almost continuously since the first recorded performance at Gray's Inn on December 28, 1594, almost certainly by members of the acting company to which Shakespeare himself belonged. Two adaptations, one called *See If You Like It* (1734) and the other *The Twins* (1762) were invariably presented till Samuel Phelps brought Shakespeare's play back on November 8, 1855. In 1864 at the Princess Theatre the brothers Webb appeared almost identical as the two Dromios.

Shakespeare Sings Again

This account of a production at Covent Garden recalls a fairly standard practice—that of tacking on songs from other plays to those of Shakespeare's plays considered less than great.

Dec. 11 [1819]. The revival of a comedy of Shakespeare, with interpolated songs, this evening, was a dramatic epoch, and it seems the favourite expedient of managers, after a run of unpopularity, to recommend them once more to the public good will. If this was the idea in which 'The Comedy of Errors' was revived, its reception has amply justified the hazard. It was attended by the most crowded house since the beginning of the season, and the audience were throughout in a unanimous temper to applaud. We will not repeat the plot, for who does not read Shakespeare? and who does not remember him? But if the managers were determined to select a play, in which their personal care was to engross the praise of the audience, they could not have found in our great author a performance more dependent upon the aids, song and scenery, to secure success. No illusion of the stage can give probability to the perpetual mutations of four persons, paired in such perfect similitude, that the servant mistakes his master, and the master his servant: the wife her husband, and the husband his wife. All this so strongly contradicts common experience, that it repels us even in description; but on the stage, with the necessary dissimilarity of countenance, voice, manner, and movement, that occurs between the actors, however disguised by dress, the improbability becomes almost offensive. Shakespeare found the story made for him, and submitted to it for the sake of those who were determined to be amused at all hazards. In his *Twelfth Night* he has allowed, partially however, the same substitution. But these were the calamities of his early day of literature, not the choice of his noble understanding. It is probable that no two human beings ever completely resembled each other; and if it might not seem touching on topics too high for this place, we may well admire that disposition of Providence, which has given to each, among the myriads of mankind, his distinctive marks, yet retained family resemblances. The line is thus mysteriously drawn which ranges the individual beside those of his blood, while it separates him from complete coincidence. The absence of this single precaution would have involved society in infinite disorder. Nothing could be safe, if any large portion of mankind were perfectly alike; but a high arrangement has secured at once the acknowledgment of kindred, and the rights of individuality. Duruset and Jones were the Antipholus of Ephesus and the Antipholus of Syracuse, and Liston and Farren were the two Dromios. All this was of course absurd, but it was borne with by the audience for the sake of the music, which was abundant, and in general happily selected. The chief burthen of the songs was laid on Miss Stephens as Adriana, and Miss Tree as Luciana, and they both sang with much applause. The songs, etc. were wholly selected from Shakespeare's plays and poems, though, we think, that selection might have been more appropriate to the scene. In actors and singers, however, the drama is most strongly cast, and bids fair to attain a higher popularity than it has ever done before, when bereft of its new musical accompaniments.

European Magazine

A Shakespeare First Night Revived

William Archer, the translator of Ibsen and for many years drama critic of The World *gives a sympathetic account of a performance of Shakespeare's play in its earliest known setting. The English Stage Society under William Poel were very largely responsible for the revival of interest in the conditions and conventions of Shakespeare's own stage as a more suitable framework for his plays than the picture-frame stage of the nineteenth century and its realistic assumptions.*

We have to thank the Benchers of Gray's Inn and the Elizabethan Stage Society (not forgetting Mr. Arnold Dolmetsch) for a very interesting and pleasant evening. There are two extant buildings in London in which we know that plays of Shakespeare's were acted during his lifetime. On Innocents' Day, December 28th, 1594, as we learn from the *Gesta Grayorum*, 'a *Comedy of Errors*, like to Plautus his *Menechmus*, was played by the players' in Gray's Inn Hall, which was even then a quarter of a century old. It is believed (but this is only a probable conjecture) that the players were the Lord Chamberlain's Company, to which Shakespeare belonged.

* * *

... the Hall undoubtedly serves the purpose of the Elizabethan Stage Society in helping us to realise the conditions of a sixteenth-century representation. And, as good luck will have it, *The Comedy of Errors*[1] is of all Shakespeare's works that which loses least and gains most in modern eyes by absence of scenery and conventionality of costume. The play is a classical farce recklessly romanticised; but it preserves so much of its classic character that the scene remains indefinite—simply 'Ephesus: a public place.' Then, again, the plot is so unblushingly extravagant that anything like illusion is from the outset impossible. To attempt it could only be to force upon us the consciousness of disillusion. The intrigue is a sort of dramatic diagram, an essay in the pure mathematics of situation. The poet seems to say, 'Admitting such-and-such inadmissible postulates, let us work out the resultant series of impossible possibilities.' Plautus is content with one pair of twins, and takes the trouble to explain at some length how the two Menæchmi came to be called by the same name. Shakespeare gives us the square of the coincidence, so to speak, by attaching indistinguishable slaves to the indistinguishable masters, and airily omits to explain why both masters are called Antipholus and both lackeys Dromio. Observe that we have here no real analogy with the case of the *Amphitruo*, in which Jupiter and Mercury miraculously assume the forms, and deliberately take the names, of Amphitryon and Sosia. There is all the difference in the world between a miracle and a coincidence. Then Shakespeare piles coincidence upon coincidence in the arrival of the father (who replaces the Prologue of the Latin comedy) and the recognition of the mother —a singularly frigid invention, and quite ineffective because quite unprepared. Thus the whole fable is so remote from even imaginable reality that we willingly dispense with all realism of presentation, and regard the stage as a sort of chess-board on which pieces and pawns (and the pieces, as in chess, are mostly

[1] Performed three times—December 6, 7, and 9 [1895].

in pairs) work out a certain problem in a given number of moves. If all Shakespeare's works were like *The Comedy of Errors*, I should willingly assent to the doctrine of the E.S.S. that we ought to get rid of scenic apparatus and revert to the bare platform of the Globe or the Blackfriars. Unfortunately for the E.S.S., but fortunately for the world at large, *The Comedy of Errors* stands alone in the abstractness, if I may call it so of its scene and matter.

Far be it from me, however, to throw cold water on the enthusiasm of the E.S.S. Though I cannot accept their principle as applied to Shakespearian productions at large, I heartily approve their practice, and hope that they will continue their interesting revivals of the more neglected plays. The costuming of *The Comedy of Errors* was excellent and really instructive, and the acting was, for amateurs, most creditable. One of the Dromios (I quite forget which) was a real comedian. It interested me to note that whereas I had always conceived it next door to impossible to find or make two pairs of actors even passably alike, as a matter of fact the two Antipholuses and the two Dromios were to me, at no great distance from the scene, actually indistinguishable. Of course, I was vaguely conscious of certain differences between them; but it would have needed a special effort of attention (from which I carefully abstained) to fix the differences in my mind so as to enable me to tell, when one of them entered, whether he was of Ephesus or of Syracuse. I was effectually enveloped in the 'general mist of error.' To this end the broad brims of the Antipholuses' hats contributed most ingeniously. The stage management might have been better— in the opening scene it was quite ridiculous—and it is hard to see why the E.S.S. should deliberately desert its strongest position in making huge and quite unnecessary cuts in the last act. On the whole, then, I remain unconverted to the general theory that scenery and accurate costume are hindrances to the proper enjoyment of Shakespeare, and that amateurs act better than actors. Strictly speaking, the comedy was not acted at all, but only more or less intelligently recited. But the effect was so picturesque and interesting that I beg to repeat in earnest a proposal which was freely mooted in jest—to wit, that the picture should be completed by the audience, too, appearing in ruffs and farthingales. The black coats and white neckties were deplorably discordant. If the Benchers of Gray's Inn should be minded to give another gaudy-night of the kind, I do not see why they should not write *Elizabethan Costume* on the cards of invitation. I am much of a masquerader myself—'parcus ludorum cultor et infrequens'—but for such a solemnity I would don doublet and hose as cheerfully as that redoubtable brigand, Mr. Tupman, squeezed himself into his green velvet jacket with a two-inch tail.

William Archer, *The Theatrical World of 1895*

The Taming of the Shrew

FROM the late 1660s till the mid-nineteenth century the play has been seen only in garbled versions, the most popular of which were John Lacy's *Sauny the Scot* (1667) and Garrick's *Catherine and Petruchio* (1754). Shakespeare did not return till Benjamin Webster and J. R. Planché brought the original play to the Haymarket on March 16, 1844.

Shakespeare Ousted

Garrick's biographer records the beginning of the period when Shakespeare's play had to make way for Garrick's adaptation. Katharine was originally played by Mrs. Pritchard, later (1756) by Mrs. Clive.

Among the plays of Shakespeare which Mr. Garrick revived, were *The Winter's Tale*, and *The Taming of the Shrew*; each of these comedies being reduced by him into three acts, and called *Florizel* and *Perdita*, and *Catherine and Petruchio*: they both pleased the audience greatly; he often introduced them to the public by a humorous prologue of his own writing, in which he criticised the various palates of the public for theatrical representation, and compared the wine of Shakespeare to a bottle of brisk champagne. *The Taming of the Shrew* was not altogether written in Shakespeare's best manner, though it contained many scenes well worth preserving. The fable was certainly of the farcical kind, and some of the characters rather exaggerated. The loppings from this luxuriant tree of the old poet were not only judicious, but necessary to preserve the pristine trunk. Woodward's Petruchio was, perhaps, more wild, extravagant, and fantastical than the author designed it should be; and he carried his acting of it to an almost ridiculous excess.

72

Mrs. Clive, though a perfect mistress of Catherine's humour, seemed to be overborne by the extravagant and triumphant grotesque of Woodward; she appeared to be overawed as much by his manner of acting, as Catherine is represented to be in the fable. In one of his mad fits, when he and his bride are at supper, Woodward stuck a fork, it is said, in Mrs. Clive's finger; and in pushing her off the stage he was so much in earnest that he threw her down; as it is well known that they did not greatly respect one another, it was believed that something more than chance contributed to these excesses.

Thomas Davies, Life of Garrick

Shakespeare Restored

J. R. Planché (1796–1880), dramatist, designer and musician recalls a notable moment of theatrical history, when Garrick's travesty of the Shrew *was laid aside in favour of Shakespeare's comedy. The play was first performed on March 6, 1844 and revived in 1847, anticipating by several decades the experiments of William Poel and The English Stage Society.*

The PLANCHE–WEBSTER production of *The Taming of the Shrew*, Haymarket, 1844.

The season 1846–47 was signalised, by the return to the stage of that charming woman and actress, Mrs. Nisbett, then Lady Boothby, and for the second time a widow but slenderly provided for.

*   *   *

Her engagement suggested the idea to me of reviving *The Taming of the Shrew*, not in the miserable, mutilated form in which it is acted under the title of *Katherine and Petruchio*, but in its integrity, with the Induction, in which I felt satisfied that excellent actor Strickland would, as Christopher Sly, produce a great effect. It also occurred to me to try the experiment of producing the piece with only two scenes—1. The outside of the little ale-house on a heath, from which the drunken tinker is ejected by the hostess, and where he is found asleep in front of the door by the nobleman and his huntsmen; and, 2. The nobleman's bedchamber, in which the strolling players should act the comedy, as they would have done in Shakespeare's own time under similar circumstances—viz., without scenery, and merely affixing written placards to the wall of the apartment to inform the audience that the action is passing 'in a public place in Padua,'—'a room in Baptista's house,'—'a public road,' etc.

Mr. Webster, to whom of course I proposed this arrangement, sanctioned it without hesitation. I prepared the comedy for representation, gave the necessary instructions for painting the two scenes, and made the designs for the dresses. One difficulty was to be surmounted. How was the play to be finished? Schlegel says that the part 'in which the tinker, in his new state, again drinks himself out of his senses, and is transformed in his sleep into his former condition, from some accident or other, is lost.' Mr. Charles Knight observes upon this: 'We doubt whether it was ever produced, and whether Shakespeare did not exhibit his usual judgment in letting the curtain drop upon honest Christopher, when his wish was accomplished, at the close of the comedy, which he had expressed very early in its progress—

''Tis a very excellent piece of work, Madame Lady—would't were done.'

Had Shakespeare brought him again on the scene in all the richness of his first exhibition, perhaps the patience of the audience would never have allowed them to sit through the lessons of 'the taming school.' We have had farces enough *founded* upon the legend of Christopher Sly, but no one has ever ventured to *continue* him. I was the last person who would have

74

been guilty of such presumption, but after studying the play carefully, I hit upon the following expedient—Sly was seated in a great chair in the first entrance, o. p., to witness the performance of the comedy. At the end of each act no drop scene came down, but music was played while the servants brought the bewildered tinker wine and refreshments, which he partook of freely. During the fifth act he appeared to fall gradually into a heavy drunken stupor, and when the last line of the play was spoken, the actors made their usual bow, and the nobleman, advancing and making a sign to his domestics, they lifted Sly out of his chair, and as they bore him to the door, the curtain descended slowly upon the picture. Not a word was uttered, and the termination, which Schlegel supposes to have been lost, was *indicated* by the simple movement of the *dramatis personæ*, without any attempt to *continue* the subject.

The revival was eminently successful, incontestably proving that a good play, well acted, will carry the audience along with it, unassisted by scenery; and in this case also, remember, it was a comedy in *five* acts, without the curtain once falling during its performance.

No such Katherine as Mrs. Nisbett had been seen since Mrs. Charles Kemble had acted it in the pride of her youth and beauty. Strickland justified all my expectations. As powerful and unctuous as Munden, without the exaggeration of which that glorious old comedian was occasionally guilty. Buckstone was perfectly at home in Grumio, and Webster, although the part was not in his line, acted Petruchio like an artist, as he acts everything.

Of the 'Induction', which had been for so many years neglected, that intelligent critic, Charles Knight, says: 'We scarcely know how to speak without appearing hyperbolical in our praise. It is to us one of the most precious gems in Shakespeare's casket. If we apply ourselves to compare it carefully with the earlier Induction upon which Shakespeare formed it, and with the best of the dramatic poetry of his contemporaries, we shall in some degree obtain a conception not only of the qualities in which he equalled and excelled the highest things of other men, and in which he could be measured with them, but of those wonderful endowments in which he differed from all other men, and to which no standard of comparison can be applied.' My restoration of this 'gem' is one of the events in my theatrical career on which I look back with the greatest pride and gratification.

J. R. Planché, Recollections and Reflections

Phelps as Sly[1]

December 6 [1856].—The 'Induction' to the *Taming of the Shrew* enables Mr. Phelps to represent, in Christopher Sly, Shakespeare's sketch of a man purely sensual and animal, brutish in appetite, and with a mind unleavened by fancy. Such a presentment would not suit the uses of the poet; it could excite only disgust; if it were not throughout as humorous as faithful. Mr. Phelps knows this; and perhaps the most interesting point to be noted in his Christopher Sly is that the uncompromising truth of his portraiture of the man buried and lost in his animal nature is throughout, by subtle touches easy to appreciate but hard to follow, made subservient to the laws of art, and the sketch, too, is clearly the more accurate for being humorous: throughout we laugh and understand.

Hamlet and Christopher Sly are at the two ends of Shakespeare's list of characters, and, with a singular skill, Mr. Phelps, who is the best Hamlet now upon the stage, banishes from his face every spark of intelligence while representing Sly. Partly he effects this by keeping the eyes out of court as witnesses of intelligence. The lids are drooped in the heavy slumberousness of a stupid nature; there is no such thing as a glance of intelligence allowed to escape from under them; the eyes are hidden almost entirely when they are not widely exposed in a stupid stare. The acting of this little sketch is, indeed, throughout most careful and elaborate. There is, as we have said, no flinching from the perfect and emphatical expression of the broader lights and shadows of the character. Christopher is, at first, sensually drunk; and when, after his awakening in the lord's house, the page is introduced to him as his lady-wife, another chord of sensuality is touched, the brute hugs, and becomes amorous. Of the imagination that, even when there are offered to the sensual body new delights of the appetite, is yet unable to soar beyond the reach already attained, Mr. Phelps, in the details of his acting, gives a variety of well-conceived suggestions. Thus, to the invitation, 'Will't please your mightiness to wash your hands?' Christopher, when he has grasped the fact that a basin is being held before him in which he must wash, enters upon such a wash as sooty hands of tinkers only can require, and, having made an end of washing and bespattering, lifts up instinctively the corner of his velvet robe to dry his hands upon.

---

[1] Samuel Phelps (1804–78) was an actor of great versatility who, as manager of Sadler's Wells for twenty years from 1843 presented authentic versions of most of Shakespeare's plays.

The stupidity of Sly causes his disappearance from the stage in the most natural way after the play itself has warmed into full action. He has, of course, no fancy for it, is unable to follow it, stares at it, and falls asleep over it. The sport of imagination acts upon him as a sleeping-draught, and at the end of the first act he is so fast asleep that it becomes matter of course to carry him away. The *Induction* thus insensibly fades into the play, and all trace of it is lost by the time that a lively interest in the comedy itself has been excited.

Henry Morley, *Journal of a London Playgoer*

Shakespeare to Daly

A light-hearted communication on the occasion of Daly's New York production of the play.

Empyrean Depths,
Ye 14th daye of Aprille,
(Newe Style), 1887.

My Dear Frende Dalye:

Inne company with my goode frende Baconne—who you maye rememberre as ye author of my playes—I occupied on yester e'en a front seat atte the One Hundredth performance of 'Ye Taming of ye Shrew' in youre most charmyng playhouse. I wolde we had so coole a place to sitte in for alle tyme.

Egad, I never knew I wrote so well, and Baconne, e'en that sour, crusty philosopher, did clappe his crumblyng fingerres till ye duste did fly from out them whenne ye curtaine fell upon act ye first.

Inne act ye seconde ye scenes did so affect me that in ye spirit I didde yelle for joy, and Baconne, too, did rolle his eyes as if ye Deville didde possesse him, and crying all ye time 'Ye gods, whatte chayres!'

The temper of ye Rehanne, deare frende, did make me gladde, and when ye Dreher walked uponne ye stage, Baconne did ask that I shulde pinche hym, lest it be a dream.

I always thought that Curtis was a man, but now that Madame Gilbert takes his lines, I'm gladde his sex is changed.

And Drewe! Ah, me! why had we not this buoyant, gladsome youth in olden tyme, with Skinner for ye Florentine, and roaryng Lewis, that our sides shulde ache for laughing!

Ah, Sir Dalye! would that we two had walked togetherre in ye dayes of good Queen Bess. How we had made thyngs humme! Ye starres! what wealth, what honours had been ours had not

77

the centuries come between us, and what greater immortality had been mine when shared with you!

I give you joy, deare frende—ay, benefactor; and in ye language of ye market place, I pray you 'Keepe it uppe!'

Thine ever, with affecsyon and gratitude,

WM. SHAKESPEARE.

P.S.—Baconne, who never yet did care for ye 'Taming of ye Shrew,' nowe claimes its authorshippe.

Life 21 April, 1887 (U.S.A.)

The Two Gentlemen of Verona

SINCE this is one of Shakespeare's early plays and one not much in critical favour, actors and producers have taken greater liberties with it than with most others. Garrick's production was of an 'improvement' by Benjamin Victor which shared the stage with Shakespeare's own play for the next fifty years. Macready, Charles Kean and Samuel Phelps all produced the play in Shakespeare's version without much success.

Shakespeare for all Seasons

This production of The Two Gentlemen *at Covent Garden had not only a pageant of the four seasons but Cleopatra's galley as well as assorted mythical personages. Frederick Reynolds (1764–1841) who wrote some 100 plays of his own, found time to ruin several of Shakespeare's, including this one, by adding his own very blank verse.*

Nov. 29 [1821]. '*The Two Gentlemen of Verona,*' was this evening revived with an abundance of music, splendid scenery, and surpassing machinery. Whether this perversion of Shakespeare into melo-drame have 'nothing of offence in it,' may be a question; but if the offence could be palliated, it must be in the case of the present play, one the feeblest and most incomplete of all the hasty works of it's great author; so much so indeed, as to have been doubted by many competent judges, if it were really his. The love of Valentine, and the inconstancy of

78

Proteus; the lofty resolution of Sylvia, and the gentle constancy of Julia, were to-night embellished with illuminated palaces and triumphant galleys; catches and glees in forests, and a blazing mountain! The first three acts were dull, with the occasional exhilaration of songs by Miss Tree and Miss Hallande; but in the fourth, the Carnival was displayed in more than its customary glories. The opening of the scene displayed the Ducal Palace and great square of Milan illuminated, golden gondolas on the river, and all the usual appendages of a foreign gala, masquers, dancing girls, and mountebanks. The pageant then commenced, with a display of the Seasons. Spring came enthroned on a pile of unblown flowers, which the nymph touched with her wand, and the buds were turned into blooms. Then came Summer in the midst of corn, which grew into golden heads at her touch. Autumn followed, with a similar conversion of leaves and stems into melting grapes and blushing apples, and Winter closed the pomp by a view of Lapland with a shower of snow; while dancing nymphs, reapers, and shivering Laplanders, filled up the intervals. Next came the elements, Earth moved on in majesty, seated in a car drawn by lions over clouds; and Air was a portrait of Juno, attended by her peacocks.— Fire had Vulcan in his forge, illuminated by showers of his own sparks; and Water was green robed, with a pair of pigmies sounding Conch shells, and seated upon Dolphins. The stage was then suddenly invaded by water, and on it's bosom rolled Cleopatra's galley, covered with silks and gilding. The Queen lay classically sofa'd upon the deck, and the Nymphs and Cupids flew and fanned about her with picturesque fidelity. This was followed by a splendid scene of the Palace of Pleasure, all gaiety and glory, which was also succeeded by a view in the Duke's gardens, with a lake, a castle, a bridge, and an artificial mountain reaching to the clouds, the explosion of which discovered a gorgeous Temple of Apollo, rich in all that is bright and brilliant; and dazzling the spectators until the drop scene covered the catastrophe. The applause which had before been most lavish, rose to enthusiasm at this spectacle, which it is but justice to say, was most magnificent. Its only fault being its too great length, which has been since remedied.

There was also rather too much music in the Play; and of this the two glees harmonized from If o'er the cruel Tyrant Love, and Pray Goody, were the most popular. Sylvia's songs, were, however, also clever compositions, and Julia's duet with Master Longhurst, displayed both to much advantage.

Jones, who bore the character which, we believe, was once

79

played by John Kemble, threw much spirit into the true lover, and bold outlaw, Valentine. Abbott played Proteus very ably, and Farren's Sir Thurio was the 'high fantastical,' both in his acting and his dress. Liston was a good Launce, and his dog Crab was a fine quiet animal of the Newfoundland breed, which bore much pulling about the stage with much equanimity. Miss Tree performed and sang most sweetly as Julia, but was tasked by too many songs, and Miss Hallande both sang and acted extremely well as Sylvia. We have spoken of the general preparation of the play, which was most costly and striking; and though something more than either song or scenery is essential to continued popularity, '*The Two Gentlemen of Verona*,' we think, discovers all the longevity, that the managers could reasonably anticipate, for its lavish expense well deserves public remuneration. The whole play is very materially transposed and altered from the original, and many of the scenes display Mr. Reynolds's blank verse in company with Shakespeare's. — What will the sterner race of critics say to this?

European Magazine

A Very Palpable Hit[1]

DEC. 6 [1821]. '*The Two Gentlemen of Verona*' had this evening rather a tragical denouement, from an accidental wound given to Mr. Abbott as Sir Proteus while fencing in the banditti scene at the close of the fifth act. From the piercing shriek of Mr. A. the injury was at first apprehended to be really dangerous, but was speedily ascertained not to have touched the eye, although the cheek was laid open by Mr. Comer's sword. The audience would not suffer the play to proceed farther, and Mr. Abbott was instantly conveyed home from the theatre in a carriage.

*　　*　　*

DEC. 17. We are equally happy in being enabled to announce the recovery and re-appearance of Mr. Abbott; and the continued success of '*The Two Gentlemen of Verona*.' The injury sustained by Mr. A. having been much less than was at first apprehended, we are gratified in congratulating both himself and the public upon his resumption of his professional exertions this evening. The temporary indisposition of Miss Hallande

---

[1] These two items concern an accident in the theatre during the run of the production described in the previous extract.

since our last notice, introduced a Miss Boyle from Dublin for a few evenings as Sylvia; and also as Zelinda in 'The Slave'; in both which characters she was very favourably received; though she is certainly far more *au fait* as an actress, than a singer. Her compass and power of voice, both appearing to us quite inadequate to sustain the vocal heroines of Covent Garden. The gorgeous spectacle attached to Shakespeare's comedy, continues to attract crowded audiences, and elicit unbounded approbation. So much so, indeed, that when gazing upon Cleopatra's galley, we forget that the Cydnus can have no business at Milan; and that Venetian Carnivals are not even yet naturalised amongst the Milanese. The last scene also by Pugh, of an opening in a forest by moonlight, forms a display of quiet tranquil beauty, that we have never seen exceeded.

European Magazine

Poor Shakespeare!

I have retained Shaw's own title to these extracts from a long and typically caustic review which shows how much better Shaw understood Shakespeare than some of the professional producers of his day. Augustin Daly (1839–99) an American, began life as a theatre critic, then became a producer-manager both in New York and London.

The Two Gentlemen of Verona. Daly's Theatre, 2 July, 1895

The piece founded by Augustin Daly on Shakespeare's *Two Gentlemen of Verona*, to which I looked forward last week, is not exactly a comic opera, though there is plenty of music in it, and not exactly a serpentine dance, though it proceeds under a play of changing coloured lights. It is something more old-fashioned than either: to wit, a vaudeville. And let me hasten to admit that it makes a very pleasant entertainment for those who know no better. Even I, who know a great deal better, as I shall presently demonstrate rather severely, enjoyed myself tolerably. I cannot feel harshly towards a gentleman who works so hard as Mr. Daly does to make Shakespeare presentable: one feels that he loves the bard, and lets him have his way as far as he thinks it good for him. His rearrangement of the scenes of the first two acts is just like him. Shakespeare shows lucidly how Proteus lives with his father (Antonio) in Verona, and loves a lady of that city named Julia. Mr. Daly, by taking the scene in Julia's house between Julia and her maid, and the scene in Antonio's house between Antonio and Proteus, and making them into one scene, convinces the unlettered audience that Proteus and Julia live in the same house with their father Antonio. Further, Shakespeare shows us how Valentine, the other gentleman of Verona, travels from Verona to Milan, the journey being driven into our heads by a comic scene in Verona, in which Valentine's servant is overwhelmed with grief at leaving his parents, and with indignation at the insensibility of his dog to his sorrow, followed presently by another comic scene in Milan in which the same servant is welcomed to the strange city by a fellow-servant. Mr. Daly, however, is ready for Shakespeare on this point too. He just represents the two scenes as occurring in the same place; and immediately the puzzle as to who is who is complicated by a puzzle as to where is where. Thus is the immortal William adapted to the requirements of a nineteenth-century audience.

In preparing the text of his version Mr. Daly has proceeded on the usual principles, altering, transposing, omitting, improving, correcting, and transferring speeches from one character to another. Many of Shakespeare's lines are mere poetry, not to the point, not getting the play along, evidently stuck in because the poet liked to spread himself in verse. On all such unbusinesslike superfluities Mr. Daly is down with his blue pencil. For instance, he relieves us of such stuff as the following, which merely conveys that Valentine loves Silvia, a fact already sufficiently established by the previous dialogue:

'My thoughts do harbor with my Silvia nightly;
    And slaves they are to me, that send them flying:
Oh, could their master come and go as lightly,
    Himself would lodge where senseless they are lying.
My herald thoughts in thy pure bosom rest them,
    While I, their king, that thither them importune,
Do curse the grace that with such grace hath blessed
        them,
    Because myself do want my servant's fortune.
I curse myself, for they are sent by me,
    That they should harbor where their lord would be.'

Slaves indeed are these lines and their like to Mr. Daly, who 'sends them flying' without remorse. But when he comes to passages that a stage manager can understand, his reverence for the bard knows no bounds. The following awkward lines, unnecessary as they are under modern stage conditions, are at any rate not poetic, and are in the nature of police news. Therefore they are piously retained.

'What halloing, and what stir, is this to-day?
These are my mates, that make their wills their law,
Have some unhappy passenger in chase.
They love me well; yet I have much to do,
To keep them from uncivil outrages.
Withdraw thee, Valentine: who's this comes here?'

The perfunctory metrical character of such lines only makes them more ridiculous than they would be in prose. I would cut them out without remorse to make room for all the lines that have nothing to justify their existence except their poetry, their humor, their touches of character—in short, the lines for whose sake the play survives, just as it was for their sake it originally came into existence.

* * *

In those matters in which Mr. Daly has given the rein to his own taste and fancy: that is to say, in scenery, costumes, and music, he is for the most part disabled by a want of real knowledge of the arts concerned. I say for the most part, because his pretty fifteenth-century dresses, though probably inspired rather by Sir Frederic Leighton than by Benozzo Gozzoli, may pass. But the scenery is insufferable. First, for 'a street in Verona' we get a Bath bun colored operatic front cloth with about as much light in it as there is in a studio in Fitzjohn's Avenue in the middle of October. I respectfully invite Mr. Daly to spend his next holiday looking at a real street in Verona, asking his conscience meanwhile whether a manager with eyes in his head and the electric light at his disposal could not advance a step on the Telbin (senior) style.[1] Telbin was an admirable scene painter; but he was limited by the mechanical conditions of gas illumination; and he learnt his technique before the great advance made during the Impressionist movement in the painting of open-air effects, especially of brilliant sunlight. Of that advance Mr. Daly has apparently no conception.

* * *

As to the elaborate set in which Julia makes her first entrance, a glance at it shows how far Mr. Daly prefers the Marble Arch to the loggia of Orcagna. All over the scene we have Renaissance work, in its genteelest stages of decay, held up as the

[1] William Telbin (1813–73) was a scene-painter for Macready at Drury Lane. His son William Lewis (1846–1931) worked for Irving at the Lyceum, among others.

perfection of romantic elegance and beauty.

*　　*　　*

As to the natural objects depicted, I ask whether any man living has ever seen a pale green cypress in Verona or anywhere else out of a toy Noah's Ark. A man who, having once seen cypresses and felt their presence in a north Italian landscape, paints them lettuce color, must be suffering either from madness, malice, or a theory of how nature should have colored trees, cognate with Mr. Daly's theory of how Shakespeare should have written plays.

Of the music let me speak compassionately. After all, it is only very lately that Mr. Arnold Dolmetsch, by playing fifteenth-century music on fifteenth-century instruments, has shown us that the age of beauty was true to itself in music as in pictures and armor and costumes. But what should Mr. Daly know of this, educated as he no doubt was to believe that the court of Denmark should always enter in the first act of *Hamlet* to the march from 'Judas Maccabæus?' Schubert's setting of 'Who is Silvia?' he knew, but had rashly used up in *Twelfth Night* as 'Who's Olivia.' He has therefore had to fall back on another modern setting, almost supernaturally devoid of any particular merit. Besides this, all through the drama the most horribly common music repeatedly breaks out on the slightest pretext or on no pretext at all. One dance, set to a crude old English popular tune, sundry eighteenth- and nineteenth-century musical banalities, and a titivated plantation melody in the first act which produces an indescribably atrocious effect by coming in behind the scenes as a sort of coda to Julia's curtain speech, all turn the play, as I have said, into a vaudeville. Needless to add, the accompaniments are not played on lutes and viols, but by the orchestra and a guitar or two. In the forest scene the outlaws begin to act by a chorus. After their encounter with Valentine they go off the stage singing the refrain exactly in the style of 'La Fille de Madame Angot.' The wanton absurdity of introducing this comic opera convention is presently eclipsed by a thunderstorm, immediately after which Valentine enters and delivers his speech sitting down on a bank of moss, as an outlaw in tights naturally would after a terrific shower. Such is the effect of many years of theatrical management on the human brain.

Perhaps the oddest remark I have to make about the performance is that, with all its glaring defects and blunders, it is rather a handsome and elaborate one as such things go.

84

Of the acting I have not much to say. Miss Rehan[1] provided a strong argument in favor of rational dress by looking much better in her page's costume than in that of her own sex; and in the serenade scene, and that of the wooing of Silvia for Proteus, she stirred some feeling into the part, and reminded us of what she was in *Twelfth Night*, where the same situations are fully worked out. For the rest, she moved and spoke with imposing rhythmic grace. That is as much notice as so cheap a part as Julia is worth from an artist who, being absolute mistress of the situation at Daly's theatre, might and should have played Imogen for us instead. The two gentlemen were impersonated by Mr. Worthing and Mr. Craig. Mr. Worthing charged himself with feeling without any particular reference to his lines; and Mr. Craig struck a balance by attending to the meaning of his speeches without taking them at all to heart. Mr. Clarke, as the Duke, was emphatic, and worked up every long speech to a climax in the useful old style; but his tone is harsh, his touch on his consonants coarse, and his accent ugly, all fatal disqualifications for the delivery of Shakespearean verse. The scenes between Launce and his dog brought out the latent silliness and childishness of the audience as Shakespeare's clowning scenes always do: I laugh at them like a yokel myself. Mr. Lewis hardly made the most of them. His style has been formed in modern comedies, where the locutions are so familiar that their meaning is in no danger of being lost by the rapidity of his quaint utterance; but Launce's phraseology is another matter: a few of the funniest lines missed fire because the audience did not catch them. And with all possible allowance for Mr. Daly's blue pencil, I cannot help suspecting that Mr. Lewis's memory was responsible for one or two of his omissions. Still, Mr. Lewis has always his comic force, whether he makes the most or the least of it; so that he cannot fail in such a part as Launce. Miss Maxine Elliot's Silvia was the most considerable performance after Miss Rehan's Julia. The whole company will gain by the substitution on Tuesday next of a much better play, *A Midsummer Night's Dream*, as a basis for Mr. Daly's operations. No doubt he is at this moment, like Mrs. Todgers, 'a dodgin' among the tender bits with a fork, and an eatin' of 'em'; but there is sure to be enough of the original left here and there to repay a visit.

Bernard Shaw—*Dramatic Opinions and Essays*

[1] Ada Rehan (1860–1916), a brilliant American actress who played many Shakespearean roles, got her stage name as a result of a printer's error; her surname was Crehan.

Henry VI,
Parts I, II and III

THERE is a sharp contrast between the popularity of these plays with the audiences of Shakespeare's own day and their comparative neglect since. *Harey the VI* performed by Lord Strange's Men at the Rose Theatre on March 3, 1592 was almost certainly *I Henry VI*, and it was presented fifteen times during the next twelve months. There appears to have been only one revival during the eighteenth century and since then the plays have nearly always been presented as mangled 'adaptations', the best known of which are John Crowne's Restoration version and J. H. Merivale's *Richard, Duke of York,* which Kean performed in 1817. Cibber also ransacked *III Henry VI* for his version of *Richard III.*

Kean's Duke of York

J. H. Merivale's adaptation, derived mainly from the second and third parts of Shakespeare's play. Kean played this at Drury Lane. Edmund Kean (?1787–1833) is perhaps the greatest actor England has ever produced. He combined a tumultuous private life with a meteoric acting career in which he played many of the great Shakespearean roles, excelling in Shylock, which he played for the first time without the traditional red wig, and Othello. Kean's acting inspired some of the finest dramatic criticism ever written, that of William Hazlitt.

On Monday, Dec. 15, [1817] the grand historical play of 'Richard Duke of York,' was performed at this Theatre, being a compilation from Shakespeare's Henry VI.; where the contention between York and Lancaster first bursts forth, until the defeat of the former by the Queen. The piece is overloaded with this mass of incident which bears it down; one plot comes close upon the heels of another, which are chiefly unfolded in narrative. Kean, as the Duke of York, sustained the principal weight of the play; we thought him, in many scenes, unusually great. Maywood personated the King, with judgment and correctness, and gave to the soliloquy, upon the field of battle, a pathos which would have been creditable to an older and more experienced actor. Mrs. Glover, as Queen Margaret, shewed a just conception of the character, Mr. Rae had but little to do in the restricted part of Suffolk, but that little was ably performed, particularly in the parting scene with Margaret, after his banishment had been pronounced by the King. The labours of Oxberry and Harley might be spared in a considerable degree, for neither Jack Cade nor Peter are very amusing characters in the manner they are here introduced, but seem brought in for the purpose only of giving a smack of the original. The 'acting' part of the Piece was well conducted throughout. The dresses were superb, and the performance was well received by a more crowded house than we have witnessed this season.

European Magazine

A Successful Revival[1]

Mr. James Anderson has rendered a service to Shakespearian drama by the restoration of *The Second Part of Henry the Sixth*, which has probably not been performed for more than two hundred and fifty years. It is true that there is but a small portion of it belonging to Shakespeare, the poet having built up his chronicle-play on the basis of two dramas published in 1594 and 1595, which treated of *The Contention of the Two Famous Houses of York and Lancaster*, together with *The True Tragedy of Richard Duke of York, and the good king Henry the Sixth*. The lines contributed by Shakespeare are distinguishable from those he found in the anonymous quartos, and thus we can trace with considerable certainty what share he had in the composition adopted by the players into his collected works. Inferior as the drama before us may be to his other histories, it is yet valuable as showing the condition in which our poet found this species of drama, and may be profitably compared with the two parts of 'Henry the Fourth,' in which Shakespeare brought it to perfection. We have not in this earlier adaptation of his any such comic inventions as Falstaff and his companions, nor indeed any creation of character at all, but a close following of the original chronicle, which, in this instance, is that of Hall, not of Holinshed, as in Shakespeare's other historical plays. We mention these particulars because Mr. Anderson, in an address to the public on his play-bill, claims the work as being altogether

---

[1] In April 1864, Part Two of Henry VI was produced as part of the celebrations connected with the tercentenary of Shakespeare's birth.

87

Shakespeare's, on the authority of the First Folio, and ignores all criticism on the point. Such as it is, he has acted wisely in producing it, particularly as it acts remarkably well, and manifestly excites interest in the audience. The multitude of characters which it comprehends exceeding the natural resources of the theatre, Mr. Anderson has doubled, tripled, and even quadrupled their representation, in the manner which he imagines must have been resorted to by Shakespeare himself when the drama was first produced. Accordingly, he performs the two leading parts himself—the Duke of York and Jack Cade, and sustains both with great animation and spirit. The latter, perhaps, he caricatures a little too much, but there cannot be a doubt of its being a truly vigorous impersonation. Bold and dashing, also, is his performance of the ambitious York, whose part he has strengthened as an acting one by incorporating with it a portion of Warwick's. In this manner it falls to Mr. Anderson's lot to describe the appearance of Duke Humphrey's body after death; and he took advantage of the situation to ensure to himself a remarkable effect, which brought down the plaudits of the house. Much praise is due likewise to other performers, particularly to Mr. Fernandez, who sustained the parts of Suffolk and Alexander Iden. The fight in the garden of the latter between him and Jack Cade was exciting, and Mr. Anderson threw considerable humour into it by indicating the weakness he suffered from a five days' fast, and buckling his belt tighter in order to strengthen himself for the task. He died boldly, like a courageous rebel of the true English type, and won our respect even in his fall. We must not close our notice without commending the Duke Humphrey of Mr. J. O'Sullivan, a new actor, late of Liverpool, who gave to the part a prominence and a force which prove him to possess as much power as skill. The same actor afterwards personated Lord Say, and further confirmed our good opinion. The paralytic infirmity which he assumed stood in decided contrast with the robust strength of the previous character, and, indeed was so marked as strongly to impress us with a sense of the actor's versatility. We cannot extend our praise to the female characters. Miss Pauncefort's Margaret was exceedingly feeble, and Mrs. St.-Henry, as the Duchess of Gloucester, was altogether unequal to the assumption. The getting-up of the drama was admirable; the scenery and costumes being in excellent keeping.

Athenaeum—April 30, 1864

Richard III

THIS has been one of the most popular plays in the Shake-spearean repertory, though for nearly 150 years it was Colley Cibber's adaptation (made by sticking together bits from five of Shakespeare's history plays) which held the stage. On February 20, 1845 Samuel Phelps presented Shakespeare's original play but sixteen years later went back to Cibber's version.

Nearly all the great tragic actors from Burbage to Henry Irving have made their mark as Richard Crookback, not forgetting Mr. Plunkett of Dublin whose début in the role is recorded in one of the following accounts.

An Early Richard

Colley Cibber (1671–1757), playwright, theatre manager, actor, poet laureate and satirical butt of Pope and Fielding, here gives an account of Samuel Sandford, an actor who played Richard on the Restoration stage before Cibber's own altered version drove Shakespeare's original from the stage.

When I first brought Richard the Third (with such alterations as I thought not improper) to the stage, Sandford was engaged in the company then acting under King William's licence in Lincoln's-Inn-Fields; otherwise you cannot but suppose my interest must have offer'd him that part. What encouraged me, therefore, to attempt it myself at the Theatre-Royal, was, that I imagined I knew how Sandford would have spoken every line of it. If therefore, in any part of it, I succeeded, let the merit be given to him. And how far I succeeded in that light, those only can be judges who remember him. In order, therefore, to give you a nearer idea of Sandford, you must give me leave (compell'd as I am to be vain) to tell you, that the late Sir John Vanbrugh, who was an admirer of Sandford, after he had seen me act it, assur'd me, that he never knew any one actor so particularly profit by another, as I had done by Sandford in Richard the Third. 'You have,' said he, 'his very look, gesture, gait, speech, and every motion of him, and have borrow'd them all, only to serve you in that character.' If therefore Sir John

89

Richard the Third, Rowe's edition, 1709.

Vanbrugh's observation was just, they who remember me in
Richard the Third, may have a nearer conception of Sandford
than from all the critical account I can give of him.

Cibber's Apology

Gentleman on Garrick

Francis Gentleman (1728–84) an Irishman, had a varied career as actor, playwright and adapter, but is best-known for his two volumes of dramatic criticism, from which this account of Garrick (who once called him 'a dirty dedicating knave') is taken. Garrick began his acting career with Richard III.

The public have set up Mr. Garrick as a standard of perfection in this laborious, difficult part; and if we consider the essentials, his claim to such distinction will immediately appear indisputable; a very deformed person never rises above, and seldom up to the middle stature; it is generally attended with an acuteness of features and sprightliness of eyes; in these three natural points our Roscius stands unexceptionable; variations of voice, and climax of expression, in both which he stands without an equal; graceful attitudes, nervous action, with a well-regulated spirit, to animate within natural bounds every passage, even from the coldest up to the most inflamed.

Mr. Garrick also preserves a happy medium, and dwindles neither into the buffoon or brute; one, or both of which this character is made by most other performers: 'tis true, there are many passages which have a ludicrous turn, yet we may rest assured, that he who occasions least laughter is most right; in respect of marking particular places with peculiar emphasis, some exceptions may be taken, or doubts raised against every person I have ever seen in the part; however, tracing minute lapses of this kind, which after all may be mere matter of opinion, would occasion too great a digression; I shall therefore only mention three which strike me most; the first is—*I am myself alone*—which words I have heard expressed in a tone of confident exultation, as if he was singularly above the rest of mankind; whereas adverting to his own unhappy composition, it should be uttered with heart-felt discontent; and indeed the three preceding lines, which exclude him from all social intercourse, should be expressive of concern.—The second passage is, where Buckingham solicits Richard for his promise, and Richard meditates, in these lines,

I do remember me, that Henry the sixth
Did prophesy, that Richmond should be king,
When Richmond was a little peevish boy.
'Tis odd—a king—perhaps—

The last line is often spoke without a tone of continuation to the word, *perhaps*, which is most evidently intended; the third place is in these lines,

> Hence, babbling dreams, ye threaten here in vain;
> *Conscience, avaunt*—Richard's himself again.

It is usual to speak this couplet in one continued climax of passion; whereas the two words marked in Italics, should be uttered in a lower tone, expressive of mental agony—Conscience being the constant disturber of his peace, and a great bar to his resolution; the latter part of the line rises to a kind of triumphant exultation, which not only varies, but gives force to the expression.

Francis Gentleman— The Dramatic Censor 1770

A Royal Comment

The occasion was Garrick's Chinese Festival which roused opposition because he imported a number of French dancers at a time when anti-French feeling was running high in England. The monarch in question is George I and the anecdote is told by Garrick's first biographer Thomas Davies, an unsuccessful actor (1712–85) who also produced two volumes of Dramatic Miscellanies.

The play commanded by His Majesty on this occasion was *Richard the Third*. After the performance Mr. Fitzherbert, father of the present Lord St. Helen's, and who had been in attendance on the Royal Person, went into the green-room, and was eagerly asked by Garrick what His Majesty thought of Richard. 'I can say nothing on that head,' replied Mr. Fitzherbert; 'but when an actor told Richard, "The Mayor of London comes to greet you," the King roused himself; and when Taswell entered buffooning the character, the King exclaimed, "Duke of Grafton, I like that Lord Mayor;" and, when the scene was over, he said again, "Duke of Grafton, that is good Lord Mayor".' Well! but the warlike bustle, the drums and trumpets, and the shouts of soldiers, must have awakened a great military genius. 'I can say nothing of that,' replied Mr. Fitzherbert; 'but when Richard was in Bosworth Field, roaring for a horse, His Majesty said, "Duke of Grafton, will that Lord Mayor not come again?"'

Davies, Life of Garrick

Offending the Audience

George Frederick Cooke (1756–1812), a wayward and often inebriate actor first played Richard at Covent Garden on 31 October, 1800 and was ever afterwards associated with the role; some preferred his portrayal to Kean's. When he died in New York Kean, who greatly admired him, had a monument erected in his memory.

GEORGE FREDERICK COOKE as Richard III, Covent Garden, 1800.

May 11, 1801

At Covent Garden Theatre, *Richard the Third* drew a large audience; with whom Mr. Cooke took a liberty that ought not to pass unnoticed. From what cause we know not; but he by no means afforded satisfaction to the audience; for, beside a negligent manner, he affected so low a tone as often to be scarcely audible. Hence he was several times desired to *speak louder*. At length his temper was soured, and he forgot himself so far as to shew something like contempt toward the quarter from which disapprobation issued; and, after pausing a few moments, he abruptly left the stage near the close of the fourth act, without finishing his speech. This disrespect was very strongly resented when he again appeared, and for a time he was not suffered to proceed. However, having manifested some contrition, the audience were pacified, and he went through the rest of the character without interruption.

If Mr. Cooke wishes to preserve any degree of estimation with the audiences of London, he will most carefully curb his temper. The unbounded liberality with which they encourage and reward histrionic merit entitles them at all times to respectful behaviour: and, without some care in this point, Mr. Cooke *may* raise a prejudice in the public mind, that talents *even great as his* will not be sufficient easily to remove.

European Magazine

Bottles on Bosworth Field

Riots in the theatre were fairly frequent, some with apparently greater justification than this.

On the 26th of December, [1801] one of those disgusting scenes of barbarous riot occurred at Covent Garden, originating from the monstrous practice of carrying spirits into the theatre, and generally providing, among the lower orders, for a few hours' entertainment, as if they were to garrison a town besieged. The play was Richard III. The first missile that threatened execution was a *wine glass*. On the entry of Betterton, as Tressel, to Murray, who acted King Henry VI. a *quart bottle* grazed his hat; the actor took it up, and walked off the stage. The indignation of the audience burst out against the villain, who was, after an obstinate resistance, secured where he sat, in the front row of the two-shilling gallery, on the King's side. Some very unlucky alterations in the performances, from indisposition, kept up the Saturnalian licence of the rabble, and the trumpets, and the shouts of Bosworth Field, could not be heard. The actors became a sort of Shrove Tuesday sport to these brutes; and they enjoyed and prolonged the agile feats of

Emery, who jumped away with singular misery, from the various *throws* at him, consisting of all the apples and oranges supplied by the fruit women. Something like this occurs in international warfare, and the merchant profitably supplies the enemy with ammunition, to be used against his country.

The farce was hurried over; the ladies would not, at last, come upon the stage; the pit took part in the tumult; the lights were extinguished, and the benches were becoming unseated, when Brandon, at the head of a few remaining soldiers, with their bayonets fixed, about *five* guardsmen, on a sudden appeared in the gallery. The glittering steel had a very calming effect upon the mischievous, and this cruel and dastardly mob slunk away in haste out of the theatre, then nearly quite dark.

James Boaden, Life of Kemble

A Letter from Elia

Charles Lamb wrote this letter to Robert Lloyd on June 26, 1801. On January 8 the following year the Morning Post *carried a longer account of Cooke in this part by Lamb.*

Cooke in *Richard the Third* is a perfect caricature. He gives you the *monster* Richard, but not the *man* Richard. Shakspeare's bloody character impresses you with awe and deep admiration of his witty parts, his consummate hypocrisy, and indefatigable prosecution of purpose. You despise, detest, and loathe the cunning, vulgar, low and fierce Richard, which Cooke substitutes in his place. He gives you no other idea than of a vulgar villain, rejoicing in his being able to overreach, and not possessing that joy in *silent* consciousness, but betraying it, like a *poor* villain, in sneers and distortions of the face, like a droll at a country fair; not to add that cunning so self-betraying and manner so vulgar could never have deceived the politic Buckingham nor the soft Lady Anne: *both* bred in courts, would have turned with disgust from such a fellow. Not but Cooke has *powers*; but not of discrimination. His manner is strong, coarse, and vigorous, and well adapted to some characters. But the lofty imagery and high sentiments and high passions of *Poetry* come black and prose-smoked from his prose Lips.

*   *   *

I want to have your opinion and Plumstead's[1] on Cooke's

[1] Plumstead was Lloyd's brother.

Richard the Third. I am possessed with an admiration of the genuine Richard, his genius, and his mounting spirit, which no consideration of his cruelties can depress. Shakspeare has not made Richard so black a Monster as is supposed. Wherever he is monstrous, it was to conform to vulgar opinion. But he is generally a Man. Read his most exquisite address to the Widowed Queen to court her daughter for him—the topics of maternal feeling, of a deep knowledge of the heart, are such as no monster could have supplied. Richard must have *felt* before he could feign so well; tho' ambition choked the good seed. I think it the most finished piece of Eloquence in the world; of *persuasive* oratory far above Demosthenes, Burke, or any man, far exceeding the courtship of Lady Anne. *Her* relenting is barely natural, after all; the more perhaps S.'s merit to make *impossible* appear *probable*, but the *Queen's consent* (taking in all the circumstances and topics, *private* and *public*, with his angelic address, able to draw the host of [piece cut out of letter] Lucifer) is *probable*; and [piece cut out of letter] resisted it. This observation applies to many other parts. All the inconsistency is, that Shakespeare's better genius was forced to struggle against the prejudices which made a monster of Richard. He set out to paint a *monster*, but his human sympathies produced a *man*.

Are you not tired with all this *ingenious* criticism? I am.

Richard itself is totally metamorphosed in the wretched *acting play* of that name, which you will see, altered by *Cibber.*

God bless you.

C. Lamb

Macready sees Kean

In 1815 Macready and his father, a provincial theatre manager saw Edmund Kean as Richard III at Drury Lane. William Charles Macready (1793–1873) one of the finest Shakespearean actors England has produced, was also responsible for several efforts to restore more of Shakespeare's text to the stage than had hitherto been heard. His Reminiscences and Diaries *present an intelligent and highly self-critical mind relentlessly bending itself to the discipline of acting, a profession he embarked upon with reluctance and gave up with relief after a long and distinguished career.*

My father and self were betimes in our box. Pope was the lachrymose and rather tedious performer of Henry VI. But when the scene changed, and a little keenly-visaged man

EDMUND KEAN as Richard III, Drury Lane, 1814 (from a painting by G. Clint).

rapidly bustled across the stage, I felt there was meaning in the alertness of his manner and the quickness of his step. As the play proceeded I became more and more satisfied that there was a mind of no common order. In his angry complaining of Nature's injustice to his bodily imperfections, as he uttered the line, 'To shrink my arm up like a withered shrub,' he remained looking on the limb for some moments with a sort of bitter discontent, and then struck it back in angry disgust. My father, who sat behind me, touched me, and whispered 'It's very poor!' 'Oh no!' I replied, 'it is no common thing,' for I found myself stretching over the box to observe him. The scene with Lady Anne was entered on with evident confidence, and was well sustained, in the affected earnestness of penitence, to its successful close. In tempting Buckingham to the murder of the children, he did not impress me as Cooke was wont to do, in whom the sense of the crime was apparent in the gloomy hesitation with which he gave reluctant utterance to the deed of blood. Kean's manner was consistent with his conception, proposing their death as a political necessity, and sharply requiring it as a business to be done. The two actors were equally effective in their respective views of the unscrupulous tyrant; but leaving to Cooke the more prosaic version of Cibber, it would have been desirable to have seen the energy and restless activity of Kean giving life to racy language and scenes of direct and varied agency in the genuine tragedy with which his whole manner and appearance were so much more in harmony. In his studied mode of delivering the passages 'Well! as you guess?'

97

and 'Off with his head! So much for Buckingham!' he could not approach the searching sarcastic incredulity, or the rich vindictive chuckle of Cooke; but in the bearing of the man throughout, as the intriguer, the tyrant, and the warrior, he seemed never to relax the ardour of his pursuit, presenting the life of the usurper as one unbroken whole, and closing it with a death picturesquely and poetically grand. Many of the Kemble school resisted conviction in his merits, but the fact that he made me feel was an argument to enrol me with the majority on the indisputable genius he displayed.

Macready's *Reminiscences*

A Gentleman Player[1]

[1816] September

Before I left Dublin an announcement appeared in the play-bills of 'Shakespeare's Historical Play of "King Richard III." The Duke of Gloster, by Mr. Plunkett, of this city, who comes before the public for the purpose of giving him a claim at a future period for a benefit in order to relieve the distressed port of Dublin and its vicinity.' The city was all alive with the promise of 'fun' which this notification held out. Mr. Plunkett was a gentleman, a barrister of the Four Courts without practice, and nearly related to Lord Fingall; but was said to have—what the Scotch call—'a bee in his bonnet.' Unlike his vulgar contemporary Coates,[2] his motives were disinterested and amiable, and his sacrifices in behalf of charity would have been without parallel could he but have known how superlatively ludicrous were his efforts in its cause. The audience that crowded the theatre were in fits of laughter from the beginning to the end, the wags in pit and gallery taking part in the dialogue. When he said in Gloster's soliloquy, 'Why, I can smile, and murder while I smile,' the response from the pit was, 'Oh! by the powers, you can!' To his question, 'Am I then a man to be beloved?' voices answered, 'Indeed, then, you are not!' At 'Off with his head!' the encore was long continued, and at the death the shouts of laughter and ironical 'bravos' drowned the remainder of the tragedy; but so satisfied was he of his triumphant success, that the next morning he called on the Lord Chief Justice Bushe to learn his opinion, and understanding that he had been unable to

[1] This episode occurred, according to Macready, in Dublin in 1816.

[2] See p. 195.

visit the theatre, Plunkett begged leave to act some of Richard's speeches before him, which, to the great annoyance of the Chief Justice, who feared the gathering of a mob about the windows, he did, and pressed the venerable judge for his verdict. The Chief Justice had no escape but in assuring him 'that he had never seen anything like it in all the performances he had ever witnessed:' which sentence, as that of the Chief Justice, Plunkett sent to the papers the next day. He was too estimable and kind-hearted a man not to excite regret in many that he should have been under such a delusion in respect to his theatrical powers.

Macready's Reminiscences

A View from Inside—

Macready's own account of how he played Richard III for the first time.

For Richard my figure was ill adapted; and there was in threatening array against me the prejudice of partisans, and the prepossession of the town in favour of Kean's admirable performance, which would denounce as presumptuous my short-comings, and thus retard my progress, if not sink me permanently in the estimation of those who had hitherto upheld me. I shrank from the perilous attempt with most determinate repugnance.

*   *   *

But the question was decided for me. On Tuesday morning, October 19th, on my way to Reynolds' house, where Mr. Harris resided when in London, to my consternation I read in the Covent Garden playbills the announcement for the following Monday of 'The historical tragedy of "King Richard III." The Duke of Gloster by Mr. Macready: his first appearance in that character.' It was with a sickening sinking of the heart I turned back to my lodgings. There was now no escape! I was committed to the public, and must undergo the ordeal. No alternative was left me but to put on, in Hamlet's phrase, a 'compelled valour,' and devote my energies of mind and body to the task before me.

*   *   *

The night of trial came (October 25th, 1819), to which I might truly apply Shakespeare's words:

'This is the night
That either makes me, or fordoes me quite.'

A crowded house testified to the public interest in the result.

99

The pit was literally jammed. The audience were evidently in a very excited state. The scene had scarcely changed to that of the White Tower, in which Gloster makes his entrance, when the applause broke out in anticipation of my appearance. This, which was intended to cheer me, rather tended to increase my nervousness. It was, however, to me like a life-and-death grapple, and I threw my whole soul into all I did. My auditors followed the early scenes with the deepest interest, frequently seizing opportunities to applaud. A friendly whisper, 'It's all going well!' from Terry, who acted Buckingham, was better than music in my ear. At the repulse of Buckingham, 'I'm busy; thou troublest me! I'm not i' the vein,' the plaudits were sudden and hearty, and loud and long; but it was in the succeeding scene that the fortune of the night was decided. At the close of the compunctious soliloquy that Cibber has introduced Tyrrel enters: with all the eagerness of fevered impatience I rushed to him, inquiring of him in short, broken sentences the children's fate; with rapid decision on the mode of disposing of them, hastily gave him his orders, and hurrying him away, exclaimed with triumphant exultation, 'Why then my loudest fears are hushed!' The pit rose to a man, and continued waving hats and handkerchiefs in a perfect tempest of applause for some minutes. The battle was won! The excitement of the audience was maintained at fever-heat through the remainder of the tragedy. The tent-scene closed with acclamations, that drowned the concluding couplet, and at the death the pit rose again with one accord, waving their hats with long-continued cheers; nor with the fall of the curtain did the display of enthusiasm relax. Connor, who played Tyrrel, the actor appointed, was not allowed to give out the play, and the practice was this evening first introduced at Covent Garden of 'calling on' the principal actor. In obedience to the impatient and persevering summons of the house, I was desired by Fawcett to go before the curtain; and accordingly I announced the tragedy for repetition, amidst the gratulating shouts that carried the assurance of complete success to my agitated and grateful heart.

Macready's Reminiscences

—And Out

The Morning Chronicle's *review of the same performance, which Macready felt described best 'the predicament in which failure would have placed me'.*

Last night was a most important one in the dramatic life of Mr. Macready. He undertook for the first time the character of Richard the Third, in Shakespeare's celebrated tragedy. The effort was hazardous in the highest degree: a failure must have stamped it as presumptuous, and in the present temper of the public mind, warm and enthusiastic as it is in admiration of Mr. Kean's admirable performance, there was no middle point between disgrace and glory. Mr. Macready's professional reputation was, in fact, at stake; he has saved and established it upon higher grounds than ever. His Richard was perfectly original; yet there was no apparent struggle after originality, no laborious effort to mark a difference in passages of small importance—the expedient of little minds to escape from their proper sphere of imitation. It was the natural unforced and unaffected effort of an intellect relying on its own powers, and making its own way undisturbed either by the wish or the apprehension of borrowing from any one. The performance had of course its unevenness. In some of the commencing scenes it was rather tame, but its distinguishing feature was that of rising in impression as the play advanced, a task which not only required the strongest mental qualifications, but such physical ones as perhaps no other actor on the stage possesses. This circumstance of itself contributed in no small degree to assist that air of novelty which certainly pervaded the whole. We found those parts which some of our most popular Richards have been obliged to slur over, from mere exhaustion, brought into prominent display. His voice, instead of suffering, seemed to acquire strength as he proceeded, and, strange to say, in a part of such exertion, was not only as audible, but as much at his command in all its tones and modulations, in the very last scene as in that which commenced his arduous task. It would be impossible, according to our present limits, to notice the various merits which an enlightened audience caught at and applauded; but justice requires that we should name a few. His courtship of Lady Anne, though by no means the most successful of his scenes, is, nevertheless, deserving of particular mention for one reason. That reason is, that it was conducted in a spirit of assumed sincerity, and with a total disregard of those sarcastic touches which tell so well in the acting, while they detract from the consistency of Richard's dissimulation. The first burst of applause, which gave an indication of complete success, was that excited by the scene in the Tower, while the assassins are murdering the children. His hurried directions for the disposal of the bodies was tragical in an eminent degree. The tent-scene was another fine display. His impetuosity and resolution, his momentary compunction and rapid recovery, were all marked in the different scenes with extraordinary fidelity and vigour. His death was also managed with the best effect; and we may say of the whole, that though we were prepared to expect much from his talents, we did not expect so much as their display impressed us with on the occasion of which we are speaking. After the conclusion of the play he was called for to announce the repetition of it himself, which he did according to the summons of the audience; and there can be but little doubt that his exertions in the part will prove attractive for a considerable time. We have studiously avoided all comparisons with another great performer of the day. It is not necessary to the reputation of either that the other should be depreciated; or if it is, we decline the ungrateful office, in respect to the public and to ourselves.

Morning Chronicle, October 26, 1819

The Younger Kean

Charles Kean (1811–68) was generally acknowledged to be a less powerful actor than his great father, but made a name for himself with his lavish and spectacular Shakespearean productions at the Princess Theatre in the 1850s. George Henry Lewes (1817–78) companion of George Eliot and a distinguished Victorian literary figure, wrote plays and dramatic criticism, in addition to acting in Shakespearean plays in an amateur group associated with Charles Dickens. (See p. 149.)

Charles Kean cannot deliver a passage with musical effect. The stubborn harshness of the voice, and the mechanicalness of his elocution, spoil even his best efforts. The tones of his father vibrate still in the memories of those who years ago trembled deliciously beneath their influence; and render even pathetic phrases powerless when spoken by his successors, because the successors cannot utter them with such 'ravishing division.' When Charles Kean as Richard delivers the speech—

Now is the winter of our discontent

no one notices it; but who can ever forget his father's look and voice? Who can forget the thrilling effect of the rich deep note upon 'buried,' when with the graceful curl of the wrist he indicated how the clouds which lowered round his head were in the deep bosom of the ocean buried?

G. H. Lewes *On Actors and the Art of Acting*

Not Suitable for Children

The four Bateman girls, daughters of the manager of the Lyceum Theatre before Irving, began their stage careers in adult parts when they were between four and eight years old. They began in America and made their English début in 1851.

KATE BATEMAN as Richmond, and ELLEN BATEMAN as Richard III, St. James's Theatre, 1851.

1851. August 30.—The discriminating Mr. Barnum has had reason to think that the English taste turns very much upon small things; and he now challenges for two miniature actors the success that attended his Tom Thumb. The 'Bateman children' are little girls respectively of eight and six, who are both pretty and clever, but whose appearance in an act of *Richard the Third* (at the St. James's Theatre) is a nuisance by no means proportioned to the size of its perpetrators. No doubt there is talent shown in it; and it is curious to hear such small imps of the nursery speak so fluently, and, strutting about easily, repeat a well-taught lesson with such wonderful aptitude. But this is the feeling of a moment, and nothing is left but the wearisome absurdity of such big words in such little mouths.

Henry Morley, *Journal of a London Playgoer*

Henry James on Henry Irving

Sir Henry Irving's Richard III. is not his first playing of the
part, but it is his first presentation of the piece. Upwards of
twenty years ago it was produced at the Lyceum by the management immediately preceding his own, and was then one of the
successes which presumably determined him to take over the
theatre from failing hands. His Richard of those days, as I remember it, strikingly showed his gifts, but he has had the artistic
patience, all these years, to leave the character alone. His gifts
have not changed, though they have visibly developed, and his
power to use them has matured. His present creation has the
benefit of this maturity, though I seem to remember that even
the earlier one, when so much of his reputation was still to come,
had that element of 'authority' which is a note by itself in an
actor's effect, independent of the particular case, and almost as
distinguishable in what he does worst as in what he does best.
What Sir Henry Irving does best, as happens in this instance, is
exactly what he does with Richard—makes, for the setting, a
big, brave general picture, and then, for the figure, plays on the
chord of the sinister-sardonic, flowered over as vividly as may be
with the elegant-grotesque. No figure could have more of this
livid complexion and Gothic angularity than, singly and simply
seen, the monster drawn by Shakespeare. Singly and simply—
in this light—Sir Henry Irving sees him, and makes him, very
obvious yet very distinguished, hold the Lyceum stage with any
of his predecessors. But I confess that, in regard to the whole
matter, the question of the better and the worse, of whether
such a Richard as this is or isn't, in his frank enjoyment of the
joke, a 'comic character,' leaves me cold compared with the
opportunity of testifying afresh to an impression now quite
wearily mature—an acute sense that, after all that has come
and gone, the represented Shakespeare is simply no longer to be
borne. The reason of this impatience is of the clearest—there is
absolutely no representing him. The attempt to make real or
even plausible a loose, violent, straddling romance like *Richard
III*—a chronicle for the market-place, a portrait for the house
wall—only emphasises what is coarse in such a hurly-burly and
does nothing for what is fine. It gives no further lift to the poetry
and adds a mortal heaviness to the prose. The thing suffers (till
it positively howls) from everything to which, in fiction—the
fiction of the theatre or any other—the present general cultiva-
tion of a closer illusion exposes it. The more it is painted and
dressed, the more it is lighted and furnished and solidified, the

less it corresponds or coincides, the less it squares with our imaginative habits. By what extension of the term can such a scene as Richard's wooing of Lady Anne be said to be represented? We can only use the word to mean that Sir Henry Irving shows his experience and his art. It leaves us doggedly defying any actress whatever to give a touch of truth, either for woe or for weal, to the other figure of the situation—leaves us weltering, at this and at the great majority of the other moments, in a sea of weak allowances from which we at last scramble ashore with (for all spoil of the wreck,) a sore sense that the more Shakespeare is 'built in' the more we are built out.

Henry James—*Harper's Weekly, January 23, 1897*

King John

T H E tradition of giving the role of Arthur to an actress goes back to the earliest recorded performance at Covent Garden in February 1737. Garrick played King John and John Philip Kemble's 1804 production gave his celebrated sister Sarah Siddons one of her most famous roles, that of Constance.

The most notable production of the play was probably by John Kemble's brother Charles at Covent Garden on November 24 1823. In 1852, Charles Kean's production at the Princess' Theatre probably took the passion for historical detail as far as it has ever gone in British theatrical history.

Garrick as King John

To enter into a long criticism upon the several merits of the actors who have represented the last masterly scene between the king and Hubert would be tedious and unprofitable. . . . Here Garrick reigned triumphant: he was greatly superior to them all. His action was more animated; and his quick transitions from one passion to another gave an excellent portrait of the turbulent and distracted mind of John. When Hubert shewed him his warrant for the death of Arthur, saying to him, at the same time,

Here is your hand and seal for what I did,

Garrick snatched the warrant from his hand; and, grasping it hard, in an agony of despair and horror, he threw his eyes to heaven, as if self-convicted of murder, and standing before the great Judge of the quick and dead to answer for the infringement of the divine command!

Davies, Dramatic Miscellanies

Mesentente Cordiale

Before we dismiss this tragedy, permit us to offer a short anecdote related by a gentleman who saw it performed at Portsmouth last war. The French party coming on with white cockades, a zealous tar shouts from the gallery, Harkee, you Mr. Mounseers, strike the white flags out of your nabs, or b— my eyes, but I'll bombard you. A general laugh went through the house, but the actors deeming it merely a transient joke, took no notice; upon which, our enraged son of Neptune gave the word fire, and immediately half a dozen apples flew, which worked the desired effect; three cheers ensued, and this incident diffused such a spirit through the house, that during the rest of the play loud huzza's attended the exits and entrances of King John's party, while King Philip and the Dauphin, notwithstanding the polite removal of their cockades, sustained many rough strokes of sea wit.

Francis Gentleman, The Dramatic Censor (1770)

Kemble's King John

Covent Garden, June 3, 1810[1]

If Mr. Kemble has not succeeded Garrick in all tragic excellence, as some of his admirers pretend, he has worthily succeeded him in one important respect, that of loving Shakspeare and keeping him before the public. The other managers of the present day have so little taste, with the exception of Sheridan who cares for no taste but that of port, that were it not for Mr. Kemble's exertions the tragedies of our glorious bard would almost be in danger of dismissal from the stage; and it does him infinite credit to have persevered in his exertions in spite of comparatively thin houses; to have added to the attractions of his poet by a splendour of scene as seasonable as well-deserved; and to have evinced so noble an attachment, and helped to keep

---

[1] This production was staged every year from 1804 to 1817.

up so noble a taste, in an age of mawkishness and buffoonery. It is in this spirit that Mr. Kemble continues to draw from Shakspeare a kind of stock play for the season, which is performed regularly once a week, as he has done with *Macbeth*, *Hamlet*, and *K. Henry the Eighth*, and is now doing again with *King John*.

* * *

The Constance of Mrs. Siddons is an excellent study for young actresses, to whom it will shew the great though difficult distinction between rant and tragic vehemence. In an inferior performer, the loudness of Constance's grief would be mere noise; but tempered and broken as it is by the natural looks and gestures of Mrs. Siddons, by her varieties of tone and pauses full of meaning, it becomes as grand as it is petrifying. Mr. Kemble's King John, with its theatrical tone of dignity and its mixture of confidence and whining, is one of his happiest performances: in the scene with Hubert he displays much knowledge of effect, and has in particular one excellent expression of the mouth, which, while he is anxiously looking for Hubert's reply to his dark hints, is breathlessly opened and gently dropped at the corners; but there is too much pantomimic rolling of the eyes. Charles Kemble, always elegant, with a chivalrous air, and possessing a strong taste for contemptuous irony, is as complete a Faulconbridge as one can desire. The effect of this and other tragedies of Shakespeare must give Mr. Kemble great satisfaction. Every person, indeed, who has a regard for the spirit and dignity of his country's literature must be gratified to see that these endeavours, founded on so just an enthusiasm, are properly rising in the public estimation. The audience assembled at *King John* last Monday was as numerous and attentive as it was respectable, and you saw what you ought to see in an English theatre—an excellent drama properly performed and properly appreciated.

Leigh Hunt — The Examiner, June 3 1810

Mr. Kemble's King John[1]

Covent Garden, December 8, 1816

We went to see Mr. Kemble's King John, and he became the part so well, in costume, look, and gesture, that if left to

[1] Hazlitt's own title. On this occasion Eliza O'Neill (1791–1872) an Irish actress who achieved fame as Juliet played Constance.

107

SARAH SIDDONS rehearsing with her father, ROGER KEMBLE and JOHN
HENDERSON, 1775 (Thomas Rowlandson).

ourselves, we could have gone to sleep over it, and dreamt that
it was fine, and 'when we waked, have cried to dream again.'
But we were told that it was really fine, as fine as Garrick, as
fine as Mrs. Siddons, as fine as Shakespeare; so we rubbed our
eyes and kept a sharp look out, but we saw nothing but a
deliberate intention on the part of Mr. Kemble to act the part

finely. And so he did in a certain sense, but not by any means as Shakespeare wrote it, nor as it might be played. He did not harrow up the feelings, he did not electrify the sense: he did not enter into the nature of the part himself, nor consequently move others with terror or pity. The introduction to the scene with Hubert was certainly excellent: you saw instantly, and before a syllable was uttered, partly from the change of countenance, and partly from the arrangement of the scene, the purpose which had entered his mind to murder the young prince. But the remainder of this trying scene, though the execution was elaborate—painfully elaborate, and the outline well conceived, wanted the filling up, the true and master touches, the deep piercing heartfelt tones of nature. It was done well and skilfully, *according to the book of arithmetic;* but no more. Mr. Kemble, when he approaches Hubert to sound his disposition, puts on an insidious, insinuating, fawning aspect, and so he ought; but we think it should not be, though it was, that kind of wheedling smile, as if he was going to persuade him that the business he wished him to undertake was a mere jest; and his natural repugnance to it an idle prejudice, that might be carried off by a certain pleasant drollery of eye and manner. Mr. Kemble's look, to our apprehension, was exactly as if he had just caught the eye of some person of his acquaintance in the boxes, and was trying to suppress a rising smile at the metamorphosis he had undergone since dinner.

William Hazlitt, *A View of the English Stage*

A Theatrical Breakthrough

J. R. Planché, who designed the costumes for Charles Kemble's production which opened at Covent Garden on November 24, 1823, describes the audience's reaction.

Never shall I forget the dismay of some of the performers when they looked upon the flat-topped *chapeaux de fer* (*fer blanc*, I confess) of the 12th century, which they irreverently stigmatized as *stewpans!* Nothing but the fact that the classical features of a Kemble were to be surmounted by a precisely similar abomination would, I think, have induced one of the rebellious barons to have appeared in it. They had no faith in me, and sulkily assumed their new and strange habiliments, in the full belief that they should be roared at by the audience. They *were* roared at; but in a much more agreeable way than they had contemplated. When the curtain rose, and discovered King John dressed as his effigy appears in Worcester Cathedral, surrounded by his barons sheathed in mail, with cylindrical helmets and correct armorial shields, and his courtiers in the long tunics and mantles of the thirteenth century, there was a roar of approbation, accompanied by four distinct rounds of applause, so general and so hearty, that the actors were astonished, and I felt amply rewarded for all the trouble, anxiety, and annoyance I had experienced during my labours. Receipts of from £400 to £600 nightly soon reimbursed the management for the expense of the production, and a complete reformation of dramatic costume became from that moment inevitable upon the English stage.

J. R. Planché, *Recollections and Reflections*

A Solid Fragment of History

February 14. [1852] There is not a play of Shakespeare's which more admits or justifies a magnificent arrangement of scene than the chronicle-play of *King John*. Its worthy presentation in an English theatre was one of the triumphs of Mr. Macready's direction of Drury Lane ten years ago, and Mr. Charles Kean now follows that example in his revival of the play at the Princess's with a devotion of care and study as well as a lavish expenditure of scenic resource which is entitled to the highest praise.

So mounted, we see in this play—what the great Marlborough saw nowhere else so satisfactorily—a solid fragment of our English history. We see revived the rude chivalric grandeur of the Middle Age, the woes and wars of a half-barbarous time, in all its reckless splendour, selfish cruelty, and gloomy suffering. In the latter features of the picture the play of *John* stands apart among Shakespeare's regal chronicles. The heart heaves and throbs beneath its coat of mail. It has a state greater than the state of kings, and a throne on which sits a higher sovereign. None of the characters of the tragedy are cast in an unyielding mould. John shrinks appalled and self-abased from the guilt he has designed, the heated iron falls from the hand of Hubert, and even Falconbridge becomes amazed, and fearful he should lose his way among the thorns and dangers of this world. Mad world, mad kings, mad composition—yet, with good and evil blended in all, the many-toned wisdom of humanity vibrates through such history as this.

Mr. Kean plays John with an earnest resolve to make apparent to the audience his mean and vacillating nature, his allegiance to 'that smooth-faced gentleman, tickling Commodity, Commodity, the Bias of the World', and the absence of dignity in his suffering. Mrs. Kean throws all her energy, and much true emotion, into Constance; and in Falconbridge Mr. Wigan makes a more sensible advance than we have yet had to record into the higher region of chivalric comedy. There is a clever child, too, in Arthur, a Miss Terry, and the minor parts are effectively presented.

Henry Morley, Journal of a London Playgoer

Titus Andronicus

THE title pages of the early quarto editions tell us that the play was performed 'sundry times' by the Lord Chamberlain's Men, but the only record before the nineteenth century is in a letter of 1596 an extract from which appears on page 16. There is also an early drawing which may be a scene from a performance but from the Restoration to the nineteenth century the play was performed, if at all, invariably in Ravenscroft's adaptation. Only three nineteenth-century performances are recorded.

Another Noble Moor

Ira Aldridge (c. 1804–67) was an American Negro actor who came to England with Kean and achieved an enormous reputation, particularly on the Continent. He chose Aaron the Moor as a part consistent with his colour, as he had chosen Othello for his London début in 1826. Two reviews of his performance are given here, the first from his London appearance, the next from his provincial tour three years later.

[I] During the past week Mr. Aldridge has appeared as Aaron in *Titus Andronicus*, a part which he has made completely and emphatically his own. *Titus Andronicus* is not a favourite play and we do not know that we ever saw it produced before on any stage. Indeed, as published in the best editions of Shakespeare's works, it would be utterly unfit for presentation, for a more dreadful catalogue of horrors and atrocities, than it consists of would be impossible to conceive . . . In fact, there are numerous internal evidences that the play is not written by Shakespeare, and we are strongly inclined to agree with Malone, Johnson, and others that it is spurious. The *Titus Andronicus* produced under Mr. Aldridge's direction is a wholly different affair; the deflowering of Lavinia, cutting out her tongue, chopping off her hands, and the numerous decapitations and gross language which occur in the original are totally omitted and a play not only presentable but actually attractive is the result.

Aaron is elevated into a noble and lofty character, Tamora, the Queen of Scythia, is a chaste though decidedly strong-minded female, and her connection with the Moor appears to be of a legitimate description; her sons Chiron and Demetrius are dutiful children, obeying the behests of their mother and—what shall we call him?—their 'father-in-law'. Old Titus himself is a model of virtue and the only person whose sanguinary character is not toned down much is Saturninus the Emperor, who retains the impurity of the original throughout. Thus altered, Mr. Aldridge's conception of the part of Aaron is excellent—gentle and impassioned by turns; now burning with jealousy as he doubts the honour of the Queen; anon, fierce with rage as he reflects upon the wrongs which have been done him—the murder of Alarbus and the abduction of his son; and then all tenderness and emotion in the gentle passages with his infant. All these phases of the character Mr. Aldridge delineated with judgement and great force of expression. He thoroughly appreciates the recondite beauties of the author, whenever they exist, and every syllable is uttered with meaning. He rants less than almost any tragedian we know—he makes no vulgar appeal to the gallery, although, at such a house as this,[1] the appeal is a tempting one—he is thoroughly natural, easy and sensible, albeit he has abundance of physique at his command when the exercise of it is required. In a word, he obviously knows what he is at, and there is as little of the 'fustian' about him as there is in anybody on the stage. We are gratified to find that his judicious impersonations appeared to be fully appreciated by the immense audience, whose orderly demeanour and rapt attention during the more thrilling parts of the tragedy were quite remarkable. Mr. Aldridge was ably supported by the rest of the excellent company . . .

The Era, April 26, 1857

[1] The Britannia, Hoxton, noted for melodrama.

[II] It was rather startling to see it announced that *Titus Andronicus* would be represented on the Brighton Stage. Its exhibition seemed impossible. It is too horrible, too revolting for the closet: and put into action could produce no accusation short of loathing. In all the rest of his works Shakespeare has recognised the true limits of tradition: he has dealt with the terrible, but stopped short of the horrible. In *Titus* there is no such restriction. It exhibits a pandemonium in which atrocity succeeds atrocity in which rapine, mutilation, murder are the incidents.

'And horror the soul of the plot'

Whether the accomplished poetic beauties or beauties of any kind were sufficient to render it desirable that such a work should be restored to the modern stage was and it remains so, an open question. Mr. Ira Aldridge tells us that being as a man of colour limited in his repertoire, he was ambitious of adding 'Aaron', the Moor to his list of characters, and therefore 'adapted' *Titus Andronicus* for modern representation. This adaptation we witnessed on Wednesday evening, and we may say that the question as to Shakespeare's tradition did not arise. Mr. Aldridge has not attempted to grapple with the difficulty presented to a modern adaptor: he has not wasted time in puzzling over the Gordian knot. He has cut it. Beyond the title, a few incidents, and some scraps of language, his *Titus* has nothing in common with Shakespeare's.

In point of fact Mr. Aldridge has constructed a melodrama 'of intense interest' of which Aaron is the hero. The character is a strong one and not unsuited to his powers, as was shown by his being twice called before the curtain during the piece. Next to the Moor, the principal part is that of Tamora with which Mrs. W. Daly did her utmost. The same may be said of Mrs. Calvert's impersonation of Lavinia which she succeeded in rendering extremely interesting.

The piece was repeated last evening.

Brighton Gazette, October 4, 1860

Love's Labour's Lost

THIS bright artificial comedy was performed before Queen Elizabeth in 1597 and seems ever since to have appealed only to a minority audience. No performances since Shakespeare's own day are known before Elizabeth Vestris' revival in 1839, and on that occasion the first night was marred by a riot. Eighteen years later Samuel Phelps staged a production which lasted for nine performances.

A First Night Fiasco

The following description of the opening night has been kindly furnished by Mr. James R. Anderson: 'Monday, Sept. 30, 1839, Covent Garden opened with Shakespeare's comedy of 'Love's Labour's Lost.' It was an interesting and a trying selection; for no one, not even the oldest actor in the theatre, had ever seen it performed. The cast was strong, including Robert Keely, Bartley, Meadows, Granby, Cooper, Vining, &c. &c., and myself as Biron; Mesdames Nisbett, Vestris, Charles, Humby, Lee, Rainforth, &c. &c. The scenery, by Grieve and Sons, was beautiful in the extreme; the dresses splendid and appropriate, sketched by Planché; the materials and harmony of colour selected and arranged by Madame Vestris herself. The comedy must have been an immense success, but for one untoward circumstance—an awful mistake in theatrical policy—namely, that of *shutting up the one shilling gallery*, and excluding 'the gods' from their time-honoured benches on high Olympus. The admission to the lower gallery had been reduced to one shilling and sixpence, in the hope to pacify and split the difference. No, sir; this sop to Cerberus could not be swallowed by the incensed deities, who would not be excluded from their old shilling gallery at 'the Garden' at any price. So, on the opening night, the enraged 'gods' filled the lower gallery to suffocation, and the demonstrations of indignation were terrific. The comedy was interrupted, often stopped, and all but 'damned' by the tremendous noise and uproar. At length, after many fruitless attempts to be heard and apologise, a man carrying a placard on a pole gave the malcontents to understand that the shilling gallery should be re-opened the following night. After three hearty cheers from the conquerors, the play was allowed to proceed and finish. This came too late, for the poor play had received its quietus in the very first act. And 'Love's Labour's Lost' appeared a most appropriate title, for it ran only a few nights.'

Charles Dickens (Ed.) *Life of Charles J. Mathews*[1] *1879*

The Comedy of Leisure[2]

Love's Labour's Lost—The Comedy of Leisure—ought to be acceptable as a relief to busy men in anxious times. It has been observed that there is only one morsel of business in the whole play, and that is mentioned to be postponed till to-morrow. The play as now acted at Sadler's Wells[3] runs daintily and pleasantly. They err who see in it only a caricature of euphuism. Euphuism, when the comedy appeared, was a language of compliment congenial to the temper of the times, and in many of its forms, while it was not less absurd than the tone of compliment conventional in our own day, it was a great deal wittier and wiser. There was room for wit in the invention of conceits, and an amusing ingenuity in their extravagance.

'Thou shin'st in every tear that I do weep;
No drop but as a coach doth carry thee.'

Shakespeare undoubtedly took pleasure in this way of frolic with the wit; it is a form of fancy, and over the whole range of fancy he was lord. Pleasant euphuisms find their way even into his graver plays, and in this play, which he devoted to a chasing of conceit through all its forms, the most poetical and the most prosy, it is manifest that he not only heartily enjoyed the sport himself, but that it must have given special pleasure to the men of his own day.

He laughed no doubt at the hollowness of all conceits, and represented them as labour lost, his sharpest satire being expressed in the part of 'Don Adriano de Armado, a fantastical Spaniard'. This is the part assumed at Sadler's Wells by Mr. Phelps.

It has a certain general resemblance to his Malvolio, inasmuch as these are both fantastical and foolish men; but

[1] Charles Mathews (1803–78) married Eliza Vestris (1797–1856); a successful actor–manager team, though this particular production was a failure.

[2] Original title.

[3] October 24, 1857.

Mr. Phelps defines clearly the essential difference between the two. One was a substantial and not ignorant steward, covering with affectations a substantial ambition to become the husband of his rich and beautiful mistress, and to be a lord. The other is a man who carries all his bravery outside. He talks conceitedly of love, and in his soul carries enshrined the image of a country drab, its best ideal. He affects finery of speech, and is so utterly destitute of ideas that to count three he must depend upon the help of a child who is his servant, and his master in all passages of wit. He carries a brave outside of clothes, but cannot fight in his shirt, because, as he is driven to admit, 'the naked truth of it is, I have no shirt'. This is the view of his character to which Mr. Phelps gives prominence by many a clever touch, such as the empty drawl on the word love, whenever Armado uses it, or the lumbering helplessness of wit displayed by the great Spaniard when magnificently and heavily conversing with the tiny Moth, in which part little Miss Rose Williams has been taught to bring out very perfectly some telling points.

We must not part from the play without praising the Biron of Mr. Henry Marston, the clever rendering of the conceits of the Schoolmaster and Curate by Mr. Williams and Mr. C. Fenton, and the Ferdinand of Mr. F. Robinson. Mrs. Charles Young—who is new to London, and has, during the last few weeks, taken honours at Sadler's Wells in two or three characters—looked and spoke like a lady as Princess of France, and Miss Fitzpatrick did fair justice to her talent as the laughing Rosaline.

Henry Morley, *Journal of a London Playgoer*

A Midsummer Night's Dream

T H E play was probably put on for the first time at court in 1595. During the years when the theatres were closed (1642–60) the comic interludes involving Bottom and Co. tended to separate from the main body and develop an independent life of their own under such titles as *The Comedy of Pyramus and Thisbe* and *The Merry Conceits of Bottom the Weaver*

(1646). Pepys as we know (p. 50) thought it 'the most insipid ridiculous play that ever I saw in my life' and operatic versions occupied the stage for nearly two centuries till Elizabeth Vestris and Charles Mathews restored most of Shakespeare's play in 1840. Samuel Phelps scored one of his greatest acting triumphs as Bottom in his Sadler's Wells production in 1853.

Poetry Versus Spectacle

Hazlitt's view that A Midsummer Night's Dream *was too delicate for the stage remained influential for a long time.*

[Covent Garden] January 21, 1816

We have found to our cost, once for all, that the regions of fancy and the boards of Covent-Garden are not the same thing. All that is fine in the play, was lost in the representation. The spirit was evaporated, the genius was fled; but the spectacle was fine: it was that which saved the play. Oh, ye scene-shifters, ye scene-painters, ye machinists and dress-makers, ye manufacturers of moon and stars that give no light, ye musical composers, ye men in the orchestra, fiddlers and trumpeters and players on the double drum and loud bassoon, rejoice! This is your triumph; it is not ours.

*   *   *

All that was good in this piece (except the scenery) was Mr. Liston's Bottom, which was an admirable and judicious piece of acting. Mr. Conway was Theseus. Who would ever have taken this gentleman for the friend and companion of Hercules? Miss Stephens played the part of Hermia, and sang several songs very delightfully,[1] which however by no means assisted the progress or interest of the story. Miss Foote played Helena. She is a very sweet girl, and not at all a bad actress; yet did any one feel or even hear her address to Hermia?

*   *   *

Poetry and the stage do not agree together. The attempt to reconcile them fails not only of effect, but of decorum. The *ideal* has no place upon the stage, which is a picture without perspective; every thing there is in the foreground. That which

[1] Including Handel's 'Hush, ye pretty warbling choir'.

117

is merely an airy shape, a dream, a passing thought, immediately becomes an unmanageable reality. Where all is left to the imagination, every circumstance has an equal chance of being kept in mind, and tells according to the mixed impression of all that has been suggested. But the imagination cannot sufficiently qualify the impressions of the senses. Any offence given to the eye is not to be got rid of by explanation. Thus Bottom's head in the play is a fantastic illusion, produced by magic spells: on the stage it is an ass's head, and nothing more; certainly a very strange costume for a gentleman to appear in. Fancy cannot be represented any more than a simile can be painted; and it is as idle to attempt it as to personate Wall or Moonshine. Fairies are not incredible, but fairies six feet high are so. Monsters are not shocking, if they are seen at a proper distance. When ghosts appear in midday, when apparitions stalk along Cheapside, then may the *Midsummer Night's Dream* be represented at Covent-Garden or at Drury-Lane; for we hear that it is to be brought out there also, and that we have to undergo another crucifixion.

Mrs. Faucit played the part of Titania very well, but for one circumstance—that she is a woman. The only glimpse which we caught of the possibility of acting the imaginary scenes properly, was from the little girl who dances before the fairies (we do not know her name), which seemed to show that the whole might be carried off in the same manner—by a miracle.

William Hazlitt—*A View of the English Stage*

Enter Mendelssohn

This production by Elizabeth Vestris and her husband Charles Mathews was in 1840. Mendelssohn wrote his famous overture for a production in Berlin thirteen years earlier by the great German Shakespearean scholar Ludwig Tieck.

A third important revival was Shakespeare's 'Midsummer Night's Dream' on a scale of great splendour, and for the first time with the overture, wedding march, and other music by Mendelssohn. When this revival was first suggested, Bartley said, 'If Planché can devise a striking effect for the last scene, the play will run for sixty nights.' I pointed out that Shakespere had suggested it himself, in the words of Oberon to his attendant fairies—

'Through the house give glimmering light,

    *   *   *

Every elf and fairy sprite
Hop as light as bird from brier,
And this ditty after me
Sing, and dance it trippingly.'

It was accordingly arranged with Grieve, the scenic artist, who is at this day still adding to his great reputation, that the back of the stage should be so constructed that at the command of Oberon it should be filled with fairies, bearing twinkling coloured lights, 'flitting through the house,' and forming groups and dancing, as indicated in the text, carrying out implicitly the directions of the author, and not sacrilegiously attempting to gild his refined gold. The result was most successful, and verified Bartley's prediction.

J. R. Planché, Recollections and Reflections

Bottom's Dream

Henry Morley saw Samuel Phelps' celebrated portrayal of Bottom on October 15, 1853.

Mr. Phelps has never for a minute lost sight of the main idea which governs the whole play, and this is the great secret of his success in the presentation of it. He knew that he was to present merely shadows; that spectators, as Puck reminds them in the epilogue, are to think they have slumbered on their seats, and that what appeared before them have been visions. Everything has been subdued as far as possible at Sadler's Wells to this ruling idea. The scenery is very beautiful, but wholly free from the meretricious glitter now in favour; it is not so remarkable for costliness as for the pure taste in which it and all the stage-arrangements have been planned. There is no ordinary scene-shifting; but, as in dreams, one scene is made to glide insensibly into another. We follow the lovers and the fairies through the wood from glade to glade, now among trees, now with a broad view of the sea and Athens in the distance, carefully but not at all obtrusively set forth. And not only do the scenes melt dream-like one into another, but over all the fairy portion of the play there is a haze thrown by a curtain of green gauze placed between the actors and the audience, and maintained there during the whole of the second, third, and fourth acts. This gauze curtain is so well spread that there are very few parts of the house from which its presence can be detected, but its influence is everywhere felt; it subdues the flesh and blood of the actors into something more nearly resembling dream-figures, and incorporates more completely the actors with the scenes, throwing the same green fairy tinge, and the same mist over all. A like idea has also dictated certain contrivances of dress, especially in the case of the fairies.

Very good taste has been shown in the establishment of a harmony between the scenery and the poem. The main feature —the Midsummer Night—was marked by one scene so elaborated as to impress it upon all as the central picture of the group. The moon was just so much exaggerated as to give it the required prominence. The change, again, of this Midsummer Night into morning, when Theseus and Hippolyta come to the wood with horn and hound, was exquisitely presented. And in the last scene, when the fairies, coming at night into the hall of Theseus, 'each several chamber bless', the Midsummer moon is again seen shining on the palace as the curtains are drawn that admit the fairy throng. Ten times as much money might have been spent on a very much worse setting of the *Midsummer Night's Dream*. It is the poetical feeling prompting a judicious but not extravagant outlay, by aid of which Mr. Phelps has produced a stage-spectacle more refined and intellectual, and far more absolutely satisfactory, than anything I can remember to have seen since Mr. Macready was a manager.

That the flesh and blood presentments of the dream-figures which constitute the persons of the play should be always in harmony with this true feeling, was scarcely to be expected. A great deal of the poetry is injured in the speaking. Unless each actor were a man who combined with elocutionary power a very high degree of sensibility and genius, it could hardly be otherwise. Yet it cannot be said even here that the poet's effects entirely failed. The *Midsummer Night's Dream* abounds in the most delicate passages of Shakespeare's verse; the Sadler's Wells pit has a keen enjoyment for them; and pit and gallery were crowded to the farthest wall on Saturday night with a most earnest audience, among whom many a subdued hush arose, not during but just before, the delivery of the most charming passages.

*   *   *

It remains for us only to speak of the success of Mr. Phelps as Bottom, whom he presented from the first with remarkable subtlety and spirit, as a man seen in a dream. In his first scene, before we know what his conception is, or in what spirit he means the whole play to be received, we are puzzled by it. We miss the humour, and get a strange, elaborate, and uncouth dream-figure, a clown restless with vanity, marked by a score of little movements, and speaking ponderously with the uncouth gesticulation of an unreal thing, a grotesque nightmare character. But that, we find, is precisely what the actor had intended to present, and we soon perceive that he was right. Throughout the fairy scenes there is a mist thrown over Bottom by the actor's art. The violent gesticulation becomes stillness, and the hands are fixed on the breast. They are busy with the unperceived business of managing the movements of the ass's head, but it is not for that reason they are so perfectly still. The change of manner is a part of the conception. The dream-figure is dreaming, there is dream within dream, Bottom is quiet, his humour becomes more unctuous, but Bottom is translated. He accepts all that happens, quietly as dreamers do; and the ass's head we also accept quietly, for we too are in the middle of our dream, and it does not create surprise. Not a touch of comedy was missed in this capital piece of acting, yet Bottom was completely incorporated with the *Midsummer Night's Dream*, made an essential part of it, as unsubstantial, as airy and refined as all the rest. Quite masterly was the delivery by Mr. Phelps of the speech of Bottom on awakening. He was still a man subdued, but subdued by the sudden plunge into a state of unfathomable wonder. His dream clings about him, he cannot sever the real from the unreal, and still we are made to feel that his reality itself is but a fiction. The preoccupation continues to be manifest during his next scene with the players, and his parting 'No more words; away; go away', was in the tone of a man who had lived with spirits and was not yet perfectly returned into the flesh. Nor did the refinement of this conception, if we except the first scene, abate a jot of the laughter that the character of Bottom was intended to excite. The mock-play at the end was intensely ludicrous in the presentment, yet nowhere farcical. It was the dream. Bottom as Pyramus was more perfectly a dream-figure than ever. The contrast between the shadowy actor and his part, between Bottom and Pyramus, was marked intensely; and the result was as quaint a phantom as could easily be figured by real flesh. Mr. Ray's Quince was very good indeed, and all the other clowns were reasonably well presented.

It is very doubtful whether the *Midsummer Night's Dream*

has yet, since it was first written, been put upon the stage with so nice an interpretation of its meaning. It is pleasant beyond measure to think that an entertainment so refined can draw such a throng of playgoers as I saw last Saturday sitting before it silent and reverent at Sadler's Wells.

Henry Morley, *Journal of a London Playgoer*

The Misadventures of Puck

Ellen Terry recalls, in appropriately whimsical fashion, two incidents which occurred during Charles Kean's 1856 production, where she played Puck at the age of nine; she does not mention that her first entrance was through a trap door seated on a mushroom.

ELLEN TERRY as Puck.

During my three years at the Princess's I was a very strong, happy, and healthy child. I was never out of the bill except during the run of 'A Midsummer Night's Dream,' when, through an unfortunate accident, I broke my toe. I was playing Puck, my second part on any stage, and had come up through a trap at the end of the last act to give the final speech. My sister Kate was playing Titania that night as understudy to Carlotta Leclercq. Up I came—but not quite up, for the man

A Midsummer Night's Dream, Princess's, 1856. ELLEN TERRY played Puck in Charles Kean's production (drawing from the original production by F. Lloyds).

shut the trap-door too soon and caught my toe. I screamed. Kate rushed to me and banged her foot on the stage, but the man only closed the trap tighter, mistaking the signal.

'Oh, Katie! Katie!' I cried. 'Oh, Nelly! Nelly!' said poor Kate helplessly. Then Mrs. Kean came rushing on and made them open the trap and release my poor foot.

'Finish the play, dear,' she whispered excitedly, 'and I'll double your salary!' There was Kate holding me up on one side and Mrs. Kean on the other. Well, I did finish the play in a fashion. The text ran something like this—

'If we shadows have offended (Oh, Katie, Katie!)
Think but this, and all is mended, (Oh, my toe!)
That you have but slumbered here,
While these visions did appear. (I can't, I can't!)
And this weak and idle theme,
No more yielding but a dream, (Oh, dear! oh, dear!)
Gentles, do not reprehend; (A big sob)
If you pardon, we will mend. (Oh, Mrs. Kean!)'

How I got through it, I don't know! But my salary was doubled—it had been fifteen shillings, and it was raised to thirty—and Mr. Skey, President of St. Bartholomew's Hospital, who chanced to be in a stall that very evening, came round behind the scenes and put my toe right. He remained my friend for life.

* * *

'Midsummer Night's Dream' at the Princess's. It was certainly a very fascinating production, and many of the effects were beautiful. I, by the way, had my share in marring one of these during the run. When Puck was told to put a girdle round the earth in forty minutes, I had to fly off the stage as swiftly as I could, and a dummy Puck was whirled through the air from the point where I disappeared. One night the dummy, while in full flying action, fell on the stage, whereupon, in great concern for its safety, I ran on, picked it up in my arms, and ran off with it amid roars of laughter! Neither of the Keans was acting in this production, but there was some one in authority to give me a sound cuff. Yet I had such excellent intentions. 'Tis ever thus!

Ellen Terry, *The Story of My Life (1908)*

Shakespeare Versus Daly

A Midsummer Night's Dream. *Daly's Theatre, 9 July, 1895*

'The Two Gentlemen of Verona' has been succeeded at Daly's Theatre by 'A Midsummer Night's Dream,' Mr. Daly is in great form. In my last article I was rash enough to hint that he had not quite realised what could be done with electric lighting on the stage. He triumphantly answers me by fitting up all his fairies with portable batteries and incandescent lights, which they switch on and off from time to time, like children with a new toy. He has trained Miss Lillian Swain in the part of Puck until it is safe to say that she does not take one step, strike one attitude, or modify her voice by a single inflexion that is not violently, wantonly, and ridiculously wrong and absurd. Instead of being mercurial, she poses academically, like a cheap Italian statuette; instead of being impish and childish, she is elegant and affected; she laughs a solemn, measured laugh, like a heavy German Zamiel; she announces her ability to girdle the earth in forty minutes in the attitude of a professional skater, and then begins the journey awkwardly in a swing, which takes her in the opposite direction to that in which she indicated her intention of going: in short, she illustrates every folly and superstition that still clings round what Mr. Daly no doubt calls 'the legitimate.' Another stroke of his is to make Oberon a woman. It must not be supposed that he does this solely because it is wrong, though there is no other reason apparent. He does it partly because he was brought up to do such things, and partly because they seem to him to be a tribute to Shakespeare's greatness, which, being uncommon, ought not to be interpreted according to the dictates of common sense. A female Oberon and a Puck who behaves like a pageboy earnestly training himself for the post of footman recommend themselves to him because they totally destroy the naturalness of the representation, and so accord with his conception of the Shakespearean drama as the most artificial of all forms of stage entertainment. That is how you find out the man who is not an artist.

*   *   *

He [Mr. Daly] certainly has no suspicion of the fact that every accessory he employs is brought in at the deadliest risk of destroying the magic spell woven by the poet. He swings Puck away on a clumsy trapeze with a ridiculous clash of the cymbals in the orchestra, in the fullest belief that he is thereby completing instead of destroying the effect of Puck's lines. His 'panoramic illusion of the passage of Theseus's barge to Athens' is more absurd that anything that occurs in the tragedy of Pyramus and Thisbe in the last act. The stage management blunders again and again through feeble imaginative realisation of the circumstances of the drama. In the first act it should be clear to any stage manager that Lysander's speech, beginning 'I am, my lord, as well derived as he,' should be spoken privately and not publicly to Theseus. In the rehearsal scene in the wood, Titania should not be conspicuously exhibited under a lime-light in the very centre of the stage, where the clowns have, in defiance of all common sanity, to pretend not to see her. We are expected, no doubt, to assume that she is invisible because she is a fairy, though Bottom's conversation with her when she wakes and addresses him flatly contradicts that hypothesis. In the fourth act, Theseus has to enter from his barge down a bank, picking his way through the sleeping Lysander and Hermia, Demetrius and Helena. The four lions in Trafalgar Square are not more conspicuous and unoverlookable than these four figures are. Yet Theseus has to make all his hunting speeches in an impossible unconsciousness of them, and then to look at them amazedly and exclaim, 'But soft, what nymphs are these?' as if he could in any extremity of absence of mind have missed seeing them all along. Most of these absurdities are part of a systematic policy of sacrificing the credibility of the play to the chance of exhibiting an effective 'living picture.'

Bernard Shaw, *Dramatic Opinions and Essays*

The Merchant of Venice

RICHARD Burbage is said to have played Shylock, possibly as a comic villain. For forty years from the beginning of the eighteenth century Shakespeare's play was abandoned in favour of an 'adaptation' by George Granville (later Lord Lansdowne) called *The Jew of Venice* which offered, among other delights, a masque of Peleus and Thetis.

Charles Macklin was the first great actor of whom we have a record as Shakespeare's Shylock, and it is fortunate that he was seen in the role by an exceptionally acute and articulate observer, George Lichtenberg. Macklin, Pope is said to have written 'is the Jew that Shakespeare drew', and since then the part has been played with distinction by a number of great actors, including Edmund Kean and Irving.

Peg Woffington's Portia

Portia was one of the many Shakespearean roles played by this celebrated actress during the seventeen years (1740–57) of her London stage career.

Portia has fallen to the lot of several capital ladies; and indeed she not only requires, but merits the exertion of eminent abilities; Mrs. Woffington, whose deportment in a male character, was so free and elegant, whose figure was so proportionate and delicate, notwithstanding a voice unfavourable for declamation, must, in our opinion, stand foremost; her first scene was supported with an uncommon degree of spirited archness; her behaviour during Bassanio's choice of the caskets, conveyed a strong picture of unstudied anxiety; the trial scene she sustained with amiable dignity, the speech upon mercy she marked as well as any body else; and, in the fifth act, she carried on the sham quarrel in a very laughable manner; to sum up all, while in petticoats, she shewed the woman of solid sense, and real fashion; when in breeches, the man of education, judgment and gentility.

Francis Gentleman, *The Dramatic Censor*

Macklin's First Shylock

Charles Macklin (?1700–97) looks back in old age on the first night of his revolutionary portrayal of Shylock not as a comic villain but as a suffering human being.

The long-expected night at last arrived, and the house was crowded from top to bottom with the first company in town. The two front rows of the pit, as usual, were full of critics, 'who, Sir (said the veteran), I eyed through the slit of the curtain, and was glad to see there, as I wished, in such a cause, to be tried by a special jury. When I made my appearance in the green-room, dressed for the part, with my red hat on my head, my picqued beard, loose black gown, &c., and with a confidence which I never before assumed, the performers all stared at one another, and evidently with a stare of disappointment. Well, sir, hitherto all was right—till the last bell rung—then, I confess, my heart began to beat a little; however I mustered up all the courage I could, and, recommending my cause to Providence, threw myself bodily on the stage, and was received by one of the loudest thunders of applause I ever before received.

'The opening scenes being rather tame and level, I could not expect much applause; but I found myself well listened to—I could hear distinctly, in the pit, the words 'Very well—very well, indeed!—this man seems to know what he is about', &c. &c. These encomiums warmed me, but did not overset me—I knew where I should have the pull, which was in the third act, and reserved myself accordingly. At this period, I threw out all my fire; and, as the contrasted passions of joy for the Merchant's losses, and grief for the elopement of Jessica, open a fine field for an actor's powers, I had the good fortune to please beyond my warmest expectations—the whole house was in an uproar of applause—and I was obliged to pause between the speeches, to give it vent, so as to be heard. When I went behind the scenes after this act, the Manager met me, and complimented me very highly on my performance, and significantly added—'Macklin, you was right at last.' My brethren in the green-room joined in his eulogium, but with different views—he was thinking of the increase of his treasury—they only for saving appearances—wishing at the same time that I had broke my neck in the attempt. The trial scene wound up the fullness of my reputation; here I was so well listened to, and here I made such a silent yet forcible impression on my audience, that I retired from this great attempt most perfectly satisfied.

'On my return to the green room, after the play was over, it was crowded with nobility and critics, who all complimented me in the warmest and most unbounded manner, and the situation I felt myself in I must confess was one of the most flattering and intoxicating of my whole life: no money, no title, could purchase what I felt; and let no man tell me after this, what fame will not inspire a man to do, and how far the attainment of it will not remunerate his greatest labours? By G–d, Sir, though I was not worthy fifty pounds in the world at that time, yet, let me tell you, I was Charles the Great for that night.'

European Magazine, April 1800

The Jew that Shakespeare Drew

George Lichtenberg (1742–1799), a German visitor to England, was one of the most acute observers of the London theatrical scene in the eighteenth century. He visited England in 1770–71 and again in 1774–75.

I saw Macklin, who is well known for his extraordinary excellence, his lawsuit, and his physiognomy, play Shylock in Shakespeare's *Merchant of Venice*. You know that Macklin as Shylock sounds as well on a playbill as Garrick as Hamlet. It was on the very evening that he played again for the first time on the conclusion of his lawsuit. When he came on the stage, he was thrice greeted with general applause, which on each occasion lasted for quite a quarter of a minute. It cannot be denied that the sight of this Jew is more than sufficient to arouse once again in the mature man all the prejudices of his childhood against this race. Shylock is not one of those mean, plausible cheats who could expatiate for an hour on the virtues of a gold watch-chain of pinchbeck; he is heavy, and silent in his unfathomable cunning, and, when the law is on his side, just to the point of malice. Imagine a rather stout man with a coarse yellow face and a nose generously fashioned in all three dimensions, a long double chin, and a mouth so carved by nature that the knife appears to have slit him right up to the ears, on one side at least, I thought. He wears a long black gown, long wide trousers, and a red tricorne, after the fashion of Italian Jews, I suppose. The first words he utters, when he comes on to the stage, are slowly and impressively spoken: 'Three thousand ducats.' The double 'th' and the two sibilants, especially the second after the 't', which Macklin lisps as lickerishly as if he

CHARLES MACKLIN as Shylock, Drury Lane, 1741.

were savouring the ducats and all that they would buy, make
so deep an impression in the man's favour that nothing can
destroy it. Three such words uttered thus at the outset give the
keynote of his whole character. In the scene where he first
misses his daughter, he comes on hatless, with disordered hair,
some locks a finger long standing on end, as if raised by a breath
of wind from the gallows, so distracted was his demeanour. Both

his hands are clenched, and his movements abrupt and convulsive. To see a deceiver, who is usually calm and resolute, in such a state of agitation, is terrible.

George Lichtenberg,
Visits to England. (Ed. Mare and Quarrell)

Macklin's Last Bow

Macklin was nearly ninety when he attempted, on May 7, 1789 to re-create his most famous role.

1789

His last attempt on the stage was on the 7th of May following, in the character of Shylock, for his own benefit. Here his imbecilities were previously foreseen, or at least dreaded by the Manager—but who knowing the state of Macklin's finances, gave, with his usual liberality, this indulgence to his age and necessities; and to prevent the disappointment of the audience (who he knew, from long experience, were always ready to assist in those liberal indulgencies to an old and meritorious servant), he had the late Mr. Ryder under-studied in the part, ready dressed to supply Macklin's deficiencies, if necessary. The precaution afterwards proved necessary.

When Macklin had dressed himself for the part, which he did with his usual accuracy, he went into the Green Room, but with such a lack-lustre looking eye, as plainly indicated his inability to perform, and coming up to the late Mrs. Pope, said, 'My dear, Are you to play to-night?'—'Good God—to be sure I am; why don't you see I am dressed for Portia?'—'Ah! very true; I had forgot—But who is to play Shylock?'—The imbecile tone of voice, and the inanity of look with which this last question was asked, caused a melancholy sensation in all who heard it—at last Mrs. Pope, rousing herself, said, 'Why you, to be sure; are not you dressed for the part?'—He then seemed to recollect himself, and, putting his hand to his forehead, pathetically exclaimed, 'God help me—my memory, I am afraid, has left me.'

He, however, after this went upon the stage, and delivered two or three speeches of Shylock in a manner that evidently proved he did not understand what he was repeating. After a while he recovered himself a little, and seemed to make an effort to rouse himself—but in vain—Nature could assist him no further—and after pausing some time, as if considering what to do, he then came forward, and informed the audience, 'That he now found he was unable to proceed in the part, and hoped they would accept Mr. Ryder as his substitute, who was already prepared to finish it.'—The audience accepted his apology with a mixed applause of indulgence and commiseration—and he retired from the stage for ever.

European Magazine, June 1801

Kean's London Début

[Drury Lane] January 27, 1814

Mr. Kean (of whom report had spoken highly) last night made his appearance at Drury-Lane Theatre in the character of Shylock. For voice, eye, action, and expression, no actor has come out for many years at all equal to him. The applause, from the first scene to the last, was general, loud, and uninterrupted. Indeed, the very first scene in which he comes on with Bassanio and Antonio, showed the master in his art, and at once decided the opinion of the audience. Perhaps it was the most perfect of any. Notwithstanding the complete success of Mr. Kean in the part of Shylock, we question whether he will not become a greater favourite in other parts. There was a lightness and vigour in his tread, a buoyancy and elasticity of spirit, a fire and animation, which would accord better with almost any other character than with the morose, sullen, inward, inveterate, inflexible malignity of Shylock. The character of Shylock is that of a man brooding over one idea, that of its wrongs, and bent on one unalterable purpose, that of revenge. In conveying a profound impression of this feeling, or in embodying the general conception of rigid and uncontrollable self-will, equally proof against every sentiment of humanity or prejudice of opinion, we have seen actors more successful than Mr. Kean; but in giving effect to the conflict of passions arising out of the contrasts of situation, in varied vehemence of declamation, in keenness of sarcasm, in the rapidity of his transitions from one tone and feeling to another, in propriety and novelty of action, presenting a succession of striking pictures, and giving perpetually fresh shocks of delight and surprise, it would be difficult to single out a competitor. The fault of his acting was (if we may hazard the objection), an over-display of the resources of the art, which gave too much relief to the hard, impenetrable, dark groundwork of the character of Shylock. It

EDMUND KEAN as Shylock, Drury Lane, 1814.

would be endless to point out individual beauties, where almost
every passage was received with equal and deserved applause.
We thought, in one or two instances, the pauses in the voice
were too long, and too great a reliance placed on the expression
of the countenance, which is a language intelligible only to a
part of the house.

The rest of the play was, upon the whole, very respectably
cast. It would be an equivocal compliment to say of Miss

Smith, that her acting often reminds us of Mrs. Siddons. Rae played Bassanio; but the abrupt and harsh tones of his voice are not well adapted to the mellifluous cadences of Shakespeare's verse.

William Hazlitt, A View of the English Stage

The Younger Kean

Charles Kean's revival was remembered more for its spectacle than for Kean's own portrayal of a role in which his father had achieved fame overnight.

[June 19, 1858]

At the Princess's *The Merchant of Venice* is the new Shakespearean spectacle. Beyond question this is the best of Mr. Kean's revivals. The literary alterations that have been made in the acted play consist only in judicious restorations of the text, which give not only more interest to the play, but also more importance to the character of Portia. Mrs. Charles Kean's Portia is known as one of the parts in which she best displays her power as an artist, while Mr. Charles Kean is

CHARLES KEAN and ELLEN TREE (Mrs. Kean), *The Merchant of Venice*, at Windsor Castle, 1848.

seldom seen to more advantage than as Shylock. The scenery is
so contrived as to suggest the whole idea of Venice, and the play
is only better understood when thus presented with the local
colouring that was in Shakespeare's mind, marked strongly by
the scene-painter. Even the interpolated dance, which in
some former revivals has appeared to me inopportune, being
introduced here, at the close of an act, as that music and dance
of masqued revellers in the street under Jessica's window,
against which Shylock had warned her to lock up his doors
and shut his house's ears, is such a show as Shakespeare might
have been content to see appended to his text.

Henry Morley, Journal of a London Playgoer

Two Shylocks?

Mr. Irving played Shylock for the first time on Saturday
night. As has been the case with every character of Shakespeare
this actor has assumed, the performance was a curiously unequal
one, but in this particular instance the inequality seemed to
arise as much from design as accident. Mr. Irving, in short,
gave us two distinct Shylocks—the one erect, composed,
dignified even in the complete overthrow of his long-cherished
purpose, and almost by his bearing compelling our sympathies
where they are most keenly raised against him; the other a
screaming, incoherent old man, who seemed to have lost his
wits together with his daughter and his ducats, and at whom
we are strongly inclined to laugh where we are really minded
to sympathise. For, we must confess, we have never been able
to share the sympathy that many commentators and critics have
lavished on Shylock's ultimate discomfiture, or to understand
in what way he was hardly treated by the Court of Venice.

*   *   *

How Mr. Irving is able to reconcile these two distinct pictures
we cannot quite understand. The Jew who pleads his case
before the Court and the Jew who scolds and rants before
Salanio and Salarino, and even before Tubal, his fellow and his
confidant, are two perfectly different men. The look, the bearing, the manner of speaking, the very voice are different. We
learn, indeed, from Salanio that Shylock's passion, on the first
discovery of his loss, was 'confused, strange, outrageous, and
variable,' and strange Mr. Irving assuredly makes it. It is only
natural, too, that before the Court, with so much at stake, he

HENRY IRVING as Shylock, Lyceum, 1879 (*Illustrated London News*, January 3, 1880).

should have put a strong restraint upon his feelings. But if the manner in which this Shylock is made to express his rage and sorrow at his double loss is the matured and carefully considered result of Mr. Irving's study of the character, we cannot understand by what method of reasoning the same character is made to assume in other conditions a complexion so completely different that it is not only the character that changes, but the very being and personality of the man himself.

The fact is, as we have tried to indicate, it is not Shylock, the Jew drawn by Shakespeare, that changes, but Mr. Irving, the actor. The conception of the character is, we conceive, consistent throughout. Not following, we need not say, Edmund Kean or any of his predecessors, but his own good judgment and intelligence, he desires to invest the character with a certain dignity that, through all the emotions of horror, contempt, or disgust that his conduct at various times may provoke, shall still command our respect. Usury is to him no more than thrift, and thrift is a virtue inculcated by the law of the Prophets of his own faith. The young spendthrifts on whose extravagance he thrives, the rich, well-honoured merchant, whom he hates with a peculiar hatred for crossing him in his own especial path, all these rail at him, spit at him, spurn him, and he accepts their insults. Yet in his heart he despises them for more than they can despise him. They are the dogs—not he. He will buy and sell and do business with them, but he will have no courtesies with them. He loves his gold better, it is true, than his daughter; but he loves his revenge more even than his gold. He will suffer much to get the Christian's money, but all the gold in Venice is lighter in the balance than one Christian life. His intense hatred of the Gentile dogs, a hatred as much national as personal, is stronger even than his avarice. It is an ancient grudge he bears; he hates them not so much because they call him Jew, but because he is a Jew. His greed may disgust us, his devilish purpose may horrify us; but we cannot despise him, and we cannot laugh at him.

This is the Shylock that Shakespeare has drawn; and this, if we are not mistaken, is the Shylock that Mr. Irving has justly set himself to present. He shows it in the earlier scenes; he shows it, and shows it with admirable skill and propriety, in the last great scene of all. But there is one part where he does not show it. In the two scenes in the third act, which we have already specified, the scene with the two young Venetians and the scene with Tubal, he falls away altogether from his purpose. Here he rants and scolds after a fashion and in a language wholly unintelligible. No Jew or Christian ever bore himself in such a manner. This arises from the actor's unfortunate and incomprehensible method of expressing any strong emotion. No one on our stage can express the passions of the mind in the face with more striking effect; but the instant he would go beyond this, no one, it is very certain, can tear a passion into such indistinguishable tatters as Mr. Irving. . . . It seems, indeed, incredible that an actor who can bear himself with such admirable propriety of voice, look, action, and gesture as Mr. Irving bore himself in his last scene should be unable to detect and to remove the extraordinary imperfections that disfigured his acting in those other passages. For than the scene in the court nothing could well have been finer. It might, perhaps, be objected that he is something too calm and composed under his defeat; but, at least, there can be no mistaking his intention. He has been so completely crushed by the suddenness of the double blow that has fallen on him in the moment of victory that he has neither life nor soul left; and this, it must be allowed, is an interpretation the text is well able to sustain. But, even if he be considered to have laid an undue stress upon this point, it in no way detracts from the general effect of his acting. Every sentence fell clear upon the ear with its proper weight and emphasis; every look had its correct significance; every gesture bore its own part. And in the earlier scenes with Bassanio and Antonio, and with his daughter, there was much that was good, despite an occasional lapse into his worse manner when a momentary flash of passion showed above his 'bated breath and whispering humbleness.' But for the rest— then, indeed, came 'the check, the change, the fall.' We have said, however, enough on this head. Where we can find so much to praise, we do not wish to insist with unnecessary pertinacity on what merits the reverse. We cannot ignore it and we cannot explain it; we can only regret it.

In Miss Terry's Portia there was no inequality. It was perfect charm throughout—a performance conceived and expressed in the highest spirit of poetry, and full of the most delightful touches of womanly wit, grace, and feeling. It has grown fuller and stronger since the days when she first surprised and de- lighted every one with it at the Prince of Wales's, and her method of elocution, always singularly sweet and pleasing, has become more clear and firmly balanced. We hardly know what feature to select for particular praise, for every feature was good. The exquisite tenderness of her manner with Bassanio over the casket, when her love almost tempts her to be for- sworn, and her fear lest he should choose wrong drives her hard to disobey her father's will; her well-bred courtliness to the Moorish Prince, the compliment of whose suit she acknowledges while she strives to conceal her distaste of the suitor; the merry humour with which she hints the design to follow her husband to Nerissa; her correct and impressive delivery of the famous speech on Mercy, and the graceful dignity of all her conduct in the court—each and all these are features on which we could gladly descant. The performance was, in truth, such as Shakespeare's self, one can imagine, would have wished to see.

For the rest, the general presentation may be accounted commendable. There were many individual defects, indeed, which could be marked if one cared to go at length through the cast, and there probably would be in these days in every cast of a play of Shakespeare's. But on the whole there was not very much fault to be found. Mr. Johnson seemed to have caught very cleverly the true spirit of Launcelot Gobbo's humour, though we doubt whether the humour of Shakespeare's clowns is ever likely to have much effect on a modern audience. Mr. Forrester made but a dull Antonio, though, to be sure, the merchant was not, in the circumstances, likely to be of a very cheerful temper. Mr. Barnes, on the other hand, was a remarkably gay and lively Bassanio, delivering his speeches with good precision and effect. It would, indeed, have been better had he contrived to temper his spirits with a little more of the dignity one may conceive as proper to a young Venetian dandy of that day, and the same may be said of his companions, Gratiano, Salarino, and the rest; but one should not, perhaps, be too critical in such matters. The piece was put upon the stage in a particularly complete and picturesque fashion.

The Times, November 3, 1879

Ellen Terry's Portia

Of the Portia we find it impossible to speak in the terms of unqualified rapture with which Miss Ellen Terry's performance has generally been greeted. We place our ideas of Portia high, — not higher, however, than Shakespeare meant them to be placed, by speaking of her as

'Nothing undervalued
To Cato's daughter, Brutus' Portia,'

by the elaborate care with which he has depicted the impression she produced on all around her, and by the way he has developed her charms of heart and mind throughout the action of the piece. She is the ideal of the high-born woman, gloriously endowed in body and in mind, and with her intellect cultivated to the highest point to which female culture could be brought.

*　　*　　*

It is in the trial scene that the character of Portia culminates. Her appearance there may surprise us; but the actress should previously have made us feel that she is equal to what she has undertaken. It is the splendid development of the splendid qualities of heart and mind, with which all we have previously heard and seen of her have made us familiar. Severe as the ordeal is to which she is exposed, the noble gravity and self-command with which she bears herself throughout the scene, should seem but a natural phase of her strong and beautiful nature. Most subtly, too, the womanly element breathes throughout her treatment of the situation, even while her penetrating look and intellectual vigour hold the Jew firmly in her grasp. She proves him, step by step, to see if he be indeed the wretch 'void of any drachm of mercy' she has been told he is; and leads him on to an avowal of the malice which nothing short of Antonio's death will appease. From that point she has him at her mercy; and, since he would have nothing but his bond to the letter, she discomfits him by holding him to the letter of his bond. The tender woman's heart, that has up to a certain point had pity for the Jew, is from that moment sternly closed against him, and she becomes as grandly stern as the mouthpiece and organ of the court in declaring the law, as she had hitherto been beautiful and persuasive in her appeals to the better feelings for which she had given Shylock credit. Her arguments are no 'pretty sophisms,' as an admiring critic of Miss Terry's Portia in one of the leading journals called them. She has law and reason on her side. The Jew is self-convicted of compassing the death of a Venetian citizen; and it is by no legal quibble, but by the laws of Venice—'thyself shall see the act,' she tells the Jew—that she defeats his purpose.[1]

If we are right in this conception of Portia, then Miss Terry's impersonation fails in its most essential point. Even those who have racked the language of panegyric in its praise have shrunk from claiming unqualified admiration for her in the trial scene. They might well do so, for at no one point in it does she indicate that she appreciates the situation, or how it should be treated. The words are spoken, but so spoken that one marvels why they should issue from the lips of one who looks so little in earnest, who takes so little note of Shylock, or Antonio, of the Doge, and

[1] We observe that Miss Terry, following the reading for the first time given upon the stage by Miss Helen Faucit, turns to the volume of the Venetian statutes, and reads from it the passage, beginning 'It is enacted in the laws of Venice,' &c. But this was only one of many touches of genius by which this great actress used to make the whole of the scene a living reality.

of the court, every one of whom it is her business to impress by the manner in which she discharges the function of determining the matter at issue, which has been delegated to her by the Duke.

We have spoken first of this scene because it is the touchstone of the actress's powers, and because our love of Shakespeare forbids us to be blinded by the attractions of either actor or actress to any failure in a due conception of the characters he has drawn for us with so firm a hand. But the shortcomings of Miss Terry, in our apprehension, begin at an earlier stage. She turns the character 'to favour and to prettiness;' but she does not even aim at the distinction and the dignity which essentially belong to it. She is not the great lady of Belmont, the self-possessed queenly creature, whose very presence turns men of ordinary mould into poets, and attracts, even while she holds them at bay in admiring reverence. She fails especially to suggest the Portia that, as Shakespeare most carefully makes us aware, would have sacrificed even her love for Bassanio, deep as we see it is, had he failed to win her by the process appointed by her father. How little this feature of the character is felt by the actress is made apparent in her treatment of the passage where she urges Bassanio to tarry, 'to pause a day or two,' before he tries his fortunes with the caskets. Throughout all this fine speech she holds him caressingly by the hand, nay, almost in an embrace, with all the unrestrained fondness which is conceivable only after he had actually won her. This, too, when all eyes are fixed upon her, and when her demeanour would have made her secret known to all the world in the last way a lady would court under any circumstances, but especially when, had her lover chosen wrong, she must have been parted from him at once and for ever.[1] There is altogether a great deal too much of what Rosalind calls 'a coming-on disposition' in

[1] If we are right in blaming the Portia, Mr. Barnes, the Bassanio of the Lyceum, must share in the blame; for a just conception of Portia, and of his position towards her, would hold him aloof from any such display of caressing physical fondness. There is something singularly incongruous in the contrast between all this 'fingering of palms,' and laying of hands on arms, before he wins her, with the exceedingly reverential manner in which Bassanio, after he has the right to 'claim her with a loving kiss,' obeys this suggestion by bending courteously over Portia's hand and kissing it. The Bassanio of the Lyceum has to contend against disadvantages of person, and a bluntness of manner, little in harmony with the characteristics of the poet's Bassanio; but he plays with so much earnestness, and speaks with such an appreciation of the significance of what he has to say, that one is well content to 'piece out his imperfections with our thoughts,' and to be content.

ELLEN TERRY as Portia, Lyceum, 1879.

Miss Terry's bearing towards her lover. It is a general fault with her, but in Portia it is painfully out of place.

A similar forgetfulness of what truth to the character and the situation demands, while the Prince of Morocco is making choice among the caskets, is visible in the far too marked demonstrativeness with which Miss Terry follows his movement from casket to casket. The room is full of people, servants, and others, any one of whom could tell in a second from Miss Terry's looks and movements when, in the words of the old game, he was hot, and when he was cold, and could have sold the information to the next wooer that arrived. It requires subtler touches than this lady seems to have at command, to indicate, without exaggerating, the emotion proper to a nature disciplined like Portia's to self-command.

There is, notwithstanding what we have said, much that is agreeable and attractive in Miss Terry's Portia, and no one will be surprised that uncritical people, who have not made their own separate study of the play, should be delighted with it. What we do wonder at, however, and most deeply regret, is the unmeasured terms of praise with which the critics of nearly all the journals have received it. Our wonder would be greater, if most of their criticisms did not at the same time show how little pains the writers had taken to make themselves masters of Shakespeare's text and of the intentions it reveals. One can only hope that Miss Terry's good sense will protect her from accepting too greedily the eulogies of undiscriminating admirers. They are certainly doing their best to spoil her.

* * *

Mr. Irving's treatment of the trial scene is excellent. He never forgets, as most Shylocks have done, that he is in the great court of Venice, and he bears himself with a restrained intensity suitable to the situation. He lays no stress upon the incident of whetting the knife, but deals with it as merely something by the way. It is in the calm, immovable rigidity of aspect, in the concentrated force which he throws into his words, that he leaves, and rightly leaves, the audience to read the triumphant inflexibility of his purpose. This contrasts finely with the momentary flashing out of a passionate delight, where Portia's words to Antonio, 'You must prepare your bosom for his knife,' seem to put within his grasp the object of his hate. It contrasts still more finely with the total collapse of mind and body, when at a glance the full significance of the words—'This bond doth give thee here no jot of blood,' bursts upon his keen intellect. In these words, and what follows, he seems to receive his death-blow. It matters little whether they strip him of his fortune, or tell him, as the condition of saving his life, that he shall presently become a Christian. His doom is written. His pulse will soon cease to beat. We feel the prop is in effect gone 'that doth sustain his life.' But he keeps a firm front to the last, and has a fine curl of withering scorn upon his lip for Gratiano, as he walks away to die in silence and alone. As he leaves the scene, we feel that we care not to know how this or that great actor of other days has treated it. This treatment is good, and it is a fitting climax to the Shylock of the previous acts.

O, si sic omnia! Oh that the same care had been bestowed upon the study of all the other characters that has been bestowed upon this—the same pains taken to make them as true to Shakespeare and to human nature! It would be idle to expect that the general run of actors and actresses should do this for themselves. This is the office of the head of a great theatre—call him manager, stage-director, or what you will. . . . And until the necessity be recognised for the presence at rehearsals of a predominating mind capable of fulfilling these functions, no theatre will ever satisfy an intelligent audience, or even do justice to the abilities of its performers.

One word in conclusion. Would it not be well for Mr Irving to set the example of trying to put a stop to the vulgar and distressing practice of recalling actors at the end of acts, or even scenes? It has long ceased to be a compliment to them, while it is simply an offence to all who deprecate so incongruous a disturbance of the illusion of the scene. We once saw Juliet in a London theatre—happily she was a foreigner, Mdlle. Stella Colas—rise from her bed in the great potion-drinking scene to curtsey to a clamorous knot of admirers. But we doubt if even this was worse than the spectacle of Shylock leading in Portia in her doctor's dress, for the same purpose, at the end of the trial scene, which may nightly be seen at the Lyceum.

Blackwood's Magazine, December 1879

The Merry Wives of Windsor

T HIS play has been far more popular with playgoers than with critics, no doubt because of the reappearance in it of Falstaff. Once again, there is the dismal story of adaptation, this time by John Dennis in *The Comical Gallant* (1702). But Shakespeare's play has more than held its own since the first recorded performance at Whitehall on November 4, 1604 and before Charles I and Queen Henrietta Maria on November 15, 1638.

A Superior Falstaff

May 17 [1815]—Mr. Bartley confirmed his fame, and his superiority over all the modern representatives of *Falstaff*, except Mr. Robert Palmer, by his performance of the roguish knight in the *Merry Wives of Windsor*, when love, founded on interest, has taken possession of his soul, and blinded his usual quickness of perception. Unlike the rest of his competitors, he never sinks into buffoonery or vulgarity. With his immortal guide, he imitates, without caricaturing nature. Rich and varied in his humour, he is just in his action, spirited in his manner. Never disgusting, he always pleases and amuses. If we were to particularise any passage, we would mention the recital which he makes of the manner in which he was conveyed out of Mrs. Ford's house, amidst foul linen, and thrown into the Thames; and, as one of the most striking in any performance, that in which he receives Mrs. Ford's last letter. Disgusted with the unfortunate result of his intrigues, and perhaps suspecting that his mistress was in the plot against him, his pride and resentment are in arms. He will not at first receive the letter, then beats it pettishly with his hand, whilst he half reluctantly opens it, and pretends to read it with total indifference. By degrees the contents revive his pride and his confidence: a complacent smile harmonises his features, and he closes the perusal with all the bursting exultation of gratified vanity, which once more betrays him into the snare. During all this, the actor was entirely left to himself; and his merits were rewarded with enthusiastic applause.

The other characters were most ably supported by their representatives.

European Magazine

Language Without Words

An account of John Henderson (1747–85) in one of the roles which brought him immediate and widespread fame.

He would sometimes delight to shew, without language, the rapid and opposite emotions, as they rise and chase each other in the mind. A masterly effort of this kind was Falstaff's reading the letter from Mrs. Ford in the presence of the 'foolish carrion' Mrs. Quickly. First, you saw, that he had 'his belly full of Ford;' —her messenger even was an object of detestation. He glanced over the beginning of the letter, and pished at its apologies. He turned again to the messenger, to see how her aid was in unison with the language of her mistress. The cudgel of Ford then seemed to fall upon his shoulders, and he shrunk from the enterprise. He read a sentence or two of the letter,—a spark of lechery twinkled in his eye, which turned for confirmation of his hopes upon love's ambassadress—and thus the images of suffering and desire, of alarm and enjoyment, succeeded one another, until at last the oil of incontinency in him settled above the water of the Thames, and the 'divinity of odd numbers determined him to risk the *third* adventure.'

James Boaden, *Life of J. P. Kemble, 1825*

In Defence of Adaptations

A review of a Drury Lane production starring William Dowton (1764–1851), an actor much admired by Hazlitt and Leigh Hunt.

A great outcry has been raised, on the revival of the *Merry Wives of Windsor*, interspersed with songs, against turning Shakespeare into opera, to which we cannot honestly contribute. If the plays which are thus garnished were so well adapted to representation in themselves as to draw houses, we should lament any interference with the wit and wisdom of the poet. But the professed idolaters of Shakspeare—those who render the largest portion of lip-homage to his genius—will scarcely contend, that all his plays are calculated to attract audiences; and if they would, empty benches and an emptier return would give them a practical answer.

*　　　*　　　*

The Merry Wives of Windsor, the Midsummer Night's Dream, and the Tempest, are only effusions of the divinest imagination under Heaven, following no guide but 'its own sweet will,' and breathing out its delicate creations, not according to the temper of the pit, but as they are inspired and clothed by plastic fancy. Is it wonderful, then, that the mere manufacture should answer the precise object for which it was contrived, better than the products of self-delighted genius?

*　　　*　　　*

There is none of his plays better adapted to this species of musical illustration than the Merry Wives of Windsor.

*　　　*　　　*

What can be more natural, if 'music be the food of love,' than that Fenton and Anne Page should breathe out their passion in simple melodies? Who should sing if the jolly dames of Windsor may not have a catch or two in the exuberance of their

145

ELIZA VESTRIS as Mrs. Page, Covent Garden, 1826.

mirth? We do not mean exactly to insinuate that Mrs. Ford
would probably sing of 'Rose-cheeked Adonis;' but Miss
Stephens's lips carry with them their own excuse for any irregu-
larity of which they may be guilty. On the whole, the introduc-
tions are judiciously contrived; and the words of the songs,
which, with one exception, are those of Shakspeare, startle the

heart with a strange pleasure, after the tawdry and inane absurdities of modern operas.

The play, thus agreeably diversified by songs, was cast with great comic and vocal strength. Dowton performed Falstaff excellently; for though inefficient in the Falstaff of Henry the Fourth, who is always triumphant over circumstances, and himself an embodied joke, he is quite equal to the Falstaff who is the butt of others. Falstaff in this comedy is 'in love,'—or rather in a passion to which a coarser name would be more appropriate, and which Mr. Dowton always expresses strongly. His manner of receiving the notes of the fair hoaxers, his disclosure of his amatory desires to Ford, his relation of the adventure of the buck-basket, and his escape as the fat woman of Brentford, were rich, unctuous, and complete. Wallack's Ford was well discriminated; he did not make the jealousy too tragic, but kept it in excellent harmony with the rest of the play. Miss Cubitt originally played and sung Mrs. Page tolerably, and Madame Vestris afterwards looked and sung in it intolerably well. But Miss Stephens in Mrs. Ford was the most charming feature of the piece. Her antique dress set off the full loveliness of her person, her arch simplicity rendered every merry jest more piquant, and her voice did justice to Shakspeare's words. Braham as Fenton happily had nothing to do but sing, and never did he sing more nobly. One beautiful ballad of Marlow, which he gave without accompaniment, was most affecting, and has commanded more applause than all the magnificent flourishes which he has indulged in for years. Harley was very ludicrous and not very extravagant as Slender; and Gattie in Doctor Caius gave as spirited a delineation as might have been expected from his Monsieur Tonson. We scarcely think the scenery was equal to the other dispositions of the piece; although no better subjects for picture could be desired than the Castle and Forest of Windsor; for the forest scenery appeared too palpable a compilation from the decorations of Kenilworth, and the view of the Castle seemed enlarged from the picture so liberally given away with the Windsor soap. In spite of this deficiency, the revived comedy has drawn a succession of brilliant houses.

Unidentified newspaper, March 1824
(Birmingham Shakespeare Library)

Applause for Shallow

Mary Cowden Clarke, who played Mistress Quickly, describes a memorable performance directed and acted in by Charles Dickens; the rest of the cast list also reads like a Who's Who *of Victorian artists and men of letters.*

The date of our first night at the Haymarket Theatre was the 15th of May, 1848; when the entertainment consisted of 'The Merry Wives of Windsor' and 'Animal Magnetism.' The 'make up' of Charles Dickens as Justice Shallow was so complete, that his own identity was almost unrecognizable, when he came on to the stage, as the curtain rose, in company with Sir Hugh and Master Slender; but after a moment's breathless pause, the whole house burst forth into a roar of applausive reception, which testified to the boundless delight of the assembled audience on beholding the literary idol of the day, actually before them. His impersonation was perfect: the old, stiff limbs, the senile stoop of the shoulders, the head bent with age, the feeble step, with a certain attempted smartness of carriage characteristic of the conceited Justice of the Peace,— were all assumed and maintained with wonderful accuracy; while the articulation,—part lisp, part thickness of utterance, part a kind of impeded sibillation, like that of a voice that 'pipes and whistles in the sound' through loss of teeth—gave consummate effect to his mode of speech. The one in which Shallow says, ''Tis the heart, Master Page; 'tis here, 'tis here. I have seen the time with my long sword I would have made you four tall fellows skip like rats,' was delivered with a humour of expression in effete energy of action and would-be fire of spirit that marvellously imaged fourscore years in its attempt to denote vigour long since extinct.

Mark Lemon's Sir John Falstaff was a fine embodiment of rich, unctuous, enjoying raciness; no caricatured, rolling greasiness and grossness, no exaggerated vulgarisation of Shakespeare's immortal 'fat knight;' but a florid, rotund, self-contented, self-indulgent voluptuary—thoroughly at his ease, thoroughly prepared to take advantage of all gratification that might come in his way; and throughout preserving the manners of a gentleman, accustomed to the companionship of a prince, 'the best king of good fellows.' John Forster's Master Ford was a carefully finished performance. John Leech's Master Slender was picturesquely true to the gawky, flabby, booby squire: hanging about in various attitudes of limp ecstasy, limp embarrassment, limp disconsolateness. His mode of sitting on the stile, with his long, ungainly legs dangling down, during the duel scene between Sir Hugh and Dr. Caius, looking vacantly out across 'the fields,' as if in vapid expectation of seeing 'Mistress Anne Page at a farm-house a-feasting,'—as promised him by that roguish wag mine Host of the Garter, ever and anon ejaculating his maudlin, cuckoo-cry of 'Oh sweet Anne Page,'—was a delectable treat. Mr. G. H. Lewes's acting, and especially his dancing, as Sir Hugh Evans, were very dainty, with a peculiar drollery and quaintness, singularly befitting the peppery but kindly-natured Welsh parson. I once heard Mr. Lewes wittily declare that his were not so much 'animal spirits,' as 'vegetable spirits;' and these kind of ultra light good-humours shone to great advantage in his conception and impersonation of Sir Hugh. George Cruikshanks as mine Ancient Pistol, was supremely artistic in 'get up,' costume, and attitude; fantastic, spasmodic, ranting, bullying. Though taking the small part of Slender's servant, Simple, Augustus Egg was conspicuous for good judgment and good taste in his presentment of the character. Over his well-chosen suit of sober-coloured doublet and hose he wore a leather thong round his neck that hung loosely over his chest; and he told me he had added this to his dress, because inasmuch as Master Slender was addicted to sport, interested in coursing, and in Page's 'fallow greyhound,' it was likely that his retainer would carry a dog-leash about him. Egg was a careful observer of costume; and expressed his admiration of mine for Dame Quickly, remarking (like a true artist) that it looked 'more toned down' than the rest of the company's, and seemed as if it might have been worn in Windsor streets, during the daily trottings to and fro of the match-making busy-body.

Charles and Mary Cowden Clarke,
Recollections of Writers, 1878

Much Ado About Nothing

K ING Charles I's copy of the play was inscribed 'Beatrice and Benedick' and these two characters in the nominal sub-plot have undoubtedly accounted for the widespread popularity of the play. It survived a Restoration adaptation by Davenant called *The Law Against Lovers* (with bits of *Measure for Measure* thrown in), though John Rich's revival of February 1721 claimed that the play had not been acted at that theatre (Lincoln's Inn Fields) for thirty years. The passion for taking bits of *Much Ado* and grafting them on to other plays continued throughout the eighteenth century, but Shakespeare's comedy was also occasionally staged more or less as written. Notable Benedick-Beatrice teams have included Garrick and Mrs. Pritchard, Charles and Fanny Kemble and Henry Irving and Ellen Terry. The roles of Dogberry and Verges, somewhat unexpectedly, do not seem to have made the reputations of any comic actors.

Monkey Tricks

Theophilus Cibber (1703–58) Colley's son, was less than enthusiastic about Garrick.

As a Theatrical Visitor then, give me leave to lay before you some of the studied absurdities or Callipedian[1] ape-tricks which are often substituted instead of the instinctive unaffected actions which simple Nature would have directed.

Of this kind is the pantomimical acting every word in a sentence: when Benedict says 'If I do, hang me in a bottle like a cat and shoot at me!', methinks this slight short sentence requires not such a variety of action as minutely to describe the cat being clapped into the bottle, then being hung up, and the further painting of the man shooting at it; but such things we have seen, nay sometimes seen applauded. Observe the golden rule of Not Too Much; this rule every actor should pay regard to.

Theophilus Cibber, *Dissertations on Theatrical Subjects, 1756*

[1] Callipedes was an actor of Aristotle's time who was apparently so affected that a rival nicknamed him the Ape.

Much Ado About Beatrice

A fairly early example of the impact of private life on public performance; I have unfortunately not been able to identify the 'errors of private character' referred to. A review of this production, by Leigh Hunt, follows.

Covent Garden Dec. 30 [1808]

Mrs. H. Johnston, after an absence of two years, resumed her station at this theatre, and performed the part of *Beatrice*, in *Much Ado About Nothing*. A report had been spread for several preceding days, that an opposition was intended to this lady's performance, by some persons who wished to visit on her public fame some supposed errors of her private character; and the expectation of this, though the circumstances alluded to were not matter of general notoriety, attracted a full house. When she first presented herself to the view of the audience, loud testimonies of disapprobation burst upon her from particular parts of the house; but the spontaneous feeling of the audience in general was highly favourable to her. The clapping, on one part, however, and the cries of *Off! Off!* blended with hisses, on the other, created such confusion, that the beginning of the first act was wholly lost to the ear. During this contention, which lasted a considerable time, Mrs. Johnston appeared strongly affected, and seemed two or three times about to swoon; but at last, with a kind of convulsive motion, she rushed forward to the front of the stage, and with uplifted hands made a silent appeal to the audience. The contention ceased; and profound silence (under an expectation that she was about to offer something in the way of excuse or explanation) was immediately restored. Nothing of the kind, however, took place: perhaps she was prevented by a very general cry of *Go on, Go on*; and the immediate entrance of Mr. Lewis, as *Benedict*, restored the house to good humour; which was only occasionally interrupted by the *Malevoli*, when they could force from any part of the dialogue of *Beatrice* constructions or allusions applicable to their purpose. Under these circumstances, much allowance is to be made for Mrs. Johnston's performance of the character; which, however, we do not think so well suited to her powers, as many others in which we have seen her, and on which she founded her former claims to public favour.

European Magazine

A Gloomy Beatrice

Covent Garden, January 3, 1808

The comedy of *Much Ado About Nothing*, which was revived at this theatre on Wednesday night, is one of those happy compounds of wit and humour which can alternately delight the fancy of the polite part of the audience, and call down the jovial roar from the galleries.

The play was altogether performed with much animation. Mr. Lewis in *Benedick* naturally provokes a comparison with Elliston, and it is pleasing to see how excellently two actors can support the same character with their own separate originality. Lewis excels in all the lighter parts of the character, Elliston in the more earnest and impassioned: in Elliston you have more of the frank soldier, more of the man of rank, more of the resolute lover; in Lewis you have more of the airy gallant, of the careless hey-day fellow, of the merry soul who turns everything into a jest: when *Benedick*'s manner is serious or when his humour acquires an additional dryness from gravity, you are intent upon the forceful style of Elliston, who is the first actor upon the stage in giving what may be called solidity to humour: Lewis, it must be confessed has no seriousness at all: when he attempts a grave surprise he exhibits a prominence of mouth that any other actor but Fawcett would reckon ludicrous; and the short breathlessness with which he chips his words as they dart forward always hinders him from expressing a natural gravity in his dialogue: but as five parts of *Benedick's* composition are mere wit and carelessness, Mr. Lewis's deficiency in seriousness is perhaps the more natural in a character of such mirthful habits. It is true that those persons who have a strong feeling of the humourous very often display more external gravity than others and perhaps more often feel a real gravity; but it will generally be found that he who is always laughing and always breaking jests is somewhat deficient in serious sensibility, for the soul generally contrives to look out of the features and manner of persons accustomed to society.

Mrs. H. Johnston reappeared after an absence of two years in the part of *Beatrice*, and perhaps it is not paying a great compliment to her performance to prefer her delivery of the harsher feelings of the character to its good-humoured levity. *Beatrice* is a very merry lady with a very good heart, she is the counterpart in short of *Benedick*, and Mrs. H. Johnston mistook

the warm satirist when she uttered her wishes of revenge against
Hero's calumniator with a gloominess and harshness of countenance bordering on malignity. I hope that one may be capable
of great severity without distorting one's temper, or manner,
or features, with mere rancour. *Beatrice* is sufficiently revenge-
ful, I allow; but there is a proud and there is a mean revenge,
there is the revenge of an ancient Spaniard and the revenge
of a North-American cannibal: none but bad hearts exhibit in
the countenance a mere disgusting malice. In some of the gayer
speeches, Mrs. H. Johnston was natural and elegant, but in
her general raillery she was a hundred times inferior to Mrs.
Jordan and Miss Duncan. The next time she hides herself
behind trees and arbours, she would do well to conceal her person as well as face. To hide the countenance and leave a long
flowing robe in view, is like the folly of the ostrich, who thinks
to escape its pursuers by thrusting its beak behind a tree and
shutting its eyes.

I could not discover what was intended by the dresses of the
gentlemen in this play. There is an astonishing disregard of
chronological propriety at the theatres, and yet they tell us that
the acting manager of Covent-Garden is a man of reading. The
time of *Much Ado about Nothing* has not been settled, if I recollect
rightly, by any of the commentators, but as it introduces a
Prince of Arragon, who visits the Governor of Messina with
familiar condescension and appears to carry his Court with him
into Sicily, it may naturally be supposed that the action is
during that period when Sicily was in possession of the House of
Arragon. The last Sicilian king of this house reigned at the
beginning of the fifteenth century, when the dresses of every
polite nation in Europe were totally different from their present
mode: the manager of Covent-Garden therefore has dressed his
Spanish prince of the 14th or 15th century like a modern
English gentleman in a blue coat, white breeches and stockings,
and an opera hat; one of his Spanish officers appears in the
exact regimentals of our present infantry, and the Italian officers
exhibit the same identical coats and breeches which their
descendants wear at this day. I do not know how Mr. Kemble
reconciles this to his studious soul, to his old affectation of
thoughtful propriety.

Leigh Hunt— The Examiner[1] (Jan. 3, 1808)

[1] William Thomas Lewis (*c.* 1748–1811), Robert Elliston (1774–1831) and
John Fawcett (1768–1837) were the subject of separate essays by Leigh Hunt
in *Critical Essays on the Performers of the London Theatres*, 1808.

Macready's Benedick

In one celebrated character in Shaksperian comedy he gained a triumph which, in its way, might fairly rank with any that he achieved in tragedy. The character was that of Benedick, which he played for his benefit. In this part his spontaneous humour, especially in the scene where he resolves to marry, roused the house to such shouts of mirth, one might have thought Keeley,[1] not Macready, was on the stage. His Benedick differed widely from that of other well-known actors. Whether it was the truest rendering of the part may be doubted, but I have seen none more effective. In the various conflicts with Beatrice there was not that eagerness of repartee, that animated enjoyment of the wit combat, nor quite that polished address (though Macready was both the soldier and the gentleman) ascribed to Charles Kemble. Macready had rather a provokingly indulgent and half-careless air towards his fair enemy. He wore a somewhat *blasé* manner to her, as of one versed in the serious business of life, and a little cynical through experience, who, nevertheless, good-naturedly consented to trifle and *badiner* with a lady for her amusement, who sometimes forgets his light *rôle* in serious thought, and then, rousing himself, returns apologetically to his recreation. In the celebrated soliloquy in the second act, after he has overheard in the arbour that Beatrice loves him, the complex expression of his face as he advanced drew roars from the house before he uttered a word. One might read there the sense of amazement, of gratification, and of perplexity as to the way of reconciling his newly-revealed passion for Beatrice with his late raillery at her and all women. His amazement was less, even, that Beatrice loved him, than that (his suspicion deepening to conviction as the soliloquy went on) he responded to her love. He evidently remembered his own recent vaunt, 'I do much wonder that one man, seeing how much another is a fool when he dedicates his behaviours to love, will, after he hath laughed at such shallow follies in others, become the argument of his own scorn by falling in love.' Accordingly, Macready, with great humour, made Benedick, in his first wish to be consistent, put his response to Beatrice rather upon the ground of pity and courtesy than of his own strong inclining: 'Love me! why it

---

[1] Robert Keeley (1793–1869) a celebrated low comedian, whose portrayal of Dogberry enchanted Dickens: 'The blunders of the old constable' he wrote 'fell from his lips with the most immovable and pompous stolidity. . . . As we write, we see again the wonderful expression of his face at the supreme moment when he was called an ass.'

must be requited. I hear how I am censured'—a shallow sophism to disguise his passion, which again called forth the heartiest mirth. His next step in reasoning, where he makes a moral aphorism the pretext for yielding to his inclinations, 'Happy are they that hear their detractions, and can put them to mending,' was not a whit less effective. In fact, the humour of the position, from his first surprise and timid regard for his consistency to the defiant scorn of ridicule at the close, was splendidly brought out. The most specious argument acquired with him the force of reason, or, if not, his will dispensed with it. It was an unopposed march, in which the victor gains audacity as he takes outwork upon outwork, until he hoists his flag from the citadel.

The success of the tragedian in this brilliant comedy was complete; yet he had so much doubted of it beforehand, he said, that he had proposed resigning Benedick to Mr. Anderson after the first night. He had had, as we have seen, similar misgivings with respect to Iago, and, previously to resuming the part in London, had been wretched with the apprehension of failure. The acclamations of the audience and the verdict of the best critics on Benedick, which proved to be one of his finest impersonations, came upon him as a shock of pleasure.

Westland Marston, *Our Recent Actors*, *1888*

Irving's Much Ado

This review of the first night of Irving's production of the play at the Lyceum on October 11, 1882, does full justice to its much praised Church scene.

[The] cathedral scene seems to an imaginative playgoer the very triumph of artistic effect pushed to the nicest point of refinement and good taste. The art here is to impress and not to shock the spectator—to soothe the mind and not disturb it. It is needless to point out the dangers ready to the hand of any one arranging such a scene for the stage. A red lamp burning before the altar, a crucifix, the use of vestments by the officiating friar, any of the determined signs of a nuptial mass, an excess of genuflexions, would have shipwrecked the whole idea and seriously endangered the beautiful in art.

But what do we get instead? The symbols severed from the soul; the suggestion without the reality. There can be no harm in the incense that fills the air as the bridal processions file to

IRVING'S *Much Ado About Nothing*, Lyceum, 1882.

the appointed spot; in the plaintive wail of the organ, with its soft and persuasive reed stop, contrasted with the secular music attendant on the bride; there can be no danger in the admirable and effective contrast of the major and the minor keys throughout this extraordinary scenic composition; a contrast of priests and courtiers, of ecclesiastical ritual and courtly solemnity; of organ and stringed band; of religion and the world. And the consequence is that there is left impressed on the memory all that is beautiful and nothing that is distasteful. That surely is the highest mission of art.

We recall old Leonato, with a look of tender love upon his face, guiding his daughter into the cathedral sanctuary; we see her crushed under the heel of a cruel suspicion, a 'broken blossom, a ruined rhyme'; we hear the passionate cry of Claudio, 'O, Hero! what a Hero hadst thou been,' and, old play as it is, know full well how many Heros and Claudios are about us in the life of to-day. We are conscious of the sudden change from gay to grave, from lively to severe, as that one sudden, impulsive, and womanlike command, 'Kill Claudio!' changes the purpose of the unreflective Benedick, and causes him to sacrifice friendship on the altar of love.

It will be found that Mr. Irving has succeeded in persuading us of three cardinal truths in connection with this most interesting play. First, that the complete unfolding of the characters of Beatrice and her lover is the mainstay of the whole plot;

secondly, that between Beatrice and Benedick there is a close affinity, that each is the other's counterpart, that they are echoes of one another as much at the outset as when they are discovered at the close writing verses to one another in secret, that the antipathy which exists is partial, and is changed by the humour of their friends to a sympathy that is real; and lastly, most important fact of all, that in this merry and enchanting comedy, a 'profound seriousness lies beneath all the superficial levity seen at first in the hero and heroine,' or, as a clever critic has put it, 'the very pair who have given the most decidedly comic character to the outset of the play, are found on the point of giving it the most tragic turn towards its close.' It is impossible to study Mr. Irving's acting as Benedick, or to sympathise fully with his masterly direction of the scene without being persuaded that he has grasped these three most important truths.

Much has been said already of the admirable humour of the new Benedick, of his inimitable delivery of Shakespeare's witty phrases, bringing them home to the dullest intelligence by the slyness of his artistic method; of his soliloquies, that seem to us masterpieces of comic expression, as full of thought, and intention, and earnestness as the thinking aloud of Hamlet himself. But there is much more than this in Mr. Irving's Benedick. There is expression—and the kind of expression may be seen by those who noticed that comical shrug of the shoulders and air of martyred resignation when the tamed Beatrice begins her old habit of chattering—but there is also seriousness.

When the cathedral scene has filled the eyes of Beatrice with tears, and Benedick has been accepted as her protector, the whole man changes. There is a moment of revolt at the words, 'Kill Claudio!' He answers, 'Ha! not for the wide world,' and Benedick means it. But he is over-persuaded, and love masters him. All the gentleman and soldier comes out in the now accepted lover. 'Think you, in your soul, that Count Claudio hath wronged Hero?' asks this fine-spirited and noble-hearted gentleman. 'Yes! as sure as I have a thought or a soul.' That assertion from his mistress is enough for Benedick. 'Enough; I am engaged. I will challenge him.' And he never breaks his word; he assumes the quarrel in all honour and honesty. Mr. Irving's Benedick is not a mere mountebank railer against womankind, not a swaggering, self-sufficient egotist; but a soldier first, a lover next, and always a gentleman.

*　　*　　*

Merriment is the abiding quality of Miss Ellen Terry's

Beatrice. She is Shakespeare's 'pleasant-spirited lady'; she was born in a 'merry hour'; we know that a 'star danced, and under that was she born'; she has a 'merry heart,' and the actress leans charmingly on this view of the character. All the people about the court love Beatrice, as well they may. They know her antipathy to the rougher sex is only skin deep, and they trick her into matrimony. She is no virago or vixen, but a smiling, chaffing, madcap girl, whose laughter and high spirits are next door to tears. How true this is of life! Laughter and tears are only divided by the narrowest channel, and the art with which Miss Ellen Terry expresses this in the scene after the cruel condemnation of her cousin is quite admirable. She wants to laugh with Benedick, but she must weep for Hero.

Most daring and original of all is her reading of the well-known outburst, 'O! God, that I were a man! I would eat his heart in the market-place.' We hold it, novel as it is, to be perfectly correct and natural in such a woman. It is not the scornful rage of a vixen, or the scream of a vulgar shrew, but a sudden, passionate sob of suppressed emotion. 'O! God, that I were a man! I would—', and then there is a long pause, as if the woman were too passionately indignant to give her thoughts utterance, but soon, with a wounded cry, and with rage expressed in the scarcely suppressed tears, come the words, 'I would eat his heart in the market-place.' When we object to unconventional readings we must remember the kind of woman presented to us.

There are many Beatrices who could not speak those lines in that particular way. But such a Beatrice as Miss Ellen Terry must have spoken them so. All who understand and have studied the style of this gay and sportive actress will guess how she could say such words as, 'No, my lord, unless I might have another for working days: your grace is too costly to wear every day,' or her answer to the question if she were born in a merry hour, 'No, sure, my lord, my mother cried.' Such sentences as these are received with a veritable shout of applause. But the audience was scarcely prepared for so excellent a delivery of the rhymed and lyrical soliloquy, 'What fire is in mine ears? Can this be true? Stand I condemned for pride and scorn so much'; and how true is the well-known Shakespearean simile as applied to this actress. 'For look where Beatrice, like a lapwing, runs close by the ground.' This is exactly how Miss Ellen Terry does run, on or off the stage.

*   *   *

The point most admired—as a rule—apart from the fantastic beauty of the scene, that put the whole attention in a period and so continually delighted the eye, was the thoroughly sound and excellent way that the comedy was being spoken. To elegance and taste was added expression, and it was Benedick himself who set the good example. So much has been said about

Mr. Irving's manner and artistic method that it is only right and just to point to his Benedick as a model of good accent and expressive delivery. This quality was even more strongly felt later on, particularly in the soliloquies, which will be remembered as Mr. Irving's most successful efforts in comedy.

The first scene of the second act introduced another welcome surprise in the Don John of Mr. C. Glenny. Now, Don John is not considered a very telling or welcome part, but instantly this young actor made his mark, not by overdoing the villain, but by making him a plausible and possible man. The speech, 'I had rather be a canker in a hedge,' roused the attention of the audience, because it was understood by the actor and intelligently delivered; with the slightest effort and in the smallest possible space Don John made his mark.

As the play proceeded the Beatrice rose gradually with the occasion. She had already shown she was Shakespeare's Beatrice, or something very like it, and there was no attempt to make acting points or to obtrude the virago. 'No, uncle, I'll none: Adam's sons are my brethren, and truly I hold it a sin to match in my kindred.' To hear Miss Terry speak that one sentence was enough to know that she understood the gay spirit of Beatrice. And it was a struggle in more senses than one for the mastery between the hero and heroine of the play. Mr. Irving and Miss Terry appeared to be vying with one another who should act the best; and though, in all probability, the prize will be awarded to the former, there was not much to choose between them until the test scene came after Hero's denunciation. . . .

In the third act, the scene in Leonato's garden was lovely in itself, both in arrangement and in colour, with its yellowing brown foliage, dim arcades of green, and old marble moss-eaten seat; but it was more remarkable still for Mr. Irving's soliloquy, in which the hesitating Benedick rails at love and lovers in general. The manner in which the actor gave a world of expression to such sentences as 'But, till all graces be in one woman, one woman shall not come in my grace,' and 'Of good discourse, an excellent musician, and her hair shall be of what colour it please God,' can only be understood by those who see and appreciate Mr. Irving's rich flow of sly humour. The audience had been presented with comedy at last and sincerely appreciated it. The introduction of Balthazar with his song, 'Sigh no more, ladies; sigh no more,' was extremely welcome, for it introduced a young singer, Mr. J. Robertson, brother of two charming sisters well-known in the musical world, who has not only a sweet and expressive voice, but well understood the grace and delicacy of this charming lyric. He did not come down to the footlights and deliver his song in a full-bodied way, as operatic tenors are wont to do, but he acted Balthazar and belonged to the scene. Of course the song was encored, for taste was in every note and line of it.

*　　*　　*

To the Don Pedro of Mr. Terriss, Mr. Forbes Robertson as Claudio makes an admirable contrast. The young man is in love, but he is never affected, he can be gay and bright in his comedy, and in pathos he feels the scene and the position. In the cathedral scene the passionate, nervous acting of the Claudio was just the note that was wanted in this very beautiful harmony of ideas. There is heart in Mr. Forbes Robertson's acting. Mention has already been made of Mr. Glenny's Don John, a nicely-conceived and artistic little bit, and what better or more picturesque Antonio could be found than Mr. H. Howe?

*　　*　　*

Dogberry and his companions fail to attract any interest whatever, but it is not the fault of Shakespeare. As usual, the public is inclined to visit the poet with the sins of the performers. A Dogberry with more pronounced humour; a Hero who should add idealism to her prettiness and more poetry to her promise; and a less modern Ursula in voice and style, would remove the only blots on a performance of singular interest and magnificent moment.

Clement Scott, The Theatre, 1884

As You Like It

THIS play was subjected to a barbarous 'improvement' in 1723 by Charles Johnson called *Love in a Forest*. Johnson left out most of the comic characters and patched up the holes thus made with bits of several other Shakespeare plays, including *Richard III*. Even when Shakespeare's own play was staged, a song from *Love's Labour's Lost* was invariably inserted. Ada Rehan made her reputation as Rosalind at the Lyceum in July, 1890.

161

Peg Woffington's Last Appearance

Tate Wilkinson (1739–1803) actor, mimic and provincial theatre manager describes the last moments of Peg Woffington's brilliant theatrical career. The date was May 3, 1757, though Wilkinson says it was May 17.

I was standing near the wing as Mrs. Woffington in Rosalind, and Mrs. Vincent in Celia, were going on the stage in the first act. Mrs. Woffington ironically said she was glad to have that opportunity of congratulating me on my stage success; and did not doubt, but such merit would insure me an engagement the following winter. I bowed but made her no answer—I knew her dislike to me,[1] and was humiliated sufficiently, and needed not any slight to sink me lower. For then, and not till then, adversity had taught me to know myself. She went through Rosalind for four acts without my perceiving she was in the least disordered, but in the fifth she complained of great indisposition. I offered her my arm, the which she graciously accepted; I thought she looked softened in her behaviour, and had less of the *hauteur*. When she came off at the quick change of dress, she again complained of being ill; but got accoutred and returned to finish the part, and pronounced in the epilogue speech, 'If it be true that good wine needs no bush—it is as true that a good play needs no epilogue,' etc. etc.—But when arrived at—'If I were among you I would kiss as many of you as had beards that pleased me.'—her voice broke, she faltered, endeavoured to go on, but could not proceed—then in a voice of tremor screamed, O God! O God! tottered to the stage door speechless, where she was caught. The audience of course applauded till she was out of sight, and then sunk into awful looks of astonishment, both young and old, before and behind the curtain, to see one of the most handsome women of the age, a favourite principal actress, and who had for several seasons given high entertainment, struck so suddenly by the hand of death in such a situation of time and place, and in her prime of life, being then about forty-four. She was given over that night, and for several days; but so far recovered as to linger till near the year 1760, but existed as a mere skeleton; *sans* teeth, *sans* eyes, *sans* taste, *sans* every thing.—Vain is Beauty's gaudy flower!

Tate Wilkinson, *Memoirs*, 1790

[1] Wilkinson had aroused Peg Woffington's resentment by his mimicry of her.

Mrs. Siddons in Comedy

Anna Seward 'the swan of Lichfield', writes of Mrs. Siddons in one of her less successful roles.

[*Lichfield, July 20, 1786*]

For the first time, I saw the justly celebrated Mrs. Siddons in comedy,—in *Rosalind*:—but though her smile is as enchanting, as her frown is magnificent, as her tears are irresistible, yet the playful scintillations of colloquial wit, which most strongly mark that character, suit not the dignity of the Siddonian form and countenance. Then her dress was injudicious. The scrupulous prudery of decency, produced an ambiguous vestment, that seemed neither male nor female. When she first came on as the princess, nothing could be more charming; nor than when she resumed her original character, and exchanged comic spirit for dignified tenderness.

One of those rays of exquisite and original discrimination, which her genius so perpetually elicits, shone out on her first rushing upon the stage in her own resumed person and dress; when she bent her knee to her father, the Duke, and said—

'To you I give myself—for I am yours;'

and when, falling into Orlando's arms, she repeated the same words,—

'To *you* I give myself—for I am *yours!*'

The marked difference of her look and voice in repeating that line, and particularly the last word of it, was inimitably striking. The tender joy of filial love was in the first; the whole soul of enamoured transport in the second. The extremely heightened emphasis on the word *yours*, produced an effect greater than you can conceive could result from the circumstance, without seeing and hearing it given by that mistress of the passions.

Anna Seward, *Letter to Miss Weston, 1786*

'As You Like It', at Coombe House

Oscar Wilde's account of an open-air production in June 1885 at Coombe House, Kingston-upon-Thames, directed by E. W. Godwin, Gordon Craig's father.

In Theophile Gautier's first novel, that golden book of spirit and sense, that holy writ of beauty, there is a most fascinating account of an amateur performance of *As You Like It* in the large orangery of a French country house. Yet, lovely as Gautier's description is, the real presentation of the play last week at Coombe seemed to me lovelier still for not merely were there present in it all those elements of poetry and picturesqueness which *le maître impeccable* so desired, but to them was added also the exquisite charm of the open woodland and the delightful freedom of the open air. Nor indeed could the Pastoral Players have made a more fortunate selection of a play. A tragedy under the same conditions would have been impossible. For tragedy is the exaggeration of the individual, and nature thinks nothing of disturbing a hero by a holly bush, and reducing a heroine to a mere effect of colours. The subtleties also of facial expression are in the open air almost entirely lost, and while this would be a serious defect in the presentation of a play which deals immediately with psychology, in the case of a comedy, where the situations predominate over the characters, we do not feel it nearly so much; and Shakespeare himself seems to have clearly recognised this difference, for while he had *Hamlet* and *Macbeth* always played by artificial light, he acted *As You Like It*, and the rest of his comedies *en plein jour*.

As You Like It at Coombe House, Kingston Hill, 1885 (from an original photograph).

The conditions then under which this comedy was produced by Lady Archibald Campbell and Mr. Godwin did not place any great limitations on the actor's art, and increased tenfold the value of the play as a picture. Through an alley of white hawthorn and gold laburnum we passed into the green pavilion that served as the theatre, the air sweet with the odour of the lilac and with the blackbird's song; and when the curtain fell into its trench of flowers, and the play commenced, we saw before us a real forest, and we knew it to be Arden. For with whoop and shout, up through the rustling fern came the foresters trooping, the banished Duke took his seat beneath the tall elm, and, as his lords lay around him on the grass, the rich melody of Shakespeare's blank verse began to reach our ears. And all through the performance this delightful sense of joyous woodland life was sustained and even when the scene was left empty for the shepherd to drive his flock across the sward, or for Rosalind to school Orlando in love-making, far away we could hear the shrill halloo of the hunter, and catch now and then the faint music of some distant horn.

One distinct dramatic advantage also was gained by the *mise-en-scene*. The abrupt exits and entrances, which are necessitated on the real stage by the inevitable limitations of space, were in many cases done away with, and we saw the characters coming gradually towards us through brake and underwood, or passing away down the slope till they were lost in some deep recess of the forest; the effect of distance thus gained being largely increased by the faint wreaths of blue mist that floated at times across the background. Indeed I have never seen an illustration at once so perfect and so practical, of the aesthetic value of smoke.

As for the players themselves the pleasing naturalness of their method harmonised delightfully with their natural surroundings. Those of them who were amateurs were too artistic to be stagy, and those who were actors too experienced to be artificial. The humorous sadness of Jacques, that philosopher in search of sensations, found a perfect exponent in Mr. Hermann Vezin; Touchstone has been so often acted as a low comedy part that Mr. Elliott's rendering of the swift sententious fool was a welcome change, and a more graceful and winning Phoebe than Mrs. Plowden, a more tender Celia than Miss Schletter, a more realistic Audrey than Miss Fulton, I have never seen. Rosalind suffered a good deal through the omission of the first act; we saw, I mean, more of the saucy boy than we did of the noble girl; and though the *persiflage* always told, the poetry was often lost; still Miss Calhoun gave much pleasure; and Lady Archibald Campbell's Orlando was a really remarkable performance. Too melancholy some seemed to think it. Yet is not Orlando love-sick? Too dreamy, I heard it said. Yet

Orlando is a poet. And even admitting that the vigour of the lad who tripped up the Duke's wrestler was hardly sufficiently emphasised, still in the low music of Lady Archibald Campbell's voice, and in the strange beauty of her movements and gestures, there was a wonderful fascination, and the visible presence of romance quite consoled me for the possible absence of robustness. Among the other characters should be mentioned Mr. Claude Ponsonby's First Lord, Mr. De Cordova's Corin, a bit of excellent acting, and the Silvius of Mrs. Webster.

As regards the costumes the colour-scheme was very perfect. Brown and green were the dominant notes, and yellow was most artistically used. There were however two distinct discords. Touchstone's motley was far too glaring, and the crude white of Rosalind's bridal raiment in the last act, was absolutely displeasing. A contrast may be striking but should never be harsh. And lovely in colour as Mrs. Plowden's dress was, a sort of panegyric on a pansy, I am afraid that in Shakespeare's Arden there were no Chelsea China Shepherdesses, and I am sure that the romance of Phoebe does not need to be intensified by any reminiscences of porcelain. Still *As You Like It* has probably never been so well mounted, nor costumes worn with more ease and simplicity. Not the least charming part of the whole production was the music, which was under the direction of the Rev. Arthur Batson. The boys' voices were quite exquisite, and Mr. Walsham sang with much spirit.

On the whole the Pastoral Players are to be warmly congratulated on the success of their representation, and to the artistic sympathies of Lady Archibald Campbell, and the artistic knowledge of Mr. Godwin, I am indebted for a most delightful afternoon. Few things are so pleasurable as to be able by an hour's drive to exchange Piccadilly for Parnassus.

Oscar Wilde
Dramatic Review, June 6, 1885

Ada Rehan

Grand Theatre, Islington 4 October, 1897

I never see Miss Ada Rehan act without burning to present Mr. Augustin Daly with a delightful villa in St. Helena, and a commission from an influential committee of his admirers to produce at his leisure a complete set of Shakespeare's plays, entirely rewritten, reformed, rearranged, and brought up to the most advanced requirements of the year 1850. He was in full force at the Islington Theatre on Monday evening last with his version of 'As You Like It' just as I don't like it. There I saw Amiens under the greenwood tree, braving winter and rough weather in a pair of crimson plush breeches, a spectacle to benumb the mind and obscure the passions. There was Orlando with the harmony of his brown boots and tunic torn asunder by a piercing discord of dark volcanic green, a walking tribute to Mr. Daly's taste in tights. There did I hear slow music stealing up from the band at all the well-known recitations of Adam, Jacques and Rosalind, lest we should for a moment forget that we were in a theatre and not in the forest of Arden. There did I look through practicable doors in the walls of sunny orchards into an abyss of pitchy darkness. There saw I in the attitudes, grace and deportment of the forest dwellers the plastique of an Arcadian past. And the music synchronized with it all to perfection, from 'La Grande Duchesse' and 'Dichter und Bauer,' conducted by the leader of the band, to the inevitable old English airs conducted by the haughty musician who is Mr. Daly's special property. And to think that Mr. Daly will die in his bed, whilst innocent presidents of republics, who never harmed an immortal bard, are falling on all sides under the knives of well-intentioned reformers whose only crime is that they assassinate the wrong people!

*   *   *

Just now she [Ada Rehan] is at the height of her powers. The plumpness that threatened the Countess Gucki has vanished: Rosalind is as slim as a girl. The third and fourth acts are as wonderful as ever—miracles of vocal expression. If 'As You Like It' were a typical Shakespearean play, I should unhesitatingly declare Miss Rehan the most perfect Shakespearean executant in the world. But when I think of those plays in which our William anticipated modern dramatic art by making serious attempts to hold the mirror up to nature— 'All's Well,' 'Measure for Measure,' 'Troilus and Cressida' and so on—I must limit the tribute to Shakespeare's popular style. Rosalind is not a complete human being: she is simply an extension into five acts of the most affectionate, fortunate, delightful five minutes in the life of a charming woman. And all the other figures in the play are cognate impostures. Orlando, Adam, Jacques, Touchstone, the banished Duke and the rest play each the same tune all through. This is not human nature or dramatic character: it is juvenile lead, first old man, heavy lead, heavy father, principal comedian and leading lady, transfigured by magical word-music. The Shakespearolators

167

who are taken in by it do not know drama in the classical sense from 'drama' in the technical Adelphi sense. You have only to compare Orlando and Rosalind with Bertram and Helena, the Duke and Touchstone with Leontes and Autolycus, to learn the difference from Shakespeare himself. Therefore I cannot judge from Miss Rehan's enchanting Rosalind whether she is a great Shakespearean actress or not: there is even a sense in which I cannot tell whether she can act at all or not. So far, I have never seen her create a character: she has always practised the same adorable arts on me, by whatever name the playbill has called her—Nancy Brasher (ugh!), Viola, or Rosalind. I have never complained: the drama with all its heroines levelled up to a universal Ada Rehan has seemed no such dreary prospect to me; and her voice, compared to Sarah Bernhardt's *voix d'or*, has been as all the sounds of the woodland to the chinking of twenty-franc pieces. In Shakespeare (what Mr. Daly leaves of him) she was and is irresistible: at Islington on Monday she made me cry faster than Mr. Daly could make me swear. But the critic in me is bound to insist that Ada Rehan has as yet created nothing but Ada Rehan. She will probably never excel that masterpiece; but why should she not superimpose a character study or two on it?

Bernard Shaw, *Dramatic Opinions and Essays*

King Richard II

APART from the famous performance at the Globe on the eve of the Essex rebellion (February 7, 1601), there are two other performances recorded before the Restoration, one of them on board H.M.S. *Dragon* off Sierra Leone on September 30, 1607. In 1680, there was a version by Nahum Tate called *The Sicilian Usurper* which failed and in 1719 another by Lewis Theobald, the great Shakespearean editor, which didn't. In 1738, Shakespeare's version came back, though it had to compete with adaptations in the nineteenth century. In 1857 Charles Kean staged a typically spectacular and enormously successful production featuring the entry of the deposed *Richard* into the city.

The Lists at Coventry

Thomas Davies recalls a production of Shakespeare's play in the mid-eighteenth century.

When this play was revived at the theatre in Covent-garden, above forty years since, the ancient ceremony which belonged to the single combat was very accurately observed, with all the decorations and arrangements proper to the appellant and respondent, the spectators and the judges. Amongst the latter, the king was seated in a throne of state. The combatants were dressed in complete armour. Two chairs, finely adorned, were placed on opposite sides of the lists: to these they retired after each of them had stood forth and spoken. Bolingbroke was acted by Ryan. Walker personated Mowbray. His helmet was laced so tightly under his chin, that, when he endeavoured to speak, nobody could understand him; and this obstacle occasioned a laugh from the audience: however, this was soon removed, and the actor was heard with attention. In their persons, dress, and demeanour, they presented something like an image of the old trial of right by duel.

Thomas Davies, *Dramatic Miscellanies*

Kean's Richard[1]

It has been supposed that this is his finest part: this is, however, a total misrepresentation. There are only one or two electrical shocks given in it; and in many of his characters he gives a much greater number. The excellence of his acting is in proportion to the number of hits, for he has not equal truth or purity of style. Richard II. was hardly given correctly as to the general outline. Mr. Kean made it a character of *passion*, that is, of feeling combined with energy; whereas it is a character of *pathos*, that is to say, of feeling combined with weakness. This, we conceive, is the general fault of Mr. Kean's acting, that it is always energetic or nothing. He is always on full stretch—never relaxed. He expresses all the violence, the extravagance, and fierceness of the passions, but not their misgivings, their help-

[1] Drury Lane, March 1815.

169

lessness, and sinkings into despair. He has too much of that strong nerve and fibre that is always equally elastic. We might instance to the present purpose, his dashing the glass down with all his might, in the scene with Hereford, instead of letting it fall out of his hands, as from an infant's; also, his manner of expostulating with Bolingbroke, 'Why on thy knee, thus low,' etc. which was altogether fierce and heroic, instead of being sad, thoughtful, and melancholy. If Mr. Kean would look into some passages in this play, into that in particular, 'Oh that I were a mockery king of snow, to melt away before the sun of Bolingbroke,' he would find a clue to this character, and to human nature in general, which he seems to have missed — how far feeling is connected with the sense of weakness as well as of strength, or the power of imbecility, and the force of passiveness.

We never saw Mr. Kean look better than when we saw him in Richard II., and his voice appeared to us to be stronger. We saw him near, which is always in his favour; and we think one reason why the Editor of this Paper[1] was disappointed in first seeing this celebrated actor, was his being at a considerable distance from the stage. We feel persuaded that on a nearer and more frequent view of him, he will agree that he is a perfectly original, and sometimes a perfectly natural actor; that if his conception is not always just or profound, his execution is masterly; that where he is not the very character he assumes, he makes a most brilliant rehearsal of it; that he never wants energy, ingenuity, and animation, though he is often deficient in dignity, grace, and tenderness; that if he frequently disappoints us in those parts where we expect him to do most, he as frequently surprises us by striking out unexpected beauties of his own; and that the objectionable parts of his acting arise chiefly from the physical impediments he has to overcome.

Of the other characters of the play, it is needless to say much. Mr. Pope was respectable in John of Gaunt. Mr. Holland was lamentable in the Duke of York, and Mr. Elliston indifferent in Bolingbroke. This alteration of Richard II[2] is the best that has been attempted; for it consists entirely of omissions, except one or two scenes which are idly tacked on to the conclusion [for Mrs. Bartley[3] to rant and whine in].

Hazlitt, A View of the English Stage

[1] *The Examiner.*
[2] By Richard Wroughton.
[3] She played the Queen.

Enter Bolingbroke[1]

CHARLES KEAN's production of Richard II, Princess's, 1857.

[I] The writer of these pages has a vivid recollection of this scene[2]—a winding street, filled with a restless crowd, every personage of which was an independent unit, acting apparently upon the impulse of the moment, laughing, jostling, fighting, neck-craning, indulging in horse-play, but never for an instant inert; the doors, windows, and balconies of the antique houses built on each side of the stage were crowded with eager spectators, some watching the vagaries of the crowd, others straining to catch the first sight of the coming pageant. At the distant sound of the trumpets, the street became a chaos, a shouting, scrambling, fighting mob, struggling for each coign of vantage, until the advanced guard, pushing back the people right and left, cleared a path. Then came the realisation of Shakespeare's fine description:—

> The rude, misgovern'd hands from window tops
> Threw dust and rubbish on King Richard's head;

[1] Princess' Theatre 1857. Charles Kean's production.
[2] The entry of Bolingbroke and the captive Richard into London, one of the highlights of Kean's production.

171

while as Bolingbroke entered upon 'his hot and fiery steed,'

> You would have thought the very windows spake,
> So many greedy looks of young and old
> Through casements darted their desiring eyes.

Nothing more perfect, more realistic than this episode has ever been seen upon any stage.

H. Barton Baker, The London Stage

*   *   *

[II] *March* 14 [1857].—*Richard II*, produced at the Princess's Theatre for the first time on Thursday night, as to its mounting is, perhaps, the most elaborate and costly spectacle that Mr. Charles Kean has yet set upon the stage, and the splendours are all unimpeachable.

*   *   *

Mr. Charles Kean has reproduced the people of the time, has restored to our eyes Richard the Second in his court, shown in their strength castles now known as ruins, reproduced with scrupulous fidelity the complete spectacle of lists set out for a tournament on Gosford Green, and has even interpolated between two acts of the play the triumph of the entry of Bolingbroke with Richard into London, which is a fine piece of stage-effect. The play gives reasonable opportunity for all these shows. They leave the mind bewildered for a time, but ultimately settle on the memory as a true picture of at least one phase of a past state of society.

Of course it is necessary to make room for stage-appointments and processions by omissions from the poetry, and *Richard II* was well chosen as a play from which certain omissions may be made without serious damage to its effect for acting purposes. Thus I hold Mr. Charles Kean to be quite justified in omitting the scenes in the fifth act founded on Aumerle's treason against Bolingbroke, though, if we consider the position of each person concerned in the episode, they contain truly the most vigorous sketch ever conceived of the domestic misery that is among the incidents of civil war. But it is to be regretted that to the necessities of the scenery two passages have been sacrificed that are most necessary to the play, and by the loss of which Mr. Charles Kean impairs greatly the success of his own efforts as an actor. At the end of the first act the curtain must fall upon the spectacle of the tournament. The scene has, therefore, to be sacrificed in which the audience is prepared for Gaunt's

172

death by tidings of his illness, and for Richard's seizure of his plate by a distinct knowledge of the King's sore poverty, his need of means to fight the Irish rebels, and his consequent wish that Gaunt may die, and leave his wealth behind him. Thus prepared, we can see with less surprise and abhorrence Richard's act of seizure in the first scene of the act that follows. Still further to soften the impression against Richard, which, if too strongly excited in the first half of the drama, would check pity in the other half, the poet has taken care to remove Gaunt from the stage to die, so that when Richard, after receiving· information of his death, turns promptly to the subject of the Irish wars and makes the seizure, he does not shock us by the rapacity and selfishness displayed while the very body of his uncle—dead but a minute since—lies before him. By the omission of the last scene in the first act, as the play is performed at the Princess's, we are brought suddenly from Gaunt in regal favour to Gaunt on his death-bed. He dies on the stage, and Richard, with the urgency of whose needs we have not been carefully impressed, becomes immediately a bird of prey beside the corpse, and loses irretrievably the goodwill of the audience. The other dangerous omission is that of the scene which should open the third act, and which immediately precedes the change of Richard's fortune, cunningly preparing us for pity by producing Bushy and Green for execution as the men who have 'misled a prince, a royal king', etc. The effect of these two omissions is to impede seriously the course of sympathy in the audience for King Richard's misfortunes, and to throw great difficulty in the way of the actor by whom it is the whole purpose of the play that sympathy shall be excited. Mr. Charles Kean could not wholly overcome this difficulty by the most careful acting, though the skill with which he marked, as the turning point in Richard's story, the revoking of Bolingbroke's sentence of banishment, went far to win some pity for his hero. Mrs. Kean, too, conquered a few kind thoughts for Richard by the pathos which she threw into his Queen's parting from him at the Tower.

By other members of the company the parts less important were efficiently sustained, and there was much to praise in Mr. Ryder's Bolingbroke. The revival earned a most complete and well-deserved success.

Henry Morley, Journal of a London Playgoer

Henry IV, Parts I and II

P ART One of *Henry IV* has always been more popular than its sequel, doubtless because in the former Falstaff appears as a heartier and more genial character. The plays have never been absent from the stage for any great length of time, and adaptations, though less brutal than in the case of some of the other Histories, have tended to chop off the historical portions in order to further inflate Falstaff. Two eighteenth-century actors James Quin and John Henderson achieved fame as Falstaff, as did Theophilus Cibber as Ancient Pistol. John Kemble's brother Stephen was celebrated for playing the Fat Knight without padding. In 1853 Samuel Phelps doubled the roles of the King and Shallow in Part Two and repeated the roles several times during the next twenty years.

True Majesty

Edward Kynaston (1619–87) was noted for his portrayal of women; Pepys once noted that he was 'clearly the prettiest woman in the whole house.'

There is a grave and rational majesty in Shakespear's Harry the Fourth, which tho' not so glaring to the vulgar eye, requires thrice the skill and grace to become and support. Of this real majesty Kynaston was entirely master; here every sentiment came from him, as if it had been his own, as if he had himself, that instant, conceiv'd it, as if he had lost the player and were the real king he personated! A perfection so rarely found, that very often in actors of good repute, a certain vacancy of look, inanity of voice, or superfluous gesture, shall unmask the man, to the judicious spectator; who from the least of those errors plainly sees the whole but a lesson given him, to be got by heart, from some great author, whose sense is deeper than the repeater's understanding. This true majesty Kynaston had so entire a command of, that when he whispered the following plain line to Hotspur,

> Send us your prisoners, or you'll hear of it!

He convey'd a more terrible menace in it than the loudest

intemperance of voice could swell to. But let the bold imitator beware, for without the look, and just elocution that waited on it, an attempt of the same nature may fall to nothing.

But the dignity of this character appear'd in Kynaston still more shining, in the private scene between the king and prince his son: there you saw majesty, in that sort of grief which only majesty could feel! there the paternal concern for the errors of the son made the monarch more rever'd and dreaded. His reproaches so just, yet so unmix'd with anger (and therefore the more piercing), opening as it were the arms of nature, with a secret wish, that filial duty and penitence awak'd, might fall into them with grace and honour. In this affecting scene I thought Kynaston shew'd his most masterly strokes of nature; expressing all the various motions of the heart, with the same force, dignity, and feeling they are written; adding to the whole, that peculiar and becoming grace which the best writer cannot inspire into any actor that is not born with it. What made the merit of this actor, and that of Betterton more surprising, was, that though they both observed the rules of truth and nature, they were each as different in their manner of acting, as in their personal form and features. But Kynaston staid too long upon the stage, till his memory and spirit began to fail him. I shall not therefore say anything of his imperfections, which, at that time, were visibly not his own, but the effects of decaying nature.

Colley Cibber, *Apology for his Life*

Hotspur in Wig and Frock

In the agreement between Quin and Garrick, in 1746, to assist each other with their mutual skill in several select plays, Quin laid his hand upon Henry IV. and called upon Garrick to give him his assistance, by exerting his talents in Hotspur: 'For you know, David, Falstaff is so weighty, that he cannot do without a lever.' The other complied, though I believe with some reluctance; for he knew that the portion of Hotspur, which best suited his animated manner of speaking, would be exhausted in the first scene of the part. The old comedian, by this manœuvre, surprised the caution of the young actor.

The person of Garrick was not formed to give a just idea of the gallant and noble Hotspur. The mechanic, or bulky, part was wanting; nor could the fine flexibility of his voice entirely conquer the high rant and continued rage of the enthusiastic warrior. He had not then acquired that complete knowledge of modulation which he was afterwards taught by more experience. During the acting of this play, he was seized with a cold and hoarseness; and, after acting Hotspur about five nights with applause, though not with that universal approbation which generally attended his performance, he fell sick, and was confined to his chamber six or seven weeks. This happened about the latter end of February; nor did he make his appearance on the stage till he acted Ranger, in the Suspicious Husband, for his benefit, in April following.

His dress in Hotspur was objected to: a laced frock and a Ramilie wig were thought too insignificant for the character.

Thomas Davies, Dramatic Miscellanies

A Flock of Falstaffs

Davies' account contains descriptions of two celebrated Falstaffs, those of James Quin (1693–1766) and John Henderson (1747–85).

The first play acted at Lincoln's-inn Fields, which fixed the attention of the public, was The merry Wives of Windsor. This comedy was so perfectly played in all its parts, that the critics in acting universally celebrated the merit of the performers. The characters were so well adapted to the abilities of the actors, that no play had been represented with equal skill and propriety at that theatre.

The great applause Quin gained in this, the feeblest portrait of Falstaff, encouraged him to venture on the most high-seasoned part of the character, in The First Part of Henry IV. Of this large compound of lies, bragging and exhaustless fund of wit and humour, Quin possessed the ostensible or mechanical part in an eminent degree. In person he was tall and bulky: his voice strong and pleasing: his countenance manly, and his eye piercing and expressive. In scenes, where satire and sarcasm were poignant, he greatly excelled; particularly in the witty triumph over Bardolph's carbuncles, and the fooleries of the hostess. In the whole part he was animated, though not equally happy. His supercilious brow, in spite of assumed gaiety, sometimes unmasked the surliness of his disposition; however, he was, notwithstanding some faults, esteemed the most intelligent and judicious Falstaff since the days of Betterton. Berry, who succeeded Quin at Drury-lane, was neither exact in his outline nor warm in his colouring. *He* was, indeed, the Falstaff of a beerhouse; while the *other* was the dignified President, w[h]ere the choicest viands and the best liquors were to be had. Love, who came next in order at Drury-lane, wanted not a good share of vis comica, and laughed with ease and gaiety. To pass by Ned Shuter's exhibition of this favourite part would be unpardonable. What Ned wanted in judgement he supplied by archness and drollery. He enjoyed the effects of his roguery with a chuckle of his own compounding, and rolled his full eye, when detected, with a most laughable effect. Woodward and Yates put on Falstaff's habit for one night only. Their respect for the judgement of the audience prevented their assuming the boldness of the character. I think their diffidence was greater than their deficiencies. These excellent comic actors might, by repeated practice, have reached the mark which they modestly despaired to hit.

The present age has, in my opinion, produced a Falstaff who has more of the pleasant and gay features of the character than any actor I have yet seen.

*   *   *

Henderson had many difficulties to conquer before he could bring Falstaff within his grapple: neither in person, voice, nor countenance, did he seem qualified for the part. By the assistance of a most excellent judgement he has contrived to supply all deficiencies. In the impudent dignity, if I may be allowed the expression, of the character, Quin greatly excelled all competitors. In the frolicksome, gay, and humorous, situations of Falstaff, Henderson is superior to every man.

From his figure, and other outward accomplishments, Falstaff seems to have courted Quin to embrace him; while Henderson was obliged to force him into his service. Quin's supercilious manner was of use to him in scenes where he wished to overawe his companions into compliance with his humour. Henderson's gay levity was best suited to midnight pleasure and riotous mirth.

The master-action of Quin was the detection of his cowardice by the prince and Poins, in the second Act; and though, in this, Henderson shews much art and true humour, yet his soliloquy in describing his ragamuffin regiment, and his enjoying the misuse of the king's press-money, are so truly excellent, that they are not inferior to any comic representation of the stage.

Davies, *Dramatic Miscellanies*

Love in Falstaff

*In a satirical poem which created a sensation in its day, Charles Churchill
pokes fun at the mannerisms of some of the leading actors.*

When Falstaff stands detected in a lye,
Why, without meaning, rowls Love's[1] glassy eye?
Why?—There's no cause—at least no cause we know—
It was the Fashion twenty years ago.
Fashion—a word which knaves and fools may use
Their knavery and folly to excuse.
To copy beauties, forfeits all pretence
To fame—to copy faults, is want of sense.

Yet, (tho' in some particulars he fails,
Some few particulars, where Mode prevails)
If in these hallow'd times, when sober, sad,
All Gentlemen are melancholy mad,
When 'tis not deem'd so great a crime by half
To violate a vestal, as to laugh,
Rude mirth may hope presumptuous to engage
An Act of Toleration for the stage,
And courtiers will, like reasonable creatures,
Suspend vain Fashion, and unscrew their features,
Old Falstaff, play'd by Love, shall please once more,
And humour set the audience in a roar.

Actors I've seen, and of no vulgar name,
Who, being from one part possess'd of fame,
Whether they are to laugh, cry, whine, or bawl,
Still introduce that fav'rite part in all.
Here, Love, be cautious—ne'er be thou betray'd
To call in that wag Falstaff's dang'rous aid;
Like Goths of old, howe'er he seems a friend,
He'll seize that throne, you wish him to defend.

Charles Churchill, The Rosciad, 1761

[1] James Love, born James Dance (1722–74) an actor and adapter of plays.
Falstaff was one of his best portrayals, which, by all accounts, is not saying
much.

John Kemble's Hotspur[1]

Covent Garden, June 1817

Again I let myself be deluded with the hope that I should see real acting, real impersonation, penetrating truth, and grasp of character, that infusion into noble poetry of life and action, which by exalting all our faculties and rousing them into harmonious exercise, offers to us perhaps the highest enjoyment which man is capable of receiving from art. But all I got for my pains was to hear some passages finely spoken, with a total breakdown and failure, as a rule, in all that is most essential. . . . Where was the humour of Hotspur, the young fiery hero, who is as brave as he is unmannerly, who out of vanity hates vanity in others; who, himself the head of the conspiracy, with the best resources in his hands, has so little self-command that he scares away the most powerful of his confederates, and who, as general, as husband, and as friend, by his fiery temper and good-humour, shows characteristics so marked and peculiar that the most careless reader never fails to have them vividly stamped upon his fancy? John Kemble declaimed leisurely, intelligently; making frequent efforts at the humour of the part, but never grasping it. Here, too, he spoke quite as slowly as in the parts I had previously seen, made two or three considerable pauses, now drawled (*klagte*), now emphasised every second or third word, one could not say why, and then ended so frequently in a sort of sing-song in all, that I thought I was again listening to one of those Protestant preachers whom one used to hear twenty years ago in provincial places indulging in this wailing, tedious *tempo*. Percy's first long story to the king Kemble seemed to take as serious earnest, only exaggerated by youthful violence. To this solemn, almost torturing slowness the ear became so accustomed, that when Percy came to the passage—

'In Richard's time—what do you call the place?
A plague upon 't!—it is in Gloucestershire—
'Twas where the madcap Duke his uncle kept,' &c.,

and he all at once spoke it with a quick, sharp utterance, like a man who suddenly cannot call a name to mind, and seeks for it with impatience, the whole house broke out into vehement applause at the sudden drop of the voice and alteration of the

---

[1] For a brief note on Tieck see his account of Kemble's Coriolanus, p. 323.

179

tempo. It is something noticeable when a thing of this kind, which is a mere matter of course, and which can be easily hit off by the mediocre actor, is received by the public with such marked admiration. This mannerism, which often shows itself in Kemble, as in other actors, capriciously and without cause, reminds one of the tragic recitation of the French, who in every scene fling out some verses at a galloping pace in succession to passages spoken with measured and exaggerated emphasis.

Ludwig Tieck, *The Nineteenth Century, February, 1880*

An Unpadded Falstaff

STEPHEN KEMBLE in *Henry IV, Part 1*, Covent Garden, 1802, who achieved notoriety as an unpadded Falstaff (from an engraving of 1825).

The acting manager of Drury Lane at that period[1] was Mr. Stephen Kemble, brother of John and Charles, and Mrs. Siddons. His obesity was so great that he played Falstaff without stuffing. I saw him do it on one occasion; but the effect was more painful than amusing. He evidently suffered under the exertion; and though his reading of the part was irre-

[1] i.e. 1818.

proachable, he lacked the natural humour, and was too ill at ease to portray the mere animal spirits of the jovial knight. But did any one ever see Sir John Falstaff except in his mind's eye? Dowton[1] was, in my opinion, the best representative in my time. His eye had the right rogueish twinkle; his laugh, the fat, self-satisfied chuckle; his large protruding under lip, the true character of sensuality; but his memory was notoriously treacherous, and the text suffered severely. He used to say to an author, 'D—n your dialogue! give me the situations.'

J. R. Planché, *Recollections and Reflections*

Coronation at Covent Garden

The coronation of George IV provided the occasion for a similar spectacle to be tacked on to Shakespeare's play. Macready records that the audience warmly applauded his performance, particularly the soliloquy on sleep.

June 25 [1821]. Our dramatic friends were indebted to the approaching Coronation for a high gratification this evening in the revival of Shakspeare's '*Second part of King Henry the Fourth*,' which the play bills informed us has not been performed during the last 20 years! at *this* Theatre, we presume, as it is certainly not quite so long since it was acted at the rival house. The cast of to night gave a new eclat to Macready in his most excellent delineation of the aged *Henry*, but we have already been lavish of our praises of that gentleman's performances in an other part of this number, and therefore merely say here, that he fully merited all our encomiums. Charles Kemble was princely as the *Prince of Wales;* Fawcett a fat *Falstaff*, if not exactly a Shaksperian one; Blanchard a blustering *Pistol*, and W. Farren, Emery, and Mrs. Davenport, fully kept up their ancient fame as *Shallow, Silence,* and *Mrs. Quickly*. The grand attraction of the evening, however, was *not* precisely the legitimate drama, as the latter portion of the Play introduced three new scenes of *Henry the Fifth*'s Coronation: first, the processional platform with it's splendid retinue; next, the magnificent inauguration in Westminster Abbey; and last, and best, the gorgeous banquet in the Hall, with the introduction of the mailed Champion, and the ceremony of his challenge. All these were set forth not only with the taste and grandeur to be expected at Covent Garden, but with almost the regal splendour of the originals. All was light and blazonry, and gold and glory;

[1] William Dowton (1764–1851) an actor famous for his portrayal of energetic old men, including Falstaff. See p. 147.

and we should despair indeed of public curiosity, and of theatrical taste, did we not prophecy a long career to the united attractions of Shakspeare's poetry, and a Coronation's magnificence.

European Magazine

Elliston's Last Falstaff

Macready describes the last performance in this role of Robert Elliston (1774–1831) a comic actor greatly admired by, among many others, Charles Lamb and Lord Byron. The date was May 11, 1826.

An interest more than ordinary attached to the reproduction of the 'First Part of King Henry IV,' from Elliston's announcement in the part of Falstaff. The play was acted on Thursday, May 11th. Elliston was an actor highly distinguished by the versatility and power of his performances, but of late years he had somewhat 'fallen from his high estate;' still such an announcement stimulated the curiosity of play-goers. His rehearsal gave me very great pleasure. I watched it most earnestly, and was satisfied that in it he made the nearest approach to the joyous humour and unctuous roguery of the character that I had ever witnessed, giving me reason to entertain sanguine hopes of a great success in its performance; but, alas! whether from failure of voice or general deficiency of power, the attempt fell ineffectively upon the audience, and the character was left, as it has been since the days of Quin and Henderson, without an adequate representative. The play was repeated on Monday, May 15th, 1826. Before the curtain rose I was in the green-room, and spoke with Elliston, who complained of being ill, and appeared so, smelling very strongly of ether. As the evening wore on he gave signs of extreme weakness, was frequently inaudible, and several times voices from the front called to him to 'speak up.' There was not on this occasion even the semblance of an effort at exertion, and in the fifth act he remained silent for some little time, then, in trying to reach the side-scene, reeled round and fell prostrate before the foot-lights. It was a piteous spectacle! A sad contrast to the triumphs of his earlier popularity! The audience generally attributed his fall to intoxication, but without just cause. He was really indisposed, and the remedy from which he sought support was too potent. He was conveyed to his dressing-room almost insensible, and never appeared upon the stage again.

W. C. Macready, Reminiscences and Diaries

Father and Son

Theophilus Cibber's most famous role was that of Ancient Pistol, while his father Colley made a memorable Shallow.

THEOPHILUS CIBBER, son of Colley Cibber, as Pistol in *Henry IV, Part 2,* Drury Lane, 1729.

Pistol is a hero, where such as Bardolph, Nym, and Peto, are the underlings. He seems to be an obvious character; and yet it must be owned that no actor, however well instructed and judicious, has gained great applause in the representation of the burlesque and boisterous humour of Pistol since it was played by Theophilus Cibber. He assumed a peculiar kind of false spirit, and uncommon blustering, with such turgid action, and long unmeasurable strides, that it was impossible not to laugh at so extravagant a figure, with such loud and grotesque vociferation. He became so famous for his action in this part, that he acquired the name of Pistol, at first as a mark rather of merit, but finally as a term of ridicule.

*   *   *

Shallow's Return

Whether he was a copy or an original in Shallow, it is certain that no audience was ever more fixed in deep attention, at his first appearance, or more shaken with laughter in the progress of the scene, than at Colley Cibber's exhibition of this ridiculous justice of peace. Some years after he had left the stage, he acted Shallow for his son's benefit. I believe in 1737, when Quin was the Falstaff, and Milward the king. Whether it was owing to the pleasure the spectators felt on seeing their old friend return to them again, *though for that night only*, after an absence of some years, I know not; but, surely, no actor or audience were better pleased with each other. His manner was so perfectly simple, his look so vacant, when he questioned his Cousin Silence about the price of ewes, and lamented, in the same breath, with silly surprise, the death of old Double, that it will be impossible for any surviving spectator not to smile at the remembrance of it. The want of ideas occasions Shallow to repeat almost every thing he says. Cibber's transition from asking the price of bullocks, to trite, but grave, reflections on mortality, was so natural, and attended with such an unmeaning roll of his small pigs-eyes, accompanied with an important utterance of tick! tick! tick! not much louder than the balance of a watch's pendulum, that I question if any actor was ever superior in the conception or expression of such solemn insignificancy.

Jonson, a year or two after Cibber had left the stage, and, when he was between seventy and eighty, undertook the part of Shallow; and though the old hound had lost almost all his teeth, he was still so staunch, that he seized his game and held it fast.

Davies, *Dramatic Miscellanies*

A Double Triumph

In his production at Sadler's Wells, Samuel Phelps played both Shallow and King Henry IV.

October 1 [1864].—Of the *Second Part of King Henry IV*, at Drury Lane, it will suffice to record that Justice Shallow is in Mr. Phelps's hands, as in Shakespeare's, anything but a merely comic character. Comic upon the surface, it is at the core terribly earnest, and was meant, with a profound seriousness under the jest, as a picture of grey hairs without honour, age looking back to a false heaven of youthful lusts that in its imbecile youth it had ill realised, instead of forward to the well-earned rest, and downward to the open grave before its feet. There is nothing more sternly earnest in Shakespeare, and more tragic in its undertone, than the dialogue between Shallow and Silence at the beginning of the second scene of the third act, and so Mr. Phelps feels it, as his acting shows. We have in this play the unhonoured age of two old men, Shallow and Falstaff; with these men on one side of him and the venerable Chief Justice on the other, Henry the Fifth speaks his closing speech, that begins,

> 'I know thee not, old man; fall to thy prayers;
> How ill white hairs become a fool and jester!'

There is a particular contrast between the unhonoured poverty of wit and soul in the old Shallow and the premature decay of the King weighted with mighty care for earthly dignities, that makes the representation of the two characters by one competent actor fully possessed with their significance a source of true artistic pleasure. It is well, also, that the untaught in dramatic art should see how far the skill of a true actor is removed from dull monotony, and through how many differing conceptions it is able faithfully to follow with its impersonation the true poet's mind.

Henry Morley, Journal of a London Playgoer

King Henry V

DURING the Christmas Revels of 1607, Richard Burbage played King Henry. We have to wait till 1735 to hear of another performance of Shakespeare's play; in the interim it had been ousted from the stage by Aaron Hill's adaptation which leaves out all the comic characters but adds a sub-plot. Garrick and Macready both played Henry in the play which was always used as a vehicle for elaborate displays of pageantry. Charles Kean's farewell production in 1859 featured his wife as Chorus in the character of Clio, the Muse of History.

King Kemble

On the 1st October [1789], Mr. Kemble acted the part of Henry V. The play had not been done for 20 years.

*　　*　　*

As far as Mr. Kemble was concerned, I do not think that even his Coriolanus exceeded his 'royal Hal.' As a *coup de théâtre*, his starting up from prayer at the sound of the trumpet, in the passage where he states his attempted atonement to Richard the Second, formed one of the most spirited excitements that the stage has ever displayed. His occasional reversions to the 'mad wag,' the 'sweet young prince,' had a singular charm, as the condescension of one who could be so terrible. Of the other performers, James Aickin and Baddeley claim a distinguished praise, in which they share, humbly, with Kemble, that is, as Exeter, and Fluellen, being unapproachable, for tenderness and humour.

James Boaden, Life of Kemble

Macready as Harry

A glimpse of Macready in a much-praised production at Covent Garden. The production was revived twenty years later when Macready was about to retire as manager of Covent Garden; it included an elaborate diorama with scenes such as the progress of the English fleet from Southampton to Harfleur.

Shakespeare's 'King Henry V.' was performed at this theatre last night. The character of that warlike and virtuous prince was sustained by Mr. Macready. In the fourth act, when the trump of battle sounds in his ear, and

'The warlike Harry, like himself,
Assumes the port of Mars,'

his performance was truly splendid. His delivery of the invocation to the 'God of battles,' and of the noble speech which unfolds the anticipated glories of 'St. Crispin's Day,' is, we venture to say, unexcelled on the stage.

Morning Herald, October 4 1819

History as Pageant

A production very much in the manner of Charles Kean's 1855 spectacle, right down to the appearance of Clio, the Muse of History as Chorus. A less serious comment on the same production will be found in the next extract.

Mr. John Coleman's production of *Shakespeare's Henry V.*, at the Queen's Theatre, is one of the best spectacles that has been

Design by Grieves and Lloyds for Charles Kean's production of *Henry V*,
Queen's, 1855.

seen in London for years, and, perhaps, one of the worst acted.
That great care has been bestowed, and an enormous amount of
capital expended upon the mounting of this revival, is evident in
every scene, and it is unfortunate that more attention was not
devoted to the casting of the numerous small but important
parts. For the scenic accessories we have nothing but praise, the
very first set of the Jerusalem Chamber rousing a burst of
applause. The next elaborate set, the Interior of Westminster
Abbey upon the occasion of the coronation of King Henry V.,
was, to our thinking, the most striking and impressive of the
whole play; the robes of the various prelates, English nobles,
etc., and the admirable grouping of all the characters on the
stage, forming a tableau of surprising grandness. The fall of
Harfleur formed Tableau II, which, in some measure, atoned
for a most execrable ballet, called 'The Falcon Chase,' which
had immediately preceded it; the stirring finish to the siege of
Harfleur, however, saved the act. Another life-like picture was
the field of Agincourt during action—the whole scene, with its
struggling combatants, riderless and maimed horses, and dead
and dying men, roused the audience to perfect enthusiasm.
Mr. Coleman being here called before the curtain on the first
representation, took the opportunity of rebuking a very noisy

but merry, gallery audience, and at the same time announced that the ballet of 'The Falcon Chase,' which had met with so chilling a reception, should not be repeated. The announcement of the 'flight' of the Falcons was received with much more favor than the 'Chase.' As a series of animated historical pictures the various scenes were unique; but, excepting the performance of Mr. Phelps, who gave a most effective impersonation of Henry IV., in the prologue, and Mr. T. Mead, who was a characteristic Pistol, the acting does not call for any detailed notice. Mr. Coleman, in the quieter scenes, gave emphasis to the lines of Henry V., though in the more telling speeches he sadly lacked force; but great commendation is due to him for the admirable taste and judgment in the stage management of a most arduous stage play. The scenery has been prepared by Messrs. Gordon & Harford, who have certainly never done better work. During the recess the theatre has been most handsomely redecorated and improved.

Charing Cross Magazine, October 1876

Magical History Tour

Perhaps it is true, as they say, that you do not see very much of Shakespeare at the Queen's Theatre, but still you do get a lot for your money. For instance, at 7.45 you see the Coronation in Westminster Abbey; at 8.30 the Siege of Harfleur; at 9.45 the Battle of Agincourt; at 10.45 Old London Bridge. And all this without moving out of your stall! Who shall say that the Drama is dead? When you know the exact moment at which you can see Mr. Coleman capering on a rocking-horse, who shall say that Shakespeare spells bankruptcy? Do not talk to me of the elevation of the Drama! When did it ever get beyond this?

The World, September 27 1876

Romeo and Juliet

THIS tragedy has been a favourite with theatre audiences ever since it was first performed. There were the usual manglings and transplants, including one by Garrick and another by Otway, but most of Shakespeare survived. Fanny Kemble made a memorable start to her career as the heroine in 1829 and, Macready made his début as Romeo nineteen years earlier at the age of seventeen.

Rival Romeos

In September 1750, the play was put on simultaneously at Drury Lane with Garrick and George Anne Bellamy and at Covent Garden with Spranger Barry and Mrs. Cibber in the title roles, provoking a contemporary quatrain:

> Well, what's tonight, says angry Ned,
> As up from bed he rouses:
> *Romeo* again! and shakes his head—
> Ah! pox on both your houses!

A character upon the stage was never supported with more luxuriant merit than this by Mess. Garrick and Barry, or Barry and Garrick; for when those inimitable performers contested it sixteen or seventeen years since, it was extremely difficult to say who should stand first; we shall offer a comparison upon strict impartiality, and leave decision to the unprejudiced reader.

As to figure, though there is no necessity for a lover being tall, yet we apprehend Mr. Barry had a peculiar advantage in this point; his amorous harmony of features, melting eyes, and unequalled plaintiveness of voice, seemed to promise every thing we could wish, and yet the superior grace of Mr. Garrick's attitudes, the vivacity of his countenance, and the fire of his expression, shewed there were many essential beauties in which his great competitor might be excelled: those scenes in which they most evidently rose above each other, are as follow— Mr. Barry the Garden scene of the second act—Mr. Garrick the friar scene in the third—Mr. Barry the garden scene in the fourth—Mr. Garrick in the first scene, description of the apothecary, &c. fifth act—Mr. Barry first part of the tomb scene, and Mr. Garrick from where the poison operates to the end.

SPRANGER BARRY as Romeo and ISABELLA NOSSITER as Juliet, Covent Garden, 1759.

Having seen this play three times at each house, during the contention, and having held the critical scale in as just an equilibrium as possible, by not only my own feelings but those of the audience in general, I perceived that Mr. Garrick commanded most applause—Mr. Barry most tears: desirous

of tracing this difference to its source; I found that as dry sorrow drinks our blood, so astonishment checks our tears; that by a kind of electrical merit Mr. Garrick struck all hearts with a degree of inexpressible feeling, and bore conception so far beyond her usual sphere that softer sensations lay hid in wonder.

Francis Gentleman, The Dramatic Censor

An Economical Performance

Goldsmith describes, perhaps accurately, his experiences with a group of strolling players. Much of the essay from which this passage is taken is derived from one in French by Marivaux.

I love a straggling life above all things in the world; sometimes good, sometimes bad; to be warm to-day, and cold to-morrow; to eat when one can get it, and drink when (the tankard is out) it stands before me. We arrived that evening at Tenterden, and took a large room at the Greyhound, where we resolved to exhibit Romeo and Juliet, with the funeral procession, the grave, and the garden scene. Romeo was to be performed by a gentleman from the Theatre-Royal in Drury-Lane; Juliet, by a lady who had never appeared on any stage before; and I was to snuff the candles: all excellent in our way. We had figures enough, but the difficulty was to dress them. The same coat that served Romeo, turned with the blue lining outwards, served for his friend Mercutio: a large piece of crape sufficed at once for Juliet's petticoat and pall: a pestle and mortar from a neighbouring apothecary's, answered all the purposes of a bell; and our landlord's own family, wrapped in white sheets, served to fill up the procession. In short, there were but three figures among us that might be said to be dressed with any propriety; I mean the nurse, the starved apothecary, and myself. Our performance gave universal satisfaction: the whole audience were enchanted with our powers, and Tenterden is a town of taste.

Oliver Goldsmith,
The British Magazine, October 1760

Macready's Début[1]

My father, to whom I of course deferred, had selected Romeo for the character of my *début*, and accordingly I was now in earnest work upon it. Frequently in the course of my solitary attempts the exclamation would escape me, 'I cannot do it;' and in some of my private rehearsals I had the discouraging remark of my father, 'that will not do,' to damp my courage and cast the gloomy shade of doubt on my exertions. Still, however, I persevered; and as the time of making the desperate plunge approached, my hopes were somewhat cheered by the encouragement of the lady who was rehearsing her part of Juliet with me (Mrs. Young from Drury Lane Theatre), and my father's admission of 'very great improvement.' By dint of practice and repeated rehearsals, alone and with the other performers, I had got by rote, as it were, every particular of place, gesture, feeling, and intonation—and well for me I had done so; for if it made my heart beat more quickly to read in the street playbills[2] the announcement of 'The part

---

[1] June 7, 1810.

[2] The playbill stated: On Thursday evening, June 7, will be presented the tragedy of 'Romeo and Juliet' (written by Shakspear). The part of Romeo by a YOUNG GENTLEMAN, being his first appearance on any stage. Friar Laurence Mr. Harley, and Juliet by Mrs. Young. The play was followed by the farce of 'The Irishman in London' (written by the father), in which the elder Macready performed the part of Murtoch Delany.

of Romeo by a young gentleman, his first appearance on any stage,' the emotions I experienced, on first crossing the stage, and coming forward in face of the lights and the applauding audience were almost overpowering. There was a mist before my eyes. I seemed to see nothing of the dazzling scene before me, and for some time I was like an automaton moving in certain defined limits. I went mechanically through the variations in which I had drilled myself, and it was not until the plaudits of the audience awoke me from the kind of waking dream in which I seemed to be moving, that I gained my self-possession, and really entered into the spirit of the character and, I may say, felt the passion I was to represent. Every round of applause acted like inspiration on me: I 'trod on air,' became another being, or a happier self; and when the curtain fell at the conclusion of the play, and the intimate friends and performers crowded on the stage to raise up the Juliet and myself, shaking my hands with fervent congratulations, a lady asked me, 'Well, sir, how do you feel now?' my boyish answer was without disguise, 'I feel as if I should like to act it all over again.'

Macready's Reminiscences

Macready on Miss O'Neill

Eliza O'Neill (1791–1872) one of the most celebrated Juliets, made her London début in the role in 1814. She retired from the stage, after five years of immense popularity, on her marriage in 1819.

In its outward graces how different was the excellence which, a night or two after, excited my enthusiastic admiration when Shakespeare's Juliet made her entry on the scene in the person of Miss O'Neill! Our seats in the orchestra of Covent Garden gave me the opportunity of noting every slightest flash of emotion or shade of thought that passed over her countenance. The charming picture she presented was one that time could not efface from the memory. It was not altogether the matchless beauty of form and face, but the spirit of perfect innocence and purity that seemed to glisten in her speaking eyes and breathe from her chiselled lips. To her might justly be ascribed the negative praise, in my mind the highest commendation that, as an artist, man or woman can receive, of a total absence of any approach to affectation. There was in her look, voice, and manner an artlessness, an apparent unconsciousness (so foreign to the generality of stage performers) that riveted the spectator's gaze; but when, with altered tones and eager glance, she inquired, as he lingeringly left her, the name of Romeo of the Nurse, and bade her go and learn it, the revolution in her whole being was evident, anticipating the worse,—

—'If he be married,
My grave is like to be my wedding-bed.'

I have heard objections to the warmth of her passionate confessions in the garden scene; but the love of the maid of sunny Italy is not to be measured and judged by the phlegmatic formalist.

'My bounty is as boundless as the sea,
My love as deep; the more I give to thee
The more I have, for both are infinite,'

is her heart's utterance. Love was to her life; life not valued, if unsustained by love. Such was the impression Miss O'Neill's conception of the character made, rendering its catastrophe the only natural refuge of a guileless passion so irresistible and absorbing. In the second act the impatience of the love-sick maid to obtain tidings of her lover was delightfully contrasted with the winning playfulness with which she so dexterously lured back to doting fondness the pettish humour of the testy old Nurse, and in rushing to her appointment at the Friar's cell, her whole soul was in the utterance of the words, 'Hie to high fortune! Honest Nurse, farewell.' The desperate alternative to which the command of Capulet that she should marry Paris reduced her, transformed the gentle girl at once into a heroine, and the distracting contention of her fears and resolution rose to a frantic climax of passion, abruptly closed by her exclamation, 'Romeo! I come! This do I drink to thee!' Through my whole experience hers was the only representation of Juliet I have seen; and as the curtain fell, I left my seat in the orchestra with the words of Iachimo in my mind. 'All of her, that is out of door, most rich! . . . She is alone the Arabian bird.'

Macready's *Reminiscences*

194

The Art of Dying

A passage from a handbook for public speakers and actors gives a fascinating glimpse of the last moments of early 19th-century Juliets. The author was Mrs. Siddons' son.

I do not know what evil genius persuades so many of our performers, the females in particular, that it is so exquisite a manœuvre to be perpetually rolling themselves on the ground. A lady acting Juliet, or any other character of that description, will sometimes fall on the boards with such violence, when she hears of the death or banishment of her lover, that we are really alarmed, lest her poor skull should be fractured by the violence of the concussion. Applause gained by arts so unnatural and so disgusting can only come from the ignorant and injudicious, who, incapable of forming a judgment on the real merit or interest of a touching situation, would be just as much concerned in the fate of a Punchinello or a Harlequin. If, on such an occurrence, an *amateur* be sometimes induced to join *his* suffrage to the general plaudit of the house, it is by a natural transition from contempt to pity: he is enchanted to find that the poor creature (who, though a most execrable actress, may be a very good girl for all that) has drawn herself out of her dangerous predicament, with all her limbs safe and sound.

Henry Siddons,
Illustrations of Gesture and Action 1811

The Many Deaths of Romeo Coates

The less than tragic début of a wealthy West Indian (1772–1848) who fancied himself as an actor.

This singular man, more than forty years ago, occupied a large portion of public attention; his eccentricities were the theme of general wonder, and great was the curiosity to catch a glance at as strange a being as any that ever appeared in English society. This extraordinary individual was a native of one of the West India Islands, and was represented as a man of extraordinary wealth; to which, however, he had no claim.

About the year 1808, there arrived at the York Hotel, at Bath, a person about the age of fifty, somewhat gentlemanlike, but so different from the usual men of the day that considerable attention was directed to him. He was of a good figure; but

The Rival Romeos. ROBERT 'Romeo' COATES and CHARLES MATHEWS, who had satirised the latter's portrayal, 1813.

his face was sallow, seamed with wrinkles, and more expressive of cunning than of any other quality. His dress was remarkable: in the daytime he was covered at all seasons with enormous quantities of fur; but the evening costume in which he went to the balls made a great impression, from its gaudy appearance; for his buttons, as well as his knee-buckles, were of diamonds. There was of course great curiosity to know who this stranger was; and this curiosity was heightened by an announcement that he proposed to appear at the theatre in the character of Romeo. There was something so unlike the impassioned lover in his appearance—so much that indicated a man with few intellectual gifts—that everybody was prepared for a failure. No one, however, anticipated the reality.

On the night fixed for his appearance, the house was crowded to suffocation. The playbills had given out that 'an amateur of fashion' would for that night only perform in the character of Romeo; besides, it was generally whispered that the rehearsals gave indication of comedy rather than tragedy, and that his readings were of a perfectly novel character.

The very first appearance of Romeo convulsed the house with laughter. Benvolio prepares the audience for the stealthy visit of the lover to the object of his admiration; and fully did the amateur give expression to one sense of the words uttered, for he was indeed the true representative of a thief stealing onwards in the night, 'with Tarquin's ravishing strides,' and disguising his face as if he were thoroughly ashamed of it. The darkness of the scene did not, however, shew his real character so much as the masquerade, when he came forward with a hideous grin, and made what he considered his bow—which consisted in thrusting his head forward, and bobbing it up and down several times, his body remaining perfectly upright and stiff, like a toy mandarin with movable head.

His dress was *outré* in the extreme: whether Spanish, Italian, or English, no one could say; it was like nothing ever worn. In a cloak of sky-blue silk, profusely spangled, red pantaloons, a vest of white muslin, surmounted by an enormously thick cravat, and a wig *à la* Charles the Second, capped by an opera hat, he presented one of the most grotesque spectacles ever witnessed upon the stage. The whole of his garments were evidently too tight for him; and his movements appeared so incongruous, that every time he raised his arm, or moved a limb, it was impossible to refrain from laughter: but what chiefly convulsed the audience was the bursting of a seam in an inexpressible part of his dress, and the sudden extrusion through the red rent of a quantity of white linen sufficient to make a Bourbon flag, which was visible whenever he turned round. This was at first supposed to be a wilful offence against common decency, and some disapprobation was evinced; but the utter unconsciousness of the odd creature was soon apparent, and then unrestrained mirth reigned throughout the boxes, pit, and gallery. The total want of flexibility of limb, the awkwardness of his gait, and the idiotic manner in which he stood still, all produced a most ludicrous effect; but when his guttural voice was heard, and his total misapprehension of every passage in the play, especially the vulgarity of his address to Juliet, were perceived, every one was satisfied that Shakespeare's Romeo was burlesqued on that occasion.

The balcony scene was interrupted by shrieks of laughter, for in the midst of one of Juliet's impassioned exclamations, Romeo quietly took out his snuff-box and applied a pinch to his nose; on this a wag in the gallery bawled out, 'I say, Romeo, give us a pinch,' when the impassioned lover, in the most affected manner, walked to the side boxes and offered the contents of his box first to the gentlemen, and then, with great gallantry, to the ladies. This new interpretation of Shakespeare was hailed with loud bravos, which the actor acknowledged with his usual grin and nod. Romeo then returned to the balcony, and was seen to extend his arms; but all passed in dumb show, so incessant were the shouts of laughter. All that went on upon the stage was for a time quite inaudible, but previous to the soliloquy 'I do remember an apothecary,' there was for a moment a dead silence; for in rushed the hero with a precipitate step until he reached the stage lamps, when he commenced his speech in the lowest possible whisper, as if he had something to communicate to the pit that ought not to be generally known; and this tone was kept up throughout the whole of the soliloquy, so that not a sound could be heard.

The amateur actor shewed many indications of aberration of mind, and seemed rather the object of pity than of amusement; he, however, appeared delighted with himself, and also with his audience, for at the conclusion he walked first to the left of the stage and bobbed his head in his usual grotesque manner at the side boxes; then to the right, performing the same feat; after which, going to the centre of the stage with the usual bob, and placing his hand upon his left breast, he exclaimed, 'Haven't I done it well?' To this inquiry the house, convulsed as it was with shouts of laughter, responded in such a way as delighted the heart of Kean on one great occasion, when he said, 'The pit rose at me.' The whole audience started up as if with one accord, giving a yell of derision, whilst pocket-handkerchiefs waved from all parts of the theatre.

The dying scene was irresistibly comic, and I question if Liston, Munden, or Joey Knight, was ever greeted with such merriment; for Romeo dragged the unfortunate Juliet from the tomb, much in the same manner as a washerwoman thrusts into her cart the bag of foul linen. But how shall I describe his death? Out came a dirty silk handkerchief from his pocket, with which he carefully swept the ground; then his opera hat was carefully placed for a pillow, and down he laid himself. After various tossings about, he seemed reconciled to the position; but the house vociferously bawled out, 'Die again, Romeo!' and, obedient to the command, he rose up, and went through the ceremony again. Scarcely had he lain quietly down, when the call was again heard, and the well-pleased amateur was evidently prepared to enact a third death; but Juliet now rose up from her tomb, and gracefully put an end to this ludicrous scene by advancing to the front of the stage and aptly applying a quotation from Shakspeare—

> 'Dying is such sweet sorrow,
> That he will die again until to-morrow.'

Thus ended an extravaganza such as has seldom been witnessed; for although Coates repeated the play at the Haymarket, amidst shouts of laughter from the playgoers, there never was so ludicrous a performance as that which took place at Bath on the first night of his appearance. Eventually he was driven from the stage with much contumely, in consequence of its having been discovered that, under pretence of acting for a charitable purpose, he had obtained a sum of money for his performances. His love of notoriety led him to have a most singular shell-shaped carriage built, in which, drawn by two fine white horses, he was wont to parade in the park; the harness, and every available part of the vehicle, (which was really handsome,) were blazoned over with his heraldic device—a cock crowing; and his appearance was heralded by the *gamins* of London shrieking out, 'Cock-a-doodle-doo!' Coates eventually quitted London and settled at Boulogne, where a fair lady was induced to become the partner of his existence notwithstanding the ridicule of the whole world.

R. H. Gronow,
Reminiscences and Recollections, 1862

Fanny Kemble's Début

On October 5, 1829 Fanny Kemble, then nineteen years old, made her début as Juliet and was an instant success.

It was one of those nights not to be forgotten in theatrical annals. The young girl herself—under twenty—coming out as the girl-heroine of tragedy, Shakespeare's Juliet; her mother, Mrs. Charles Kemble, after a retirement from the stage of some years playing (for this especial night of her daughter's *début* and her husband's effort to re-establish the

FANNY KEMBLE as Juliet, Covent Garden, 1829 (drawing by John Hayter).

attraction of Covent Garden Theatre) the part of Lady Capulet; her father, Charles Kemble, a man much past fifty years of age, enacting with wonderful spirit and vigour the mercurial character of Mercutio; combined to excite into enthusiasm the assembled audience. The plaudits that overwhelmed Mrs. Charles Kemble, causing her to stand trembling with emotion and melted into real tears that drenched the rouge from her cheeks, plaudits that assured her of genuine welcome given by a public accustomed to a long esteem for the name of Kemble, and now actuated by a private as well as professional sympathy for her—these plaudits had scarcely died away into the silence of expectancy, when Juliet had to make her entrance on the scene. We were in the stage-box, and could see her standing at the wing, by the motion of her lips evidently endeavouring to bring moisture into her parched mouth, and trying to summon courage for advancing; when Mrs. Davenport, who played in her own inimitable style the part of the Nurse, after calling repeatedly 'Juliet! what, Juliet!' went towards her, took her by the hand, and pulled her forward on to the stage—a proceeding that had good natural as well as dramatic effect, and brought forth the immediately recognizant acclamations of the house. Fanny Kemble's acting was marked by much originality of thought and grace of execution. Some of the positions she assumed were strikingly new and appropriate, suggestive as they were of the state of feeling and peculiar situation in which the character she was playing happened to be. For instance, in the scene of the second act, where Juliet is impatiently awaiting the return of her nurse with tidings from Romeo, Fanny Kemble was discovered in a picturesque attitude standing leaning on the back of a chair, earnestly looking out of a tall window opening on to a garden, as if eager to catch the first approach of the expected messenger. . .

Charles and Mary Cowden Clarke,
Recollections of Writers

Not Acted but Costumed

It has the advantage of that splendid scenic presentation which Mr. Irving understands so well, and which converts the play from a splendid and delicate poem into a gorgeous and over-weighted spectacle. Mr. Irving does these things very handsomely; he is a most liberal and intelligent manager. It may, indeed, not be thought a proof of his intelligence that he himself should play the hero, or that he should entrust the girlish Juliet to the large, the long, the mature Miss Terry. Miss Terry has great charm; she is what the French call, in artistic parlance, a 'nature'; she is almost always interesting, and she is often a delightful presence: but she is not Juliet; on the contrary! She is too voluminous, too deliberate, too prosaic, too English, too unversed in the utterance of poetry. How little Mr. Irving is Romeo it is not worth while even to attempt to declare; he must know it, of course, better than anyone else, and there is something really touching in so extreme a sacrifice of one's ideal. It remains to be ascertained why he should have wished to bring out the play. Mr. Irving is not a Romeo; Miss Terry is not a Juliet; and no one else, save Mrs. Stirling, is anything in particular. Was it for Mrs. Stirling, then, that this elaborate undertaking was set on foot? She plays the Nurse, and plays it very well—too well, almost, since it is pushed forward, out of its relations to the total. Mrs. Stirling, to-day a very old woman, is a rich and accomplished actress; she belongs to a more sincere generation; she knows her art, and it is from her rendering of the garrulous, humorous, immoral attendant of the gentle Juliet that the spectator receives his one impression of the appropriate and the adequate. It was probably for the spectacle that Mr. Irving took the play in hand, and the spectacle has richly rewarded him. It is the last word of stage-carpentering, and is full of beautiful effects of colour and costume. The stage is crowded with figures; there are at moments too many; the play moves slowly through a succession of glowing and deceptive pictures. The fault of all this splendour of detail is that, in the homely phrase, it puts the cart before the horse. The play is not acted, it is costumed; the immortal lovers of Verona become subordinate and ineffectual figures. I had never thought of *Romeo and Juliet* as a dull drama; but Mr. Irving has succeeded in making it so. It is obstructed, interrupted; its passionate rapidity is chopped up into little tableaus. In a word, it is slow,—mortally slow; for much of the dialogue is incomprehensibly spoken, and the rest ineffectively. To make this enchanting poem tame,—it was reserved for the present management of the Lyceum to accomplish that miracle.

Henry James,
Atlantic Monthly, August 1882

Twelfth Night

PEPYS saw the play three times and didn't enjoy it once. In 1741, Macklin gained fame as Malvolio and Mrs. Pritchard as Viola. The play has always been vulnerable to musical prettification and this tendency increased alarmingly throughout the 19th century. Notable Violas included Ellen Tree (Charles Kean's wife) in a spectacular production in 1850 and Ada Rehan in 1894.

Mrs. Jordan's Olivia

Dorothy Jordan (1762–1816) was a celebrated comic actress who appeared as Phoebe in As You Like It *in 1777 and as Rosalind in the same play (her last stage appearance) in 1814. In between she played many Shakespearian comic heroines, including Beatrice and Helena.*

Those who have only seen Mrs. Jordan within the last ten or fifteen years, can have no adequate notion of her performance of such parts as Ophelia; Helena, in All's Well that Ends Well; and Viola in this play. Her voice had latterly acquired a coarseness, which suited well enough with her Nells and Hoydens, but in those days it sank, with her steady melting eye, into the heart. Her joyous parts—in which her memory now chiefly lives— in her youth were outdone by her plaintive ones. There is no giving an account how she delivered the disguised story of her love for Orsino. It was no set speech, that she had foreseen, so as to weave it into an harmonious period, line necessarily following line, to make up the music— yet I have heard it so spoken, or rather *read* not without its grace and beauty—but, when she had declared her sister's history to be a 'blank,' and that she 'never told her love,' there was a pause, as if the story had ended—and then the image of the 'worm in the bud' came up as a new suggestion— and the heightened image of 'Patience' still followed after that, as by some growing (and not mechanical) process, thought springing up after thought, I would almost say, as they were watered by her tears. So in those fine lines—

Write loyal cantos of contemned love—
Hollow your name to the reverberate hills—

there was no preparation made in the foregoing image for that which was to follow. She used no rhetoric in her passion; or it was nature's own rhetoric, most legitimate then, when it seemed altogether without rule or law.

Charles Lamb, *On Some of the Old Actors*

A Magnificent Malvolio

Robert Bensley (1742–1817) played at Drury Lane and Covent Garden for some thirty years from 1765. Malvolio was one of his best parts.

The part of Malvolio, in the Twelfth Night, was performed by Bensley, with a richness and a dignity, of which (to judge from some recent castings of that character) the very tradition must be worn out from the stage. No manager in those days would have dreamed of giving it to Mr Baddeley, or Mr

Parsons; when Bensley was occasionally absent from the theatre, John Kemble thought it no derogation to succeed to the part. Malvolio is not essentially ludicrous. He becomes comic but by accident. He is cold, austere, repelling; but dignified, consistent, and, for what appears, rather of an over-stretched morality. . .

*　　*　　*

Bensley accordingly threw over the part an air of Spanish loftiness. He looked, spake, and moved like an old Castilian. He was starch, spruce, opinionated, but his superstructure of pride seemed bottomed upon a sense of worth. There was something in it beyond the coxcomb. It was big and swelling, but you could not be sure that it was hollow. You might wish to see it taken down, but you felt that it was upon an elevation. He was magnificent from the outset; but when the decent sobrieties of the character began to give way, and the poison of self-love, in his conceit of the Countess's affection, gradually to work, you would have thought that the hero of La Mancha in person stood before you. How he went smiling to himself! with what ineffable carelessness would he twirl his gold chain! what a dream it was! you were infected with the illusion, and did not wish that it should be removed! you had no room for laughter! if an unseasonable reflection of morality obtruded itself, it was a deep sense of the pitiable infirmity of man's nature, that can lay him open to such frenzies—but in truth you rather admired than pitied the lunacy while it lasted—you felt that an hour of such mistake was worth an age with the eyes open. Who would not wish to live but for a day in the conceit of such a lady's love as Olivia? Why, the Duke would have given his principality but for a quarter of a minute, sleeping or waking, to have been so deluded. The man seemed to tread upon air, to taste manna, to walk with his head in the clouds, to mate Hyperion. O! shake not the castles of his pride— endure yet for a season bright moments of confidence—'stand still ye watches of the element,' that Malvolio may be still in fancy fair Olivia's lord— but fate and retribution say no— I hear the mischievous titter of Maria— the witty taunts of Sir Toby—the still more insupportable triumph of the foolish knight—the counterfeit Sir Topas is unmasked—and 'thus the whirligig of time,' as the true clown hath it, 'brings in his revenges.' I confess that I never saw the catastrophe of this character, while Bensley played it, without a kind of tragic interest.

Charles Lamb, On Some of the Old Actors

Kemble's Revival

March 3, 1811, Covent-Garden

Of the numerous revivals of late, which do so much credit to Mr. Kemble, the principal have been Shakspeare's *Twelfth Night*, Jonson's *Every Man in His Humour*, Massinger's *New Way to Pay Old Debts*, and Addison's *Cato*. . . .

Twelfth Night, though it has passages of exquisite delicacy, and two scenes of irresistible humour, is perhaps the last in rank of Shakspeare's more popular dramas.

*   *   *

It is only a pity that the elegant part of this drama is inferior to the coarse in point of probability. *Viola*'s patient devotion for the Duke is interesting, particularly as he is not aware of it; and there is something extremely touching and gratifying, not only in viewing the disinterestedness with which she pleads his cause to *Olivia*, but still more so in anticipating the amends she is to make him for the latter's disdain. But the disguise of women in male attire, though it continues, and is likely to continue, welcome in the spectators from causes unconnected with dramatic decorum, always strikes one as a gross violation of probability, especially if represented as accompanied with delicacy of mind. In Shakspeare's time, when there were no female performers, the personal absurdity was avoided; and this circumstance probably gave rise, in other nations as well as ours, to the fondness for representing women as boys and pages. It may also have encouraged, and in some measure lessened, the still greater absurdity of bringing together two persons perfectly resembling each other, as in the play before us, and in the *Comedy of Errors*—a trick however, which it is impossible to render complete without resorting to the masks of the ancient stage. In our own times, it could hardly be rendered bearable, even by selecting counterparts of equal size and general appearance; but when the managers of Covent-Garden present us with Mr. Brunton as the facsimile of a delicate little lady, shorter at least by the head and shoulders, they bring the absurdity to its climax: Mr. Brunton, in spite of his effeminate air and voice, becomes by the contrast a rough and sturdy gallant; and nothing can be more ridiculous than to see the persons on the stage affecting an *unaffected* astonishment at the double likeness, and exclaiming,

205

> An apple, cleft in two, is not more twin
> Than these two creatures!

With the exception of the distaste caused by these aggravated inconsistencies, the comedy goes off with some spirit, though certainly not well performed upon the whole. Miss Booth's representation of Viola is touchingly correct—feminine, feeling, intelligent. The modesty of her dress is suitable to the delicacy of the character; and the breathless timidity she exhibits in her forced duel with Ague-cheek is nicely discriminated, on the one hand, from a powerful expression, unsuitable to a delicate female, and on the other, from a comic extravagance, unnatural to such a person actually suffering. Mr. Blanchard's Ague-cheek is deservedly applauded for the impotence of its gaiety and the utter weakness of its pretence, in every respect. Perhaps the best touches in his performance are the extravagant and at the same time feeble bursts of laughter with which he acknowledges the clown's bon mots. But the part of a simpleton, having little thought to express and scarcely any variety to put in action, is no great trial of comic power. It is well known that there is scarcely an actor, serious or comic, of any powers of expression, who cannot imitate an idiot. Mrs. C. Kemble in Olivia, and Mr. Emery in Sir Toby, must, I am afraid, be content on this occasion with the old newspaper praise of being respectable. The clown of Fawcett is not unentertaining, but it wants quaintness, and a greater affectation of humility in the midst of its insolence. Duke Orsino is represented by Mr. Barrymore, formerly of Drury-Lane Theatre, who, after some years absence from a company in which he is wanted, has returned to the metropolis and been engaged in one that has no need of him. His parts were already sustained, with at least equal merit, by Mr Egerton, who, if he has not so tragic an air, can hardly be denied more judgment. Mr. Barrymore has a good and powerful voice, an imposing step, and a face which, though not handsome or dignified, is by no means deficient in intelligence; but his enunciation is snappish in the very midst of its pompousness; his manner at all times theatrical; and in short, he has little or no variety, either in tone, look, or gesture. His delivery of the exquisite lines that open the play,

> If music be the food of love, play on, &c. &c.

was like that of a mouthing schoolmaster hastening to finish the passage that he might proceed to lecture upon it—that is to say, upon what he neither feels nor understands. The orchestra were in excellent accompaniment; and when the Duke called for 'the strain again,' because 'it had a dying fall,' gave it with as much indifference, and with as little of the *dying* in it, as if they thought his Highness was joking.

Leigh Hunt—The Examiner

Peacocks, Pavilions and Poetry

This spectacular production at Covent Garden, in addition to a masque with a lady in a shell, boasted 'Songs, Glees and Choruses, the poetry selected entirely from the Plays, Poems and Sonnets of Shakespeare'.

Covent Garden

Nov. 25, 1820. '*Twelfth Night*' was again performed this evening, to an unusually crowded house. The beauty of the music, and the richness and variety of the scenery are high materials of popularity, even if the Drama was of an inferior rank. But a play of *Shakspeare* must abound in all that poetry has of splendour, and character of truth, and brought forward as '*Twelfth Night*' now is, we conceive that the power of the great author is supplied with another triumph, not abated or dishonoured by the association of delicious music, and romantic scenery. The play was to night performed admirably well. Though Miss Love had taken Miss Greene's part of the Lady Olivia, it suffered no deterioration in her hands. Farren's Malvolio was equally good in the earlier scenes as it had been, and in the latter where the interest had flagged, he exerted himself with as much spirit as the character would bear. But the self admiring steward is facetious only while under the spells of his vanity; and when he comes to their castigation, he grows as dull as his own dungeon. Liston's Sir Andrew is not among his happiest performances. But his humour makes its way, and the carousing scene is equal to any piece of idiot festivity on the stage. The drunkenness which makes his eyes dim and his feet tremble, without making his idiotism more senseless, is admirably conceived, and his attempt to light his pipe was amusingly unsuccessful as it could be, without a more direct imitation of Mathews. Sir Toby has now grown a greater favourite with the audience, as he has thrown more of ease into his part; he is, indeed, a kind of Falstaff, and ought to be played in some measure in the jocularity of the fat Knight. Miss M. Tree's Viola was still pretty and piquant, and if she could infuse more tenderness into her recitation, she would make a perfect representative of one of the most touching of the characters of Shakspeare. Viola's whole dialogue overflows with graceful disguise, the exquisite finesses of a spirit deeply enamoured, and a constant fear of betraying itself. She scarcely makes a speech in which there might not be detected some allusion to her own anxieties, and the charm of the character is almost entirely founded on this struggle between passion and delicacy, the study to conceal her thoughts, and the overwhelming fondness which renders concealment next to impossible. The Masque was again received with the greatest applause. It is certainly merely a pageant, and the plot altogether escapes the audience; but it has clouds ascending and descending, pavilions and peacocks, palaces of rocks and curtains of sea-weeds, and Miss Dennett enthroned in a shell, a theatric Lady of the Lobster. All this is so shewy, and the colourman and the carpenter have such an undisputed triumph, that we cannot but hope the adaptation of these plays will be carried on in the same spirit, and meet, and merit the same success.

European Magazine

A Castilian Castellan

1857, *January* 24.—For the past fortnight the four nights a week dedicated at Sadler's Wells to Shakespeare have been occupied by performances of *Twelfth Night*—last acted here five years ago—in which comedy the part of Malvolio is that sustained by Mr. Phelps . . .

The aspect and behaviour of the pit and gallery at Sadler's Wells during the performance of one of Shakespeare's plays cannot fail to impress most strongly every visitor who is unaccustomed to the place. There sit our working-classes in a happy crowd, as orderly and reverent as if they were at church, and yet as unrestrained in their enjoyment as if listening to stories told them by their own firesides. Shakespeare spoke home to the heart of the natural man, even in the same words that supply matter for nice judgment by the intellect; he was as a cook, who, by the same meat that feeds abundantly the hungry, tickles with an exquisite delight the palate of the epicure. It is hard to say how much men who have had few advantages of education must in their minds and characters be strengthened and refined when they are made accustomed to this kind of entertainment.

*   *   *

Malvolio lives at Sadler's Wells in bearing and attire
modelled upon the fashion of the Spaniard, as impassive in
his manner as a Spanish king should be. In one of the first
sentences addressed to him we are told his character: 'O, you
are sick of self-love, Malvolio, and taste things with a distempered appetite.' Such a man is the Malvolio we see. When in
his tasting of Maria's letter he betrays his distempered appetite
for greatness, we are not allowed to suppose for a moment
that he loves his mistress. Seeing that, as Maria says, 'it is his
ground of faith that all that look on him love him', he accepts
easily the hope of greatness thrust upon him, and his rejoicing
is in the love of Olivia, not in the way of sympathy, but as a
way to 'sitting in his state, calling his officers about him in his
branched velvet gown'. Such a man, as Mr. Phelps represents
him, walks not with a smirk and a light comic strut, but in the
heaviness of grandeur, with a face grave through very empti-
ness of all expression. This Malvolio stalks blind about the
world; his eyes are very nearly covered with their heavy lids,
for there is nothing in the world without that is worth noticing,
it is enough for him to contemplate the excellence within;
walled up in his own temple of the flesh, he is his own adorer.
If his ears are assailed with irreverences by the fool, he counts
the fool as naught, and is moved therefore but to the expression
of a passing shade of pity for his ignorance. Upon the debase-
ment of Sir Toby and Sir Andrew he looks down with very
calm disdain. When in the latter half of the play he has been
bidden, as he thinks, by her who will thrust greatness upon
him, to be opposite with a kinsman, surly with servants, and,
if he entertain her love, to let it appear in his smiling; though
he had been practising behaviour to his shadow, all the smile
he can produce is one of intense satisfaction with himself, and
all the surliness but a more open expression of disdain for those
who do not pay him homage. When locked up as a madman
he is sustained by his self-content, and by the honest certainty
that he has been notoriously abused; and when at last he, for
once, opens his eyes on learning how he has been tricked,
they close again in happy self-content, and he is retiring in state
without deigning a word to his tormentors, when, as the fool
had twitted him by noting how 'the whirligig of time brings
in his revenges', he remembers that the whirligig is still in
motion. Therefore, marching back with as much increase of

speed as is consistent with magnificence, he threatens all—
including now Olivia in his contempt—'I'll be revenged on
the whole pack of you!'

Other Malvolios seen by the playgoers of this generation
have been more fantastical and caused more laughter—
although this one causes much—but the impression made by
them has been less deep. Few who have seen or may see at
Sadler's Wells the Spanish-looking steward of Countess
Olivia, and laughed at the rise and fall of his *château en Espagne*,
will forget him speedily. Like a quaint portrait in which there
are master-strokes, his figure may dwell in the mind for years.

Henry Morley, Journal of a London Playgoer

'Twelfth Night' at the Lyceum

*An appreciative account of Irving's Malvolio, which was not generally
popular. Ellen Terry, who played Viola, called the production 'dull,
lumpy and heavy'.*

On Tuesday night of this week, July 8th, another Shaksperian
revival saw the footlights at the one theatre in London where
we are sure to have a loving and a painstaking presentation of
any of the Master's plays. The play was 'Twelfth Night,' or
as you call it by its second title, 'What you will.'

Let me admit that the impression made by the play as a
whole is that of a disjointed drama. It does not hang well
together. It is not what a manager of to-day would call a good
acting play. This is even true after all the necessary trans-
positions of scenes and speeches that had to be performed, and
that have been performed with great skill, ere the comedy as
written was presentable on the modern stage. But with all its
disjointed nature the play's *disjecta membra* are so beautiful
that, in the study at all events, the incoherence and incon-
sequence of 'Twelfth Night' are forgotten, and even in
representation they are largely hidden by the wealth of good
things in the sweet play.

As to the whole of the general arrangements nothing is to be
said but in terms of praise, with one great exception. It is
difficult to speak in words that will not appear exaggerated of
the scenery, the dresses, the staging of the play. As to all these,
they are full of a beauty and a poetry in harmony with the
piece and with the very names of Illyria, of Olivia, and of

Viola. As an instance of the extreme care with which all is done, take this. One of the scenes, the 'Market Place,' the first scene of the 4th act, is before the audience literally for only two or three minutes. It is painted with as much elaboration and finish as if it were to be the setting of all the action of a long play. And I am fain to mention specially a front-cloth that intervenes again only for a few minutes between Orsino's palace and Olivia's garden (two full stage sets). It is the scene in which Sebastian and his sea captain, 'the good Antonio, the honest Antonio,' of this play are first met. Only a front cloth as it is, the effect produced by the skill, I am not sure that I ought not to write by the genius, of Hawes Craven, the artist, is of great depth and efficiency.

But there is one great exception to the general finish of this fascinating performance. Of all the Shaksperian plays, 'Twelfth Night' is the most musical. Not alone in the sweet sounding names of its two women or in that melody of words and thoughts that they, Orsino, and all true lovers make. The play is so rich in actual song and music, and alas! most of this is cut out in the Lyceum representation. The Clown (O rare Will Shakspere!) is a singing character. Four songs fall to his lot in the written version. Two of these are incomparable, 'O Mistress mine,' and 'Come away, come away, death.' Neither of these was sung on Tuesday night, and I am not able to say that S. Calhaem, who played the part of the Clown, atoned by any other great excellence for his incapacity to sing. As Shakspere wrote the comedy it begins and ends with music. As Henry Irving puts it on the stage, the exigencies of the re-arrangement of scenes relegate the music that is first the food and then the sad remembrancer of Orsino's love to the 3rd scene of the play. The end song of the comedy is wisely retained, and with all the men and women singing merrily 'with a hey ho, the wind and the rain,' the curtain falls on them and the memory of Malvolio. All Shakspere lovers ought to be grateful to Henry Irving for restoring in the drunken night scene the catch that Shakspere meant Sir Toby and his two companions to sing, 'Hold thy peace,' the music of which is known to all glee lovers.

One or two more little grumbles about general things, and I may turn to the analysis of the two chief characters. So careful a stage-manager as Henry Irving ought not to allow more than one pronunciation of the same word by different members of his company in one evening. The word 'notable' appeared in two distinct forms on the night of the first performance. A second point is the comparative dearth of laughter throughout. This is due to the cause which I think the most serious indictment that can be formed against the manager of the Lyceum. His characters, after the great primary ones, are not filled by quite worthy artists. I know that it is a far cry from him and Ellen Terry in Shaksperian comedy parts to any other actor or actress that we have at present with us. The interval between these two and the rest of their possible helpers is not greater than that between the characters of Malvolio and Viola on the one hand, and those of Sir Toby and Olivia on the other. I cannot but think that there are men and women more capable of filling the so-called secondary parts than some at least of the supporters of Irving at the Lyceum. For a proof, let me record that the scenes between Sir Toby and Andrew Aguecheek went without a solitary laugh. David Fisher, as Sir Toby, missed altogether the rich, unctuous, racy, rollicking, anger-forbidding humor of the part. Francis Wyatt, as Andrew Aguecheek, was a fop more than a fool. The vacuous, serene, self-contemplative stupidity of the younger knight was never caught. Even in the garden scene, not one of the interlocutory phrases of these two unworthy worthies and their practical joke-companion hit the mark, the mark that Shakspere aimed at, and that actors ought to help him in attaining, a burst of laughter at every one of these compound asides to relieve the mutual tension due to the close following of the reading of the letter by Malvolio. These laughter reliefs are in the present representation of the play the more needful on account of the way in which Irving treats the character of Malvolio.

Ere I turn to a brief note on his conception of that character, and his execution of the conception, let me say a word or two of Ellen Terry. You in America last winter and spring fell in love with her (as an actress) as if you had been Englishmen, or even Irishmen. When you see her as Viola-Cesario, you will be more in the depths than ever. Her first appearance, when the curtain rises for the first time, and she is seen high up on a rock looking out over a sea still sullen from the angry storm that had hunted for her life all night, a sea stained with the red of a sunrise recalling to her human blood that may be that of her lost brother Sebastian, from that moment to the end when she has learnt that at last she is to be 'her master's mistress,' the old inexpressible charm of Ellen Terry charmed us all again. That gesticulating forefinger was as much to the fore as in former parts, and one or two of the loveliest lines were not, I think, wholly understood by their fair deliverer. Thus the tender pathetic 'She had better love a dream' was given lightly and nearly jestingly. It moved to laughter and not to tears. And the double-meaning answer to the Duke's question:

> 'My life upon't, young though thou art, thine eye
> Hath stay'd upon some favor that it loves:
> Hath it not, boy?'

was so spoken as to make me think that the actress had only seen one side of it. The reply is: 'A little by your favor,' and when we remember that the answer is not only to her lord, but to her lord and master and lover, the beautiful thought's-play in the heart of the boy-woman comes home to us when it has not apparently to Ellen Terry.

But with these one or two exceptions the part is deliciously played. It demands no great strength. It asks only for grace, sweetness, and delicate touches of pathos, and with all these it is furnished. Her turn of the body and face from the sea to the land when first Orsino's name is named, the meaning, unconscious as it were in her question, 'Who's she?' when Olivia is first mentioned, the fun in the duel scene with her co-partner in fear, Andrew Aguecheek, and above all the mixture of emotions in the plea 'Let me see your face' to her veiled rival, all this was as excellent as it could be. Especially was this last phrase given as one may think Shakspere would have had it given. He alas! never saw his women characters played by any but growing boys speaking 'with a reed voice,' a thought as pathetic as that Homer never saw the faces of the crowds to whom he sung his songs, and that Beethoven never heard the music of his later years. The blending of anxiety, expectation, jealousy, dread in the request 'Let me see your face' led up finely to the half despair in look and voice when the face, once seen, she knew how fair her rival was, how hopeless her own case.

As to the Malvolio, I hardly know how to write. I fear my readers will think me one of the unreasoning mad Irving worshippers who, like Christians with Jesus Christ, detract from the true and noble nature of the man, with all its beautiful faults, by talking of absolute perfection. I have written as unfavorably of our greatest actor as almost any critic. But I hope that as I have never been blind to his faults, and they are many and great, so I have never been blind to his virtues. These are more in number and much greater in magnitude. And now, after this preliminary personal explanation, let me say at once that the Malvolio of Irving is, to my thinking, among the very highest of his creations. And more than that. It is to me a revelation. I have studied the play long and carefully, and I may fairly say that I know it nearly by heart. But until Tuesday night I did not know the character of Malvolio. So new was the conception, so startling, so thoroughly carried out, and withal so true, that I confess to being staggered. Unfortunately, the majority of the audience without a doubt, either did not understand at what Irving was aiming, or, if they understood, did not agree with his reading. My own impression is that they did not in the least degree comprehend what he meant to convey. And this, from no fault of his, but from the novelty of idea, and from the natural denseness of English audiences.

I must pass rapidly over everything in the treatment of Malvolio save the one new and tremendous notion. I would like to tell you by what subtle and variable and ever-consistent touches the low birth of the steward was hinted, to call all the little gestures and pieces of business so full of meaning with which the impersonation abounds, such as the impatience with which he hears that the youth from the Count is here with more love-messages for his mistress, the almost familiar tone of the old servant with that same mistress on the words 'He *has* been told so' in the same scene, the unobtrusive yet most suggestive business when Olivia gave him the ring for Cesario. Nor can I dwell on all the details of the long letter-scene with its humor less forced than is the wont of most actors in this part. Only one little thing seemed to me, hyper-critic that I am, to be wanting in the scene. The 'demure travel of regard' is surely a line in which the word might be suited to the action, the action to the word.

The gradual growth of the great idea in his mind that Olivia loved him was shown as I believe none other could show it, and with that growth came as gradually the first indication of the new line he meant to take. He intended us to pity Malvolio, to weep for if not with him. From the moment when we see how completely he, the sport of others, is self-deceived, a feeling of incipient sympathy takes hold on us. At the end of the scene his exit was not with a pompous swaggering strut, Malvolio passed out with his face buried in his hands, strangely moved, overwhelmed with his good fortune. Then we began to see what real pain this foolish jest of Maria was, like most foolish jests, about to cause. But how much and how real the pain, was not conceived until Malvolio was seen in prison. The scene is so arranged, with a wall, that of his cell, built down the centre line of the stage, that we see both his tormentors and the man himself. On the right hand are Maria and the plaguing clown. On the other lies Malvolio. He is in darkness. The mental and physical horror of darkness and the longing yearning for deliverance from a prison cell were never so realised, I think, before. And with all this agony (it is literally agony) there is the sense of the grievous wrong done to him, and the utter hopelessness of redress. My readers may be inclined to smile at me, but I declare in all seriousness the effect of this scene from the comedy of 'Twelfth Night' on me was that of the intensest tragedy.

The critics, as a rule, do not appear to grasp what Irving intended them to grasp any better than did the first night audience. When it dawns slowly on them, controversy will set in as to whether this reading of Malvolio is true, or whether the old, broadly humorous one, that only moves men to inextinguishable mirth, is right. For my part, I have decided, or rather Irving has decided for me. His conception may be new to us of to-day. I believe it would be old to Shakspere.

Edward Aveling, Our Corner July 1884 (U.S.A.)

Troilus and Cressida

THE 'Epistle to the Reader' in the 1609 edition tells us that the play was 'never clapper-clawed with the palms of the vulgar' and this situation apparently remained unchanged till Charles Fry revived the play in June 1907. From 1679 till 1734 Shakespeare's play had to yield the stage to Dryden's adaptation *Truth Found Too Late* and there seem to have been no 19th-century performances. J. P. Kemble prepared a version for production at the end of the 18th century, but it was never performed.[1]

---

[1] See 'The Darkened Stage' by Jeanne T. Newlin in *The Triple Bond* ed. Joseph Price (1975).

Measure for Measure

ADAPTATIONS by Davenant and Gildon held the
stage till 1738 when Mrs. Siddons appeared as Isabella, a
role in which she excelled. Like the other 'dark comedies'
this has not been performed often till the 20th century, but
William Poel made it the first production of his Elizabethan
Stage Society at the Royalty Theatre in November, 1893.

Mrs. Siddons as Isabella

*Mrs. Siddons' London début as Portia in 1775 had been unpromising.
She returned in 1781, this time to a chorus of praise. Isabella was one of
her greatest roles, though one would not guess it from this review of the
first night's performance.*

November 3, 1783 Drury-Lane.

Shakespeare's Measure for Measure, was performed, for the
purpose of introducing Mrs. Siddons in the part of Isabel.

In Measure for Measure there are three situations in which
the powers of Isabel are to be displayed; when she petitions
Angelo for the life of her brother, and rejects with a virtuous
resolution the condition of his deliverance; when she rejects
with horror and most extreme detestation the solicitations of
her brother to submit to that condition; and when she pleads
her cause, under the most disadvantageous circumstances,
against Angelo, before the Duke.

Shakespeare has pointed out the general manner in which the
part is to be performed; and we think Mrs. Siddons has not
conceived it in that stile of truth and superiority which her
friends ascribe to her.

—For in her youth
(that of Shakespeare's Isabel)
There is a prone and speechless dialect!
Such as move men!

Of this general effect of her appearance we see nothing in
Mrs. Siddons. An ample atonement, however, is made, at
least to a great part of the audience, by artificial variations of
voice and countenance, in the interesting points of the situations
already mentioned. She rejects the proposal of Angelo, and the

solicitations of Claudio, to sacrifice her virtue with looks of indignation, and tones of hatred, which have a happy effect, as they succeed the soothing voice of intreaty and consolation. The performance of the whole part, though correct and striking in Mrs. Siddons's stile of acting, which we may possibly more particularly delineate when Mrs. Crawford appears, will not enlarge her pretensions to public opinion and regard.

Some of the other parts were performed by persons whose abilities have undergone almost every species of trial, and whose theatric estimation is very honourably ascertained. Such are Messrs. Smith, Palmer, Brereton, Lewes, and Aickin. Mrs. Ward and Miss Barnes are useful appendages of a theatre.

European Magazine

Pathos and Grandeur

Eliza O'Neill succeeded Mrs. Siddons in the role of Isabella, when the play was revived at Covent Garden.

Feb. 8, 1816 'Measure for Measure'. The infinity of Shakespeare's genius is no where more comprehensive than in the machinery of this play. He fathoms the depth of the human heart: not as a moral inquisitor; but by combining those secret sympathies which invest distinct degrees and attributes in society with the eloquence of truth. In the heroine, Miss O'Neill soars beyond her accustomed sphere with an eagle's flight. To the pathos of intense feeling, she adds the grandeur of lofty declamation: with tenderness of thought, she harmonizes sublimity of expression. She embellishes Isabella with that seductive bloom of loveliness and divinity of grace which is visibly reflected by the chaste mirror of her illustrious author's mind.—Why do we pause?—From a conscious inability to illustrate the dignity of our theme. Let us, therefore, by analogy, speak the oracular opinions of Dr. Johnson, who tells us that Pope was not content to satisfy—he ever desired to excel: he courted not the candour, but invited the criticism of the learned: he weighed words with minute attention: he examined sentences with punctilious study: he *earned* the *immortality* of his fame. This we consider to be the talisman which gives a prevailing constancy to all Miss O'Neill's dramatic efforts, and approximates them to perfection. Native genius is wild as it is luxuriant; but judgment will teach it to collect and to combine: energy, to animate and to amplify: the one introducing the aid of personal diligence: the other, that

217

of classic vigour. Hence the vast chasm that separates the intellectual endowments of Miss O'Neill and Mr. Kean. We will not form selections. The spirit of Shakspeare lives and breathes in the tempting youth, the tender solicitudes, the exalted enthusiasm of his new Isabella!—We beheld Mr. Young, after his accident, with a warmth of satisfaction that relieved our previous anxiety, and we rejoice in his restored health. The philosophic Duke was personated with a calm and manly dignity: Mr. Terry communicated force to the character of Angelo: Mr. C. Kemble was most impressive in Claudio: and Mr. Jones enacted an entertaining Impertinent. Emery, however, is a stranger to Shakspeare. He plays Barnardine as ridiculously as he has played Caliban; and gives to both the birth, parentage, and education of a Yorkshire loon. We must not forget Liston's clown—Pompey exemplified his text. We conclude by insisting that with all its *delicate* imperfections, 'Measure for Measure' is a very fine play, and we exult at its re-introduction to the stage.

European Magazine

Barnadine

A glimpse of a minor character played by a leading comic actor, John Emery (1777–1822). He played Barnardine in the Siddons' farewell season in 1811 and again in 1816.

When I saw Emery crawl from his den with the straws sticking in his clotted hair and filthy garments, growling out his remonstrance at being disturbed from his sleep, I absolutely started! I had read the play often, and the character was familiar to me as that of a depraved, abandoned wretch; but here was a real, sombre splendour thrown upon it by the power of genius, and, with an oppressed chest, I sighed, 'Oh, nature! Oh, Shakspeare! who shall ever know the end or depth of your beauties?'

William Robson, The Old Playgoer, 1845

Back to Shakespeare?

15th November, 1893

It is to be hoped that some means may be found of preserving for future use the excellently painted scene, representing the interior of an Elizabethan theatre, in which the Shakespeare

Reading Society gave their performances of *Measure for Measure* at the Royalty last week. .... A whole essay, nay, a whole book, might be written in criticism of details of the Royalty scene. I may even confess that I have made some collections towards such a book, and am therefore in a position to say, with a certain confidence, that Mr Minton Taylor has shown both learning and ingenuity in his reconstructive effort. On the whole, and taking into acccount the somewhat restricted space at his command, I doubt if he could have done better. The gallants, smoking their Elizabethan clay pipes on their sixpenny stools on the stage, certainly contributed to the illusion; but I fear it was very seldom that the ruffling blades of the Court and the Inns of Court conducted themselves with such propriety. To make the realism perfect they should have called for and consumed burnt sack in the midst of the performance, exchanged banter with the citizens in the 'yard,' and between-whiles quarrelled among themselves. It would not have been amiss if one of them had casually run another through the body.

So much for the scene. As for the play, *Measure for Measure* was certainly not the best that could have been selected to illustrate the artistic advantages and drawbacks of the early theatre. In the first place, the Elizabethan costumes worn by the actors were not essentially different from those in which a manager of to-day would dress the play. It would have been much better (if possible) to have selected, say, a Roman play, and let us see how Brutus and Antony looked in slashed doublets and trunk-hose. (But soft! Did they already use 'shapes' in classical pieces on the Elizabethan stages? I really forget, and my authorities are not at hand.) In the second place, there is no other play of Shakespeare's in which so much of the dialogue is absolutely unspeakable before a modern audience. Therefore large cuts were inevitable; and having begun to cut, the actors went on with a sweeping hand, and made huge excisions for the mere sake of brevity. Now the chief interest of such an experiment would have been to speak as nearly as possible the whole text of the play, and see how close the performance could be brought to the traditional 'two hours' traffic' of the Shakespearian stage. It was note-worthy that, despite the enormous excisions, and despite the fact that 'business' was (quite properly) reduced to a minimum, and that some of the actors (quite improperly) recited their verses so fast as to be totally unintelligible, the two hours' limit was on Thursday night exceeded by five or ten minutes. In the third place, *Measure for Measure* happens to be one of the plays

219

in which there is no necessity for using the upper stage. There is not a single stage-direction: 'Enter So-and-so, above,' nor is there any passage in which it seems in the least degree probable that a stage-manager of the period would have brought the upper stage into requisition. On Thursday night, then, it was used in a quite arbitrary fashion, and once or twice in contradiction to the text. This was, of course, a pity. It would have been much more interesting to have seen the upper stage employed in one of the numerous scenes to which it belongs of necessity.

As the performers withhold their names on the playbill, it is to be presumed that they deprecate criticism of their individual efforts. I shall only remark, then, that a Shakespeare Reading Society ought surely to set an example to the professional stage in meticulous respect for the poet's text; whereas several of the performers simply improvised at will when their memory failed them, and not one paid any great attention to the metre. For the rest, the Duke and Lucio both looked and spoke well, the Isabella showed intelligence and sincerity, and the Claudio was strikingly handsome, both in features and figure. His admirable stage-face reminded me strongly of the portraits of Charles Kemble.

William Archer, *The Theatrical World for 1893*

All's Well That Ends Well

THE first recorded performance was in 1741 and had David Garrick as Bertram. The play has not often been staged since, though John Kemble revived it at the end of the 18th century and Samuel Phelps in the middle of the 19th. The celebrated Peg Woffington made an impressive Helena in 1742 and Theophilus Cibber was very popular as Parolles in the same production.

The Unfortunate Comedy[1]

The part of Parolles was, by Fleetwood, the manager,

[1] Drury Lane, October 1742.

promised to Macklin; but Theophilus Cibber, by some sort of artifice, as common in theatres as in courts, snatched it from him, to his great displeasure. Berry was the Lafeu, and Chapman the Clown and Interpreter. *All's well that ends well* was termed, by the players, the unfortunate comedy, from the disagreeable accidents which fell out several times during the acting of it. Mrs. Woffington was suddenly taken with illness as she came off the stage from a scene of importance. Mrs. Ridout, a pretty woman and a pleasing actress, after having played Diana one night, was, by the advice of her physician, forbidden to act during a month. Mrs. Butler, in the Countess of Rousillon, was likewise seized with a distemper in the progress of this play.

All's well that ends well, however, had such a degree of merit, and gave so much general satisfaction to the public, that, in spite of the superstition of some of the players, who wished and entreated that it might be discontinued, upon Mr. Delane's undertaking to act the King after Milward's decease, it was again brought forward and applauded.

Cibber's Parolles, notwithstanding his grimace and false spirit, met with encouragement. This actor, though his vivacity was mixed with too much pertness, never offended by flatness and insipidity. Chapman was admirable in the clowns of Shakspeare. Berry's Lafeu was the true portrait of a choleric old man and a humourist. Milward was, in the King, affecting; and Delane, in the same part, respectable.

Davies, Dramatic Miscellanies

All's Far From Well

All's Well was one of G.B.S's favourite Shakespeare plays, and one which clearly influenced the conception of the mature Shavian heroine, in relentless pursuit of the chosen male.

When I saw 'All's Well' announced for performance by the Irving Dramatic Club,[1] I was highly interested, especially as the performers were free, for once, to play Shakespeare for Shakespeare's sake. Alas! at this amateur performance, at which there need have been none of the miserable commercialisation compulsory at the regular theatres, I suffered all the vulgarity and absurdity of that commercialism without its efficiency. We all know the stock objection of the Brixton

[1] Performed at St. George's Hall, 22 and 24 January 1895.

Family Shakespeare to 'All's Well'—that the heroine is a lady doctor, and that no lady of any delicacy could possibly adopt a profession which involves the possibility of her having to attend cases such as that of the king in this play, who suffers from a fistula. How any sensible and humane person can have ever read this sort of thing without a deep sense of its insult to every charitable woman's humanity and every sick man's suffering is, fortunately, getting harder to understand nowadays than it once was. Nevertheless 'All's Well' was minced with strict deference to it for the members of the Irving Dramatic Club. The rule for expurgation was to omit everything that the most pestiferously prurient person could find improper. For example, when the non-commissioned officer, with quite becoming earnestness and force, says to the disgraced Parolles: 'If you could find out a country where but women were that had received so much shame, you might begin an impudent nation,' the speech was suppressed as if it were on all fours with the obsolete Elizabethan badinage which is and should be cut out as a matter of course. And to save Helena from anything so shocking as a reference to her virginity, she was robbed of that rapturous outburst beginning

'There shall your master have a thousand loves—
A mother and a mistress and a friend,' etc.

But perhaps this was sacrificed in deference to the opinion of the editor of those pretty and handy little books called the Temple Shakespeare, who compares the passage to 'the nonsense of some foolish conceited player'—a criticism which only a commentator could hope to live down.

The play was, of course, pulled to pieces in order that some bad scenery, totally unconnected with Florence or Rousillon, might destroy all the illusion which the simple stage directions in the book create, and which they would equally have created had they been printed on a placard and hung up on a curtain. The passage of the Florentine army beneath the walls of the city was managed in the manner of the end of the first act of Robertson's 'Ours,' the widow and the girls looking out of their sitting-room window, whilst a few of the band gave a precarious selection from the orchestral parts of Berlioz's version of the Rackoczy March. The dresses were the usual fancy ball odds and ends, Helena especially distinguishing herself by playing the first scene partly in the costume of Hamlet and partly in that of a waitress in an Aerated Bread shop, set off by a monstrous auburn wig which could by no stretch of imagination be taken for her own hair. Briefly, the whole play was vivisected, and the fragments mutilated, for the sake of accessories which were in every particular silly and ridiculous. If they were meant to heighten the illusion, they were worse than failures, since they rendered illusion almost impossible. If they were intended as illustrations of place and period, they were ignorant impostures. I have seen poetic plays performed without costumes before a pair of curtains by ladies and gentlemen in evening dress with twenty times the effect: nay, I will pledge my reputation that if the members of the Irving Dramatic Club will take their books in their hands, sit in a Christy Minstrel semicircle, and read the play decently as it was written, the result will be a vast improvement on this St. George's Hall travesty.

Perhaps it would not be altogether kind to leave these misguided but no doubt well-intentioned ladies and gentlemen without a word of appreciation from their own point of view. Only, there is not much to be said for them even from that point of view. Few living actresses could throw themselves into the sustained transport of exquisite tenderness and impulsive courage which makes poetry the natural speech of Helena. The cool young woman, with a superior understanding, excellent manners, and a habit of reciting Shakespeare, presented before us by Miss Olive Kennett, could not conceivably have been even Helena's thirty-second cousin. Miss Lena Heinekey, with the most beautiful old woman's part ever written in her hands, discovered none of its wonderfully pleasant good sense, humanity, and originality: she grieved stagily all through in the manner of the Duchess of York in Cibber's 'Richard I I I.' Mr. Lewin-Mannering did not for an instant make it possible to believe that Parolles was a real person to him. They all insisted on calling him *parole*, instead of Parolles, in three syllables, with the *s* sounded at the end, as Shakespeare intended: consequently, when he came to the couplet which cannot be negotiated on any other terms:

'Rust, sword; cool, blushes; and, Parolles, thrive;
There's place and means for every man alive,'

he made a desperate effort to get even with it by saying:

'Rust, rapier; cool, blushes; and, *parole*, thrive,'

and seemed quite disconcerted when he found that it would not do. Lafeu is hardly a part that can be acted: it comes right if the right man is available: if not, no acting can conceal the makeshift. Mr. Herbert Everitt was not the right man; but he made the best of it. The clown was evidently willing to relish his own humor if only he could have seen it; but there are few actors who would not have gone that far. Bertram (Mr. Patrick Munro), if not the most intelligent of Bertrams, played the love scene with Diana with some passion. The rest of the parts, not being character studies, are tolerably straightforward and easy of execution; and they were creditably played, the king (Mr. Ernest Meads) carrying off the honors, and Diana (Mrs. Herbert Morris) acquitting herself with comparative distinction. But I should not like to see another such performance of 'All's Well' or any other play that is equally rooted in my deeper affections.

Bernard Shaw, Dramatic Opinions and Essays

Julius Caesar

T HOMAS Platter saw the play at the Globe in 1599 (p. 18) and it has been continuously popular ever since except for the last quarter of the 18th century. Brutus and Mark Antony are of course the starring roles; though many distinguished actors have portrayed Cassius, among them Macready and Charles Mayne Young in the early 19th century. The 1881 production in London by the visiting Saxe-Meiningen company won wide acclaim for the staging of the crowd scenes.

All The Conspirators

Thomas Davies, himself an (unsuccessful) actor, recalls some of the actors in the early years of the 18th century.

Bowman, who had acted this part of Ligarius more than fifty years, was advanced above the age of fourscore when I saw him perform it; he assumed great vigour and a truly Roman spirit. The applause which he obtained, and justly merited, was not relished by Quin, who neglected to pay that attention to the character which he ought. This is a fault which

I have observed in some principal actors, who have treated their inferiors of the stage with disregard, because they were below them in rank as comedians, though the parts they acted demanded observance to be paid them, at least before the public, to support that stage-deception, without which a play loses its effect.

*   *   *

Julius Caesar was, in the opinion of the elder Mills, the part in tragedy which his son William acted with most propriety. I remember to have seen him perform it; and, though he was in general a snip-snap speaker, a manner which Mr. Garrick very happily mimicked in 'The Rehearsal', when speaking before Mills himself, yet in Caesar he gave such an idea of the part as Shakespeare intended.

*   *   *

Wilks,[1] who above fifty years since acted Mark Antony, as soon as he entered the stage, without taking any notice of the conspirators, walked swiftly up to the dead body of Caesar and knelt down; he paused some time before he spoke; and, after surveying the corpse with manifest tokens of the deepest sorrow, he addressed it in a most affecting and pathetic manner. A graceful dignity accompanied the action and deportment of this actor.

*   *   *

The action of Wilks in Antony, from the beginning to the end of the oration, was critically adapted to produce the intended consequences of the speaker. His address through the whole was easy and elegant; but his voice wanted that fulness and variety, requisite to impress the sentiments and pathos with which the speech abounds: besides, Wilks was apt to strike the syllables too forcibly as well as uniformly. Mr. Barry's fine person and pleasing manner were well adapted to Mark Antony, but his utterance in recitation was not sufficiently sonorous, nor his voice flexible enough, to express the full meaning of the author in the opening of the address. When roused by passion, Barry rose superior to all speakers. His close of the harangue was as warm and glowing as the beginning was cold and deficient.

The only man, in my memory, whose powers were perfectly

---

[1] Robert Wilks (1665–1732) was a popular actor who succeeded in both tragedy and comedy. From 1711 until his death he was a joint manager of Drury Lane Theatre.

suited to all parts of this celebrated harangue, was William Milward, who, from enjoying a full-toned and harmonious pipe, was frequently tempted to sacrifice sense to sound. On particular occasions, and in some parts, he was known to be a judicious and accurate speaker. In Mark Antony he had every thing for him which nature could bestow, person, look, voice; his action and address were easy without art, and his deportment, though not absolutely perfect, was far from ungraceful: he opened the preparatory part of the oration in a low but distinct and audible voice; for nothing can atone for the want of articulation; to be heard is the first lesson the actor should be master of; nor can I applaud the apology of Baron, the French Roscius, who, on his opening Racine's Iphigenia in a whispering tone, when called upon by a spectator to speak louder, replied, *if he did he should not act in character*. Milward, I say, began low, and, by gradual progress, rose to such a height, as not only to inflame the populace on the stage, but to touch the audience with a kind of enthusiastic rapture; when he uttered the following lines:

> — — But were I Brutus,
> And Brutus Antony, there were an Antony
> Would ruffle up your spirits, and put a tongue
> In every wound of Caesar, that should move
> The stones of Rome to rise and mutiny.

It is scarcely to be conceived with what acclamations of applause this was accompanied.

Thomas Davies, *Dramatic Miscellanies*

Young's Cassius

In John Kemble's Covent Garden revival, which opened in February 1812, Kemble himself played Brutus while Charles Mayne Young (1777–1856) was a notable Cassius.

April 5, 1812

The most prominent attraction in the performance of *Julius Caesar* is the Cassius of Mr. Young. It is full of fire, and yet marked with the nicest discrimination—a rare combination, in which this actor promises to excel all his contemporaries, and of which the passage in his conference with Brutus, beginning 'I know that virtue to be in you,' would alone be a finished specimen. This speech is a string of varieties, from the commonest colloquial familiarity to the loftiest burst of passion;

and Mr. Young passes from one to another with the happiest instantaneousness of impression—from an air of indifference to one of resentment, from anecdote to indignant comment, from the subdued tone of sarcastic mimicry to the loud and impatient climax of a jealousy wrought up into rage. The transition in particular from the repetition of Caesar's sick words to the contemptuous simile they occasion, and from that again to the concluding burst of astonishment, accompanied with a start forward and a vehement clasp of the hands, is exceedingly striking. As there is no single passage in Shakspeare more various in expressing the shades of passion and discourse, so I do not remember a speech delivered on the stage by which the actor more nearly approaches to the ideal picture of the person he represents. There is none therefore that deserves better to be recorded as one of the uniques of its day; and if Mr. Young proceed in this manner to study his part *ambitiously*, and to read his part with that searching and patient eye which will alone enable us to catch all the pith and scope of his eloquence, I repeat with still greater confidence than before that he will soon oust Mr. Kemble from the throne which his grave cant has usurped, and place in it a proper being of flesh and blood, who feels and speaks like a susceptible creature.

The next performance in merit is certainly that of Anthony by Mr. Charles Kemble, who in pronouncing the celebrated speech over the dead body of Caesar manages with great nicety the difficult point of insinuating the sarcasms against the conspirators without coming broadly to them at once. He also looks the character to perfection, as Shakspeare has represented it; and so do Messrs. Young and Kemble theirs, with the exception of their respective ages, which ought to look the reverse of what they appear, for Cassius was an old man compared with Brutus. With respect to Mr. Kemble's performance, it is excellent as far as philosophic appearance and manner can make it so, and his general conception of the character is just and impressive; but Brutus, who affected pithiness of speech, never thought of recommending it by a drawling preachment; and really this artificial actor does so dole out his words, and so drop his syllables one by one upon the ear, as if he were measuring out laudanum for us, that a reasonable auditor, who is not to be imposed upon with the multitude in general, has no alternative between laughing or being disgusted.

But in the name of all that is serious and fitting, let us have a more endurable Caesar by next year, if the play keep possession so long. Shakspeare has distorted and tumified Caesar's character enough, as it is; but what little remained of familiarity and of gentlemanly bearing in it, Mr. Egerton is determined to make all of a piece with the rest. Every action is lofty, every look tragic, every turn of step and of feature imperial and bluff. When Caesar, upon a representation of Anthony's, that Cassius was not a dangerous man, pleasantly wishes that 'he were fatter,' Mr. Egerton takes it in the light of a serious and impassioned desire, and mouths out the words like a stage-tyrant who wishes a man in his grave; and when Anthony is familiarly requested to step on the other side of him, because the ear at which he is standing is deaf, he delivers the request with as much dignity, and motions him round with as much mysterious solemnity, as if he were asking him to defend his other side from an assassin.

Leigh Hunt, *The Examiner*

The Killing of Caesar

Tieck saw the Kemble production of 1812 five years later, the last year during which it was performed.

As my anticipations were no longer vague, so was my enjoyment greater. The play itself, too, being narrower in its range, and more easily understood, was altogether better given. Brutus, it is true, was not acted, but only declaimed with intelligence. The celebrated quarrel scene between him and Cassius (Mr. Young) produced but little impression; for scenes of this kind Kemble's voice is much too weak. The orations were well spoken. Charles Kemble, brother of the famous actor, delivered his speech as Antony with great energy, only there was too much malignant bitterness in his laugh at its close, when he saw the people roused, showing a false interpretation of the poet's purpose! Here was an instance of what we often see—that an inferior talent infuses too much of itself into the poet, and thereby drags him down to a lower level. Much may be introduced well and properly in the plays of other writers, which is quite out of place where Shakespeare is concerned.

The scene of the mob, with its rising turbulence and its calming down again, was very well given. On this occasion, too, the costumes were satisfactory.

*   *   *

228

The stage was deep, and Caesar sat upon a chair in the extreme background. When the petition was presented, and rejected by him, the conspirators arranged themselves in a well-defined pyramid, of which Caesar formed the apex, while Brutus stood well forward in the proscenium to the left. Casca is the first to stab him; then Caesar turns to the right and receives a second blow from the second of his enemies; again he staggers in affright to the left, a few steps forward, and receives a fresh wound, then the same to the right: now the free space on the stage grows larger, and this strange movement of the mortally wounded man becomes more extraordinary and unnatural, but he still goes on staggering across the stage five or six times, so as to be stabbed by the conspirators, who remain quietly standing, until he receives his death-blow from Brutus, and falls forward, exclaiming: '*Et tu, Brute!*' This scene, arranged like the most formal ballet, lost all dignity; and it was rendered outrageous by its pretentious solemnity. It was even impossible to laugh at it. . . . To what will not men become accustomed! I believe, of all the native audience there was not one who was disturbed by this grotesque piece of stage business.

Ludwig Tieck,
The Nineteenth Century, February 1880
(Theodore Martin)

The Meiningen Court Company

The Meiningen Court Company was formed as a private resident company attached to the court by the Duke of Saxe-Meiningen (1826– 1914). The company, under its director Ludwig Chronegk was especially noted for its skilful handling of crowd scenes and for accuracy of historical detail. On its visit to London in 1881, the Meiningen Company performed (in German) Twelfth Night and The Winter's Tale as well as Julius Caesar and several non-Shakespearean plays.

The effect produced on the mind by the acting of the German Court Company in 'Julius Caesar' is not at all dissimilar to that harmony of detail and mechanical effort observed in the Passion Play at Oberammergau last year. Nor is the comparison irrelevant or unfair when we look closely into it. The venerable pastor Daisenberger in the Bavarian Highlands and the Grand Duke of the German principality are alike actuated by an enthusiasm. One desires to edify the Christian world, the other to revive the artistic glories of Weimar. Both are leading spirits, and give forth the infection

The SAXE-MEININGEN PLAYERS in Julius Caesar, Drury Lane, 1881
(*Illustrated London News*, June 4, 1881).

of their enthusiasm. They take vast pains to secure perfection;
they urge upon the players the immense value of rehearsals,
accuracy, industry, and research; their motto is that no
trouble is too great for the subject-matter in hand; and the
result in both cases is the perfection of mechanical excellence
rather than the glow of apparent inspiration. In point of stage
management the Passion Play, with all its astounding
difficulties, its groupings, its crowds, its tableaux and processions, was a most remarkable and creditable effort; nothing
went wrong, everyone knew where to go and what to do, the
performance lasted from eight o'clock in the morning until six
at night and there was not a blunder perceptible or a hitch

visible. Yet through all there was a sense of rigid uniformity that became positively wearisome.

* * *

The pictures were marvellous, but there was no soul in them; the artists were drilled, not inspired. The same kind of effect is observed when the curtain draws up on 'Julius Caesar,' and one of the first results of Herr Chronegk's manipulation is shown. It is certainly a crowd full of movement, action, variety, and change. The colours are almost faultless, the groupings fascinate the eye. Something is always going on; men and women change places; they converse in dumb show; one leaps upon the pediment of a statue to see the procession of the advancing Caesar, another strains his eyes to catch the first glimpse of the coming procession. But what is the result? The crowd gradually becomes of superior instead of sub-ordinate importance. We are looking at the citizens instead of listening to Brutus, Cassius, and Casca. Our attention is taken off the play to observe its detail; we do not feel the existence of a crowd, but its corporeal presence is forced upon us, and, instead of saying 'How naturally that is done!' we point out how cleverly it is accomplished. Now this is surely incorrect in art. Everything that is obtrusive is *ipso facto* inartistic; the best-dressed man or woman is one whose costume is scarcely remembered, and Shakespeare has himself had something to say about minor effects that are forced in front of the picture. We believe that a play can be as much over stage-managed as under stage-managed, and there have been recent instances in our own theatres where excess of care and laboured attention to minutiae have produced exactly the opposite effect to what was intended.

* * *

In the great scene where Marcus Antonius inflames the passions of the citizens over the dead body of Caesar, there is, however, a dramatic purpose in the crowd, and it would be affectation not to admire the skill of Herr Ludwig Barnay, or the result of Herr Chronegk's system of training. Take, for instance, the clever but natural idea of the first words of Mark Antony's speech being drowned in the murmur and confusion. What old-fashioned actor, accustomed to ladle out the well-known 'Friends, Romans, countrymen, lend me your ears,' would have tolerated the innovation? Yet the triple appeal justifies the interruption, and warrants that shrug of the

231

shoulders from Herr Barnay when, in spite of all efforts he cannot get a hearing, the 'Peace ho! let us hear him,' having been drowned beforehand. The thing that has so astonished English audiences is the power obtained of crescendo and diminuendo effects as in music. The passions surge and swell, subside, or increase, according to the will and power of the speaker. The unanimity is wonderful, if anything too wonderful. The yells come out like an electric shock with startling and sudden effect; the arms and hands are shot out as if they had been pulled by wires. In timing, unison, and precision such an effect has seldom been seen on any stage, and the only fault that can possibly be found with it is that the sense of training is too obvious; the hand of the drillmaster is too often seen, and we think occasionally more of the cleverness of the result than the nature of the scene. It is the most difficult thing in the world, no doubt, to hit off the precise balance between feeble effort and successful endeavour, for the dramatist is often himself responsible for solecisms. A crowd does not speak a long sentence unanimously, 'all' cannot deliver a sentiment in time. They may assent or differ together, but no more. Acting, doubtless, is a mixed art of mechanism and individual expression, and stage crowds must be trained; but there is danger when the training is so positive and absolute as this.

*   *   *

We want mechanical regularity, it is true, no business is worth anything without it; the most natural-looking actors are studied to a fault; but we do also want individual expression, and in the play of 'Julius Caesar' only Marcus Antonius and Casca stood out as artists of any marked thought and intelligence. The allusion to Casca reminds us how wonderfully well all the details of the murder of Caesar were managed. Everyone naturally knew what was coming; but no one could conceive how it was to be done. It must be remembered that, much as the lovers of art in Germany admire and appreciate the enthusiasm of the Meiningers, and their whole-souled devotion to the drama, still critical opinion is divided as to the value of their method. When they first left their quiet home in 1874, and burst upon the world at Berlin, as a recent writer observes, 'at once the whole theatrical world of that city was stirred up and divided into Meiningen and anti-Meiningen, just as they are divided into Wagnerian and anti-Wagnerian; for the Meiningen Company also had and has still its strong opponents. They contended that the pompous scenery and splendid get-up of the whole overshadowed the ingenuity of the acting; that, moreover, the introduction of most minute details, such as a particular ancient lamp of unquestionable historical exactness in "Julius Caesar," a lamp that was a work of art in itself, might easily draw the attention of the audience from the play itself to this insignificant detail.' This is precisely the danger of ultra-realism, and we have had so many warnings that we are not likely to forget them. But in the art of stage management as shown by Herr Chronegk, though we have much to admire, we have very little to imitate.

Daily Telegraph, June 3, 1881

Hamlet

BURBAGE was the first Hamlet and since then this most popular of Shakespearean roles has been played by every important tragic actor. Davenant's Restoration adaptation of the play was less drastic than usual, though he made heavy cuts. There is an almost continuous record of performances, though none at the Elizabethan or Jacobean court, which some consider significant. Many Hamlets have been actresses, among them Sarah Bernhardt.

Betterton Remembered

Colley Cibber recalls Betterton in his prime. In the next extract is an account of Betterton in his seventies still playing Hamlet.

Betterton was an actor, as Shakespear was an author, both without competitors! form'd for the mutual assistance and illustration of each other's genius! How Shakespear wrote, all men who have a taste for nature may read, and know—but with what higher rapture would he still be *read*, could they conceive how Betterton *play'd* him! Then might they know. the one was born alone to speak what the other only knew to write! Pity it is, that the momentary beauties flowing from an harmonious elocution, cannot like those of poetry be their own record! That the animated graces of the player can live no

233

Frontispiece to Rowe's edition of Hamlet, 1709. Betterton may be represented in the title-role.

longer than the instant breath and motion that presents them; or at best can but faintly glimmer through the memory, or imperfect attestation of a few surviving spectators. Could *how* Betterton spoke be as easily known as *what* he spoke; then might you see the muse of Shakespear in her triumph, with all her beauties in their best array, rising into real life, and charming her beholders. But alas! since all this is so far out of the reach of description, how shall I shew you Betterton? Should I therefore tell you that all the Othellos, Hamlets, Hotspurs, Mackbeths, and Brutus's whom you may have seen since his time, have fallen far short of him; this still should give you no idea of his particular excellence. Let us see then what a particular comparison may do! whether that may yet draw him nearer to you?

You have seen a Hamlet perhaps, who, on the first appearance of his father's spirit, has thrown himself into all the straining vociferation requisite to express rage and fury, and the house has thunder'd with applause; tho' the mis-guided actor was all the while (as Shakespear terms it) tearing a passion into rags.—I am the more bold to offer you this particular instance, because the late Mr. Addison, while I sate by him, to see this scene acted, made the same observation, asking me with some surprise, if I thought Hamlet should be in so violent a passion with the Ghost, which tho' it might have astonish'd, it had not provok'd him? for you may observe that in this beautiful speech, the passion never rises beyond an almost breathless astonishment, or an impatience, limited by filial reverence, to enquire into the suspected wrongs that may have rais'd him from his peaceful tomb! and a desire to know what a spirit so seemingly distrest, might wish or enjoin a sorrowful son to execute towards his future quiet in the grave? This was the light into which Betterton threw this scene; which he open'd with a pause of mute amazement! then rising slowly to a solemn, trembling voice, he made the ghost equally terrible to the spectator as to himself! and in the descriptive part of the natural emotions which the ghastly vision gave him, the boldness of his expostulation was still govern'd by decency, manly, but not braying; his voice never rising into that seeming outrage, or wild defiance of what he naturally rever'd. But alas! to preserve this medium, between mouthing, and meaning too little, to keep the attention more pleasingly awake, by a temper'd spirit, than by mere vehemence of voice, is of all the master-strokes of an actor the most difficult to reach. In this none yet have equalled Betterton.

Cibber's *Apology*

. . . all his Visage Wanned

This account of Betterton strangely recalls Hamlet's soliloquy on the actor, II ii.

The following account of Betterton's amazing feeling will furnish a proof, that, when the player is truly impressed with his character, he will, in the representation of fear and terror, assume a pallid hue, as well as the contrary complexion from different emotions:

'I have lately been told, by a gentleman who has frequently seen Betterton perform Hamlet, that he observed his countenance, which was naturally ruddy and sanguine, in the scene of the third act where his father's ghost appears, through the violent and sudden emotion of amazement and horror, turn, instantly, on the sight of his father's spirit, as pale as his neckcloth; when his whole body seemed to be affected with a tremor inexpressible; so that, had his father's ghost actually risen before him, he could not have been seized with more real agonies. And this was felt so strongly by the audience, that the blood seemed to shudder in their veins likewise; and they, in some measure, partook of the astonishment and horror with which they saw this excellent actor affected.'

Davies, *Dramatic Miscellanies*

Garrick's Hamlet

Garrick first played Hamlet at Goodman's Fields on December 9, 1741. Murphy describes his performance at Drury Lane the following year.

To do justice to such a character, it was necessary that the talents of the actor should be as various as those of his great master. When Garrick entered the scene, the character he assumed, was legible in his countenance; by the force of deep meditation he transformed himself into the very man. He remained fixed in a pensive attitude, and the sentiments that possessed his mind could be discovered by the attentive spectator. When he spoke, the tone of his voice was in unison with the workings of his mind, and as soon as he said, '*I have that within me which [sur] passes shew,*' his every feature confirmed and proved the truth. The soliloquy, that begins with, '*O that this too, too solid flesh would melt,*' brings to light, as it were by accident, the character of *Hamlet*. His grief, his

236

DAVID GARRICK as Hamlet, Drury Lane, 1754.

anxiety, and irresolute temper, are strongly marked. He does
not as yet know that his father was poisoned, but his mother's
marriage excites resentment and abhorrence of her conduct.
He begins with it, but as Smith observes in his excellent notes
on *Longinus*, he stops for want of words. Reflections crowd upon
him, and he runs off in commendation of his deceased father.
His thoughts soon turn again to his mother; in an instant he
flies off again, and continues in a strain of sudden transitions,

237

taking no less than eighteen lines to tell us, that in less than two months, his mother married his father's brother, *'But no more like his father, than he to Hercules.'* In all these shiftings of the passions, his voice and attitude changed with wonderful celerity, and, at every pause, his face was an index to his mind. On the first appearance of the ghost, such a figure of consternation was never seen. He stood fixed in mute astonishment, and the audience saw him growing paler and paler. After an interval of suspence, he spoke in a low trembling accent, and uttered his questions with the greatest difficulty. An attempt to trace him through the whole play, would lead to a long dissertation. His directions to the players were given *con amore.* He thought it a lecture on his own school of acting, and certainly had in his eye some performers of that day, when he said, 'There be players that I have seen play, and heard others praise, and that highly,—not to speak it profanely, that having neither the accent of Christian, Pagan, or man, have so strutted, and bellowed, that I thought some of nature's journeymen made men, and not made them well, they imitated humanity so abominably.' It will be easily conceived, that he, who so perfectly represented the real madness of *Lear,* should know how to assume the counterfeit appearance of it in his interview with *Ophelia.* The closet-scene with his mother was highly interesting, warm, and pathetic. He spoke daggers to her, till her conscience turned her eyes inward on her own guilt. In the various soliloquies, which have never been equalled by any writer, ancient or modern, Garrick proved himself the proper organ of Shakespeare's genius.

Arthur Murphy, Life of Garrick

To Be Or Not To Be

Hamlet, who is in mourning, as I have already reminded you, appears here, having already begun to feign madness, with his thick hair dishevelled and a lock hanging over one shoulder; one of his black stockings has slipped down so as to show his white socks, and a loop of his red garter is hanging down beyond the middle of the calf. Thus he comes on to the stage sunk in contemplation, his chin resting on his right hand, and his right elbow on his left, and gazes solemnly downwards. And then, removing his right hand from his chin, but, if I remember right, still supporting it with his left hand, he speaks the words 'To be or not to be,' &c., softly, though, on account of the absolute silence (not because of some particular talent of the man's, as they say even in some of the newspapers), they are audible everywhere.

*   *   *

Ophelia's dress, likewise, after she has lost her reason, is disordered, as far as propriety allows. She was played by Mrs. Smith, a young woman and a good singer, who is admirably suited to the part (although she has not enough vivacity for several others that she takes). Her long flaxen hair hung partly down her back, and partly over her shoulders; in her left hand she held a bunch of loose straw, and her whole demeanour in her madness was as gentle as the passion which caused it. The songs, which she sang charmingly, were fraught with such plaintive and tender melancholy that I fancied that I could still hear them far into the night, when I was alone. Shakespeare makes this whole scene so moving as to cause one actual pain and leave a sore place in the heart, which goes on throbbing until one could wish never to have seen poor, unhappy Ophelia. I wish that Voltaire might have been here and heard Mrs. Smith's interpretation of Shakespeare! This remarkable man would, I believe, almost have repented of what he said against these scenes. I am sure that if I had written any such thing— of course with the wit of a Voltaire and his influence on weak minds—and had afterwards seen what I have been seeing, I should, forsooth, have asked the forgiveness of Shakespeare's spirit in the newspapers. Voltaire has, however, gained one victory at Drury Lane. The gravediggers' scene is omitted. They retain it at Covent Garden. Garrick should not have done this. To represent so ancient and superb a piece in all its characteristic rude vigour in these insipid times, when even in this country the language of nature is beginning to yield to fine phrases and conventional twaddle, might have arrested this decline, even if it could not put a stop to it.

Lichtenberg, Visits to England

Hannah More Writes Home

Adelphi, 1776.

I imagine my last was not so ambiguous but that you saw well enough I staid in town to see Hamlet, and I will venture to say, that it was such an entertainment as will probably never again be exhibited to an admiring world. But this general panegyric can give you no idea of *my* feelings; and particular praise would be injurious to his excellences.

In every part he filled the whole soul of the spectator, and transcended the most finished idea of the poet. The requisites for Hamlet are not only various, but opposed. In him they are all united, and as it were concentrated. One thing I must particularly remark, that, whether in the simulation of madness, in the sinkings of despair, in the familiarity of friendship, in the whirlwind of passion, or in the meltings of tenderness, he never once forgot he was a prince; and in every variety of situation, and transition of feeling, you discovered the highest polish of fine breeding and courtly manners.

Hamlet experiences the conflict of many passions and affections, but filial love ever takes the lead; *that* is the great point from which he sets out, and to which he returns; the others are all contingent and subordinate to it, and are cherished or renounced, as they promote or obstruct the operation of this leading principle. Had you seen with what exquisite art and skill Garrick maintained the subserviency of the less to the greater interests, you would agree with me, of what importance to the perfection of acting, is that consummate good sense which always pervades every part of his performances.

To the most eloquent expression of the eye, to the hand-writing of the passions on his features, to a sensibility which tears to pieces the hearts of his auditors, to powers so unparalleled, he adds a judgment of the most exquisite accuracy, the fruit of long experience and close observation, by which he preserves every gradation and transition of the passions, keeping all under the control of a just dependence and natural consistency. So naturally, indeed, do the ideas of the poet seem to mix with his own, that he seemed himself to be engaged in a succession of affecting situations, not giving utterance to a speech, but to the instantaneous expression of his feelings, delivered in the most affecting tones of voice, and with gestures that belong only to nature. It was a fiction as delightful as fancy, and as touching as truth.

Hannah More,
Memoirs and Correspondence, 1834

The Ghost

The Ghost is most admirably written; and according to the idea I form of supernatural utterance, adapted to supernatural appearance. Mr. Quin[1] has never been excelled, nor by many degrees equalled; solemnity of expression was his excellence in tragedy, and, if I may be allowed the remark, his fault. Tho' not directly to my purpose at present, I cannot help observing that Shakespeare's fame as an actor, was disputed only because he wrote, as plainly appears, for the mode of speaking, Mr. Garrick, by most excellent example, has established; he certainly, as a judge and lover of nature, despised the titum-ti, monotonous sing-song then fashionable, and indeed equally admired, till within less than these last thirty years; for this reason, he was judged to be but a middling performer, except in the Ghost; and there, with propriety, no doubt, he assumed pomposity, which, on other occasions, less commendable, would have rendered him a very popular actor. — Want of action in the Ghost throws a damp on the narration; if a spirit can assume corporeal appearance, there can be no reason to suppose imaginary arms motionless, no more than imaginary legs; however, some peculiarity in this point, as well as the tones of expression, should be observed.

Francis Gentleman, The Dramatic Censor

Kemble's First Appearance

Kemble made his London début at Drury Lane on September 30, 1783. Having described the first night, Boaden goes on to discuss a number of 'points' in Kemble's performance, comparing it with Garrick's; two of these occur in the later part of this extract.

On Mr. Kemble's first appearance before the spectators, the general exclamation was, 'How very like his sister!' and there was a very striking resemblance. His person seemed to be finely formed, and his manners princely; but on his brow hung the weight of 'some intolerable woe.' Apart from the expression called up by the situation of Hamlet, there struck me to be in him a peculiar and personal fitness for tragedy. What others assumed, seemed to be inherent in Kemble. 'Native, and to the manner born,' he looked an abstraction, if I may so say, of the characteristics of tragedy.

The first great point of remark was, that his Hamlet was decidedly original. He had seen no great actor whom he could

[1] James Quin (1693–1766) was a representative of the older declamatory school of acting which Garrick challenged. 'If that young fellow is right,' Quin said of Garrick, 'I and the rest of the players have been all wrong.'

have copied. His style was formed by his own taste or judgment, or rather grew out of the peculiar properties of his person and his intellectual habits. He was of a solemn and deliberate temperament—his walk was always slow, and his expression of countenance contemplative—his utterance rather tardy for the most part, but always finely articulate, and in common parlance seemed to proceed rather from organization than voice.

*　　*　　*

Having drawn his sword, to menace the friends who prevented him from following the Ghost, every Hamlet before Mr. Kemble presented the point to the phantom as he followed him to the removed ground. Kemble, having drawn it on his friends, retained it in his right hand, but turned his left towards the spirit, and drooped the weapon after him—a change both tasteful and judicious. As a defence against such a being it was ridiculous to present the point.—To retain it unconsciously showed how completely he was absorbed by the dreadful mystery he was exploring.

The *kneeling* at the descent of the Ghost was censured as a *trick*. I suppose merely because it had not been done before: but it suitably marked the filial reverence of Hamlet, and the solemnity of the engagement he had contracted. Henderson saw it, and adopted it immediately,—I remember he was applauded for doing so.

These two great actors[1] agreed in the seeming intention of particular disclosure to Horatio—

'Yes, but there *is*, Horatio,—and much offence too.'

turned off upon the pressing forward of Marcellus to partake the communication. Kemble *only*, however, prepared the way for this, by the marked address to Horatio, 'Did you not speak to it?'

In the scene with Polonius, where Hamlet is asked what is the matter which he reads, and he answers, 'Slanders, sir,' Mr. Kemble, to give the stronger impression of his wildness, tore the leaf out of the book. Even this was remarked, for he was of consequence enough, at first, to have every thing he did minutely examined.

A critic observed that, in the scene with Rosencrantz and Guildenstern, he was not only familiar, but gay and smiling; and that he *should* be quite the reverse, because he tells them

[1] i.e. Kemble and Garrick.

that he 'has lost all his mirth,' &c. This was pure mis-apprehension in the critic. The scene itself ever so slightly read would have set him right. Hamlet, from playing on Polonius, turns to receive gaily and with smiles his *excellent friends*, his *good lads*, who are neither the *button on fortune's cap*, nor the *soles of her shoe*. And it is only when the conception crosses him that they were sent to sound him, that he changes his manner, puts his questions eagerly and importunately, and, having an eye upon them, gives that account of his disposition, which rendered it but a sleeveless errand which they came upon.

Boaden, Life of J. P. Kemble

Mr. Kean's Hamlet[1]

Last Saturday was rendered somewhat memorable in the annals of the Drama, by the event of Mr. Kean's appearance, on that evening, for the first time, in this metropolis at least, in the arduous character of Hamlet.

This tragedy, although it be pregnant with numerous beauties, is so full of errors, that it was difficult to understand many of its passages clearly in its original state; but since such a herd of commentators have undertaken to write glossaries and cloudy notes, in order to explain the true meaning of the author, it hath become very nearly inexplicable. Under these circumstances we think that Mr. Kean was unwise, if not presumptuous, in mangling this distorted drama, still more, by omitting various fragments of the dialogue that were necessary to sustain the true directions of the plot. At the termination of the second act, when Hamlet hath been ruminating upon the possible diabolism of the visiting spirit, and has resolved upon the performance of a play before the *King*, in order to try the effect that an assimilating catastrophe may produce externally upon his functions, he is made to say, and that very properly,

> 'I'll have grounds
> More relative than this. The play's the thing
> Wherein I'll catch the conscience of the king.'

Yet Mr. Kean thought fit to leave out the whole of the first line in this declaration, though the strong sense that is included in that very line is the qualification and basis of all his future resolutions! This, in the saucy jargon of the day, may be

[1] Original title.

EDMUND KEAN as Hamlet, Drury Lane, 1814.

called 'a new reading,' but as it is a proceeding that is deeply injurious to common sense, we must enter our protest against such destructive novelties.

In the most important scene with Ophelia, previous to the play, Mr. Kean became *practically amorous*, and kissed the lady's hand, for which deviation from rectitude many thoughtless spectators cheered him! We do repeat, that they absolutely cheered him, though the deed should have been reprobated, because it tended to give *the lie circumstantial* to what the King is made to utter to Polonius immediately after they had been listening, *sub silentio*, in order to ascertain whether his ascribed dementation arose from the love he bore towards Ophelia, or not. The exclamation of the disappointed King runs thus:

'Love! his affections do not that way tend.'

In the play scene, he left out the whole of that illustrative conversation with Ophelia, beginning with:

'My Lord, you are as good as a chorus, &c.'

and during the mimic representation, Mr. Kean so far forgot that inalienable delicacy, which should eternally characterise a gentleman in his deportment before the ladies, that he not only exposed his *derrière* to his mistress, but positively crawled upon his belly towards the King like a wounded snake in a meadow, rather than a Prince openly indulging himself in moral speculation in the saloon of a royal palace!

In the consequent scene with Rosencrantz and Guildenstern, when the pipe is introduced, Mr. Kean favoured us with another 'new reading,' for, instead of saying the instrument, when duly used,

'Will discourse most eloquent music,'

which is perfectly rational and correct, he substituted

'most eloquent *harmony*'

which is sheer nonsense, as harmony, critically speaking, is the delightful issue of several sounds in concord. In regard to Mr. Kean's emphasis, it was generally proper, and sometimes very erroneous. He appeared to us to labour more sedulously to be singular in his manner, than just, which is a scenic vice that is gaining ground too rapidly. Many of his speeches are marred by a drawling sententiousness that fatigued the ear, and some of his words were too powerfully accented. When he questioned the Ghost of his murdered father, in the first act, his tone was partially indecorous, and unmingled with that awe and reverence which such a vision would naturally inspire in a loving and beloved son. It was so far from being tremulous that, in addressing the sacred phantom, he exclaimed,

'Art thou a spirit of health, or goblin damn'd?'

laying such a violent and unnecessary stress upon the word *damn'd*, as if he felt some triumph at the supposition!

His action was sometimes true, and sometimes faulty; sometimes in accordance with his princely dignity, and sometimes vulgar and inelegant. He hath acquired an habitude of bending his body, that is ungraceful; and recurs too often to the trick of patting his forehead. When the Ghost first appeared, Mr. Kean started, as is usual; but when the Ghost first spoke, he stood as unmoved, as if he had been accustomed to hold a colloquy with such sepulchral visitors, and that the circumstance of their being oracular, had nothing extraordinary in its nature!

When the Spirit descended, calling out, in a depth of pathos,

'Farewell—remember me,'

Mr. Kean did not look, with any sort of astonishment, of recollective fondness upon the spot of his preternatural departure to another world: but walked over it towards the orchestra, with as little apparent regret, as an inconsiderate young heir might display when treading over the atoms of a deceased parent.

In pronouncing the word *contumely*, in the celebrated soliloquy, he chose to divide it into four distinct syllables, that seemed to hop after each other like limping relatives; as thus:— Con-*tu*-me-ly! This was another effort of new reading, and certainly did not pass off without exciting a burst of 'bravos' from many of the auditors, who appeared to be loud in their acclamations, in proportion as he departed from the prescribed institutes of speech!

In the fencing scene with Laertes, Mr. Kean exhibited much grace and address, and was loudly and in this instance, most deservedly applauded.

His dress, in the fifth act, when he wears a scarlet cloak, approximated strongly to the ludicrous.

We observed that Mr. Kean reposed for security only, upon the lower tones of his voice, from which he seldom deviated: and this was judicious in him, as his upper tones are unmanageable, and not unfrequently discordant.

Morning Herald, March 14, 1814

Tieck on Kemble

Nearly thirty-five years after his début, Kemble played Hamlet at Covent Garden, where Ludwig Tieck saw him on the night of June 21, 1817.

It was obvious (are his words) that the artist must have played this part in his youth with very different power, but no doubt he played it then upon the same lines. It would hardly be possible for any man of talent altogether to fail in this infinitely suggestive character, which reveals almost every aspect of humanity, and gives expression to the most diversified emotions in scenes of such various interest. What Kemble brought prominently out was the sad, the melancholy, the nobly suffering aspect of the character. He gave way to tears much too often, spoke many of the scenes—that with the players, for instance—admirably, and moved and bore himself like a man of high blood and breeding. But, as usual, there was almost no distinction between the lighter and heavier parts of the play; and then, again, the distinction between prose and verse was nowhere marked. The great passionate scenes passed off almost flatly; at least, that where the ghost appears was quite ineffective. In such passages as the opening of the first monologue—

'Oh, that this too solid flesh would melt!'

Kemble lingers for some seconds on the 'Oh!' with a strongly tremulous cadence.

When Hamlet, speaking of the rugged Pyrrhus, says:

'If it live in your memory, begin at this line; let me see, let me see!
      The rugged Pyrrhus, like the Hyrcanian beast—
'Tis not so; it begins with Pyrrhus——'

there was a general burst of applause throughout the house, because this forgetfulness, this seeking after the beginning of the verse, was expressed in such a natural way. And, indeed, when one has been listening for a length of time to a slow, measured, wailing rhythm, regularly interrupted by considerable pauses, and by a succession of highly pitched inflections, one is quite taken by surprise on hearing once more the tones of nature, and the manner of everyday conversation.

I have seen nothing new in this impersonation, neither have I learned anything except that Hamlet, after he has stabbed the king, while saying—

'Here, thou incestuous, murd'rous, damned Dane,
  Drink off this potion! Is thy union here?'

thrusts the poisoned chalice to the king's mouth, and forces him, as he dies, to drink it, which I take to be the right thing. A good effect, too, was produced in this scene by the king being seated some steps above the stage. These words, so explained and acted, brought vividly to my mind Macbeth's imagery in the monologue of the last scene of the first Act:

> 'This even-handed justice
> Commends the ingredients of our poison'd chalice
> To our own lips.'

Ludwig Tieck—
The Nineteenth Century, February 1880
(Theodore Martin)

Actor Hisses Actor

In 1846, Macready was hissed while playing Hamlet by an American actor Edwin Forrest (1806–72) who blamed Macready for his own unpopularity on the London stage in the previous year. In 1849, Macready nearly lost his life in a riot involving Forrest in New York.

MACREADY as Hamlet, Haymarket, 1849.

Edinburgh, March 2nd.—Acted Hamlet really with particular care, energy, and discrimination; the audience gave less applause to the first soliloquy than I am in the habit of receiving, but I was bent on acting the part, and I felt, if I can feel at all, that I had strongly excited them, and that their sympathies were cordially, indeed enthusiastically, with me. On reviewing the performance, I can conscientiously pronounce it one of the very best I have given of Hamlet. At the waving of the handkerchief before the play, and 'I must be idle,' a man on the right side of the stage—upper boxes or gallery, but said to be upper boxes—hissed! The audience took it up, and I waved the more, and bowed derisively and contemptuously to the individual. The audience carried it, though he was very staunch to his purpose. It discomposed me, and alas! might have ruined many; but I bore it down. I thought of speaking to the audience, if called on, and spoke to Murray about it, but he very discreetly dissuaded me. Was called for, and very warmly greeted. Ryder came and spoke to me, and told me that the hisser was observed, and said to be a Mr. W——, who was in company with Mr. Forrest! The man writes in the *Journal*, a paper depreciating me and eulogising Mr. F., sent to me from this place.

Macready's Diaries

A French Hamlet

G. H. Lewes recalls the Hamlet of Charles Albert Fechter (1824–79) a bilingual actor who played Hamlet in 1861.

Intellectually and physically his Hamlet so satisfies the audience, that they exclaim, 'How natural!' Hamlet is fat, according to his mother's testimony; but he is also—at least in Ophelia's eyes—very handsome—

> The courtier's, soldier's, scholar's eye, tongue, sword,
> The glass of fashion and the mould of form,
> The observed of all observers.

Fechter is lymphatic, delicate, handsome, and with his long flaxen curls, quivering sensitive nostrils, fine eye, and sympathetic voice, perfectly represents the graceful prince. His aspect and bearing are such that the eye rests on him with delight. Our sympathies are completely secured. All those scenes which demand the qualities of an accomplished comedian he plays to perfection. Seldom have the scenes with the players, with Polonius, with Horatio, with Rosenkrantz and Guildenstern, or the quieter monologues, been better

CHARLES FECHTER as Hamlet, Lyceum, 1861.

played; they are touched with so cunning a grace, and a manner so *natural*, that the effect is delightful. We not only feel in the presence of an individual, a character, but feel that the individual is consonant with our previous conception of Hamlet, and with the part assigned him in the play. The passages of *emotion* also are rendered with some sensibility. His delightful and sympathetic voice, and the unforced fervour of his expression, triumph over the foreigner's accent and the foreigner's mistakes in emphasis. This is really a considerable triumph; for although Fechter pronounces English very well for a Frenchman, it is certain that his accent greatly interferes with the due effect of the speeches. But the foreign accent is as nothing compared with the frequent error of emphasis; and *this* surely he might overcome by diligent study, if he would consent to submit to the rigorous criticism of some English friend, who would correct him every time he errs. The sense is often perturbed, and sometimes violated, by this fault. Yet so great is the power of true emotion, that even *this* is forgotten directly he touches the feelings of the audience; and in his great speech 'O what a rogue and peasant slave am I!' no one hears the foreigner.

G. H. Lewes, On Actors and the Art of Acting

Hamlet at the Lyceum

'The king for my money!' exclaimed Partridge, after he had been taken to the playhouse by Mr. Jones to see one David Garrick enact Hamlet, Prince of Denmark.[1] 'The King for my money: he speaks all his words distinctly, half as loud again as the other. Anybody may see he is an actor.' Had the schoolmaster of Little Baddington visited the Lyceum Theatre last Monday night he would probably have repeated his criticism of the last century; for to those who consider sound rather than sense the distinctive mark of a good actor, Mr. Irving's presentation of Hamlet will not recommend itself. His voice is weak, uncertain, and at times, almost unmusical in its weakness. His pronunciation is blurred by his own peculiar mannerism, and his utterance—now and then, but very rarely—is indistinct. As in the days of Mr. Partridge, so now the king has the best of it, at least, in volume of voice. But fortunately we do not all of us demand a 'robustious fellow' to deliver in full round tones the soliloquies of the Danish Prince; nor a bold and amorous hero of romance, a chivalrous gallant whose attractions lie more in the beauty of his body than the beauty of his soul. A scholar rather than a soldier, a poet rather than a statesman, a thinker rather than a man of action, a mind prone to self-analysis and 'thinking too precisely on the event', unstable from the delicacy of its mechanism, suspicious from its knowledge of human nature, with all its purest beliefs upset by the discovery of a mother's guilt—a dreamy philosopher whose exquisite supersensitive organisation, strung up to tension point 'in its weakness and its melancholy', the slightest breath causes to vibrate. Such is the Hamlet some

[1] In Fielding's *Tom Jones*.

conceive Shakespeare to have drawn, and to them Mr. Irving's interpretation of the part cannot fail to be acceptable.

So much has been said and written by foreigners, as well as by Englishmen, about this particular creation since its appearance in October 1874, that the subject seems well-nigh exhausted. Mr. Irving's admirers, however, must have remarked with pleasure last Monday evening many fresh touches and details which the last four years have added to the original picture. It has been said that the character of Hamlet is so varied in its complexion as to require three or four actors to represent it rightly; rather does it seem like an organ over whose many stops the player should have easy and instant control, now discoursing the sweet tones of the flute, now the reedy music of the hautbois; and nothing, to carry on the simile of the organ, is more peculiarly individual to the nature of Hamlet than the manner in which he at times shuts up with a snap, as it were the poetic or philosophic stops and pulls out the fantastic or cynical. This side of a many-sided mind, most difficult to portray, yet most important for a happy result, Mr. Irving has distinctly worked up and improved since his earlier performances. The general outlines of the picture remain such as they were originally conceived; and whatever their opinion may be as to its execution, few people can witness the performance of this character without an intense admiration for the beauty and truth of the actor's conception.

In Miss Ellen Terry, Mr. Irving has a decided acquisition as a member of his company, and the public as a recruit to the ranks of the poetic drama. Grace, tenderness, and, above all, Nature are hers; and exacting indeed must the critic be who would desire a better representative for the part of Ophelia. Mr. Bellew is excellent as Osric, Miss Pauncefort and Mr. Chippendale intelligent as the Queen and Polonius, nor is the Gravedigger undeserving of a favourable word. But in approval of the other actors there is not much to be said. One can only hope that as time goes on the new manager of the Lyceum may be enabled to gather round him a company worthy of the principal performers. The new scenery of the play especially deserves praise. Nothing could be better than the churchyard scene, with its distant landscape, or the grand impressive rock from which the Ghost speaks his well-known lines. The dresses, too, are in admirable taste, and when time has toned down their brand-new look (it does seem improbable that the whole court of Denmark should have ordered their clothes on the same day) will leave little to be desired.

Mr. Irving has now a great chance before him, and one which, in the interests of dramatic art, it is to be hoped he will not throw away. He has shown a wisdom in the choice of Miss Terry which argues well for the future of his management. These two artists together should be capable of great things; and it must be the sincere wish of all true lovers of art that in future years we may be able to write of them as Fielding wrote of Garrick and Clive and Cibber:— 'They formed themselves upon the study of nature only, and not on the imitations of their predecessors. Hence they have been able to excel all who have gone before them; a degree of merit which the servile herd of imitators can never possibly arrive at.'

Vanity Fair, Jan. 11, 1879

A Classical Hamlet

Sir Johnston Forbes Robertson (1853–1937) actor and painter, studied under Samuel Phelps and was held to be one of the greatest Hamlets of the 19th century.

2 October, 1897

The Forbes Robertson 'Hamlet' at the Lyceum is, very unexpectedly at that address, really not at all unlike Shakespeare's play of the same name. I am quite certain I saw Reynaldo in it for a moment; and possibly I may have seen Voltimand and Cornelius; but just as the time for their scene arrived, my eye fell on the word 'Fortinbras' in the programme, which so amazed me that I hardly know what I saw for the next ten minutes. Ophelia, instead of being a strenuously earnest and self-possessed young lady giving a concert and recitation for all she was worth, was mad—actually mad. The story of the play was perfectly intelligible, and quite took the attention of the audience off the principal actor at moments. What is the Lyceum coming to? Is it for this that Sir Henry Irving has invented a whole series of original romantic dramas, and given the credit of them without a murmur to the immortal bard whose profundity (as exemplified in the remark that good and evil are mingled in our natures) he has just been pointing out to the inhabitants of Cardiff, and whose works have been no more to him than the word-quarry from which he has hewn and blasted the lines and titles of masterpieces which are really all his own? And now, when he has created by these means a reputation for Shakespeare, he no sooner turns his back for a moment on London than Mr. Forbes Robertson competes with him on the boards of his own theatre by actually playing off against him the authentic Swan of Avon. Now if the result had been the utter exposure and collapse of that impostor, poetic justice must have proclaimed that it served Mr. Forbes Robertson right. But alas! the wily William, by literary tricks which our simple Sir Henry has

254

never quite understood, has played into Mr. Forbes Robertson's hands so artfully that the scheme is a prodigious success.

* * *

Mr. Forbes Robertson is essentially a classical actor, the only one, with the exception of Mr. Alexander, now established in London management. What I mean by classical is that he can present a dramatic hero as a man whose passions are those which have produced the philosophy, the poetry, the art, and the statecraft of the world, and not merely those which have produced its weddings, coroner's inquests, and executions. And that is just the sort of actor that Hamlet requires. A Hamlet who only understands his love for Ophelia, his grief for his father, his vindictive hatred of his uncle, his fear of ghosts, his impulse to snub Rosencrantz and Guildenstern, and the sportsman's excitement with which he lays the 'mousetrap' for Claudius, can, with sufficient force or virtuosity of execution, get a great reputation in the part, even though the very intensity of his obsession by these sentiments (which are common not only to all men but to many animals), shows that the characteristic side of Hamlet, the side that differentiates him from Fortinbras, is absolutely outside the actor's consciousness. Such a reputation is the actor's, not Hamlet's.

* * *

It is in fact not possible for any actor to represent Hamlet as mad. He may (and generally does) combine some notion of his own of a man who is the creature of affectionate sentiment with the figure drawn by the lines of Shakespeare; but the result is not a madman, but simply one of those monsters produced by the imaginary combination of two normal species, such as sphinxes, mermaids, or centaurs. And this is the invariable resource of the instinctive, imaginative, romantic actor. You will see him weeping bucketsful of tears over Ophelia, and treating the players, the gravedigger, Horatio, Rosencrantz and Guildenstern as if they were mutes at his own funeral. But go and watch Mr. Forbes Robertson's Hamlet seizing delightedly on every opportunity for a bit of philosophic discussion or artistic recreation to escape from the 'cursed spite' of revenge and love and other common troubles; see how he brightens up when the players come; how he tries to talk philosophy with Rosencrantz and Guildenstern the moment they come into the room; how he stops on his country walk with Horatio to lean over the churchyard wall and draw out the gravedigger whom he sees singing at his trade; how even his fits of excitement find expression in declaiming scraps of poetry; how the shock of Ophelia's death relieves itself in the fiercest intellectual contempt for Laertes's ranting, whilst an hour afterwards, when Laertes stabs him, he bears no malice for that at all, but embraces him gallantly and comradely; and how he dies as we forgive everything to Charles II. for dying, and makes 'the rest is silence' a touchingly humorous apology for not being able to finish his business. See all that; and you have seen a true classical Hamlet. Nothing half so charming has been seen by this generation. It will bear seeing again and again.

Bernard Shaw,
Dramatic Opinions and Essays

Sarah Bernhardt, 1899

The charm of the two best French Hamlets consist in that dominant note of comedy, that rare vein of humour, that eccentric capriciousness which are in the very veins of Hamlet.

Never were the scenes with Polonius and with Rosencrantz and Guildenstern played so admirably as by Sarah Bernhardt. Fechter ran her close, but Sarah Bernhardt was the better of the two. In the love scene with Ophelia, the divine Sarah has only had one rival—Henry Irving—but here the French temperament scored off the English, because the brain of the French actress is so quick, her changes so vivid, her alertness so admirable.

The opening of the love scene, when Ophelia is discovered, after the grand soliloquy 'To be or not to be,' was quite perfect in its earnestness and pathos. Hamlet has been meditating on death, suicide, the future state, the end of everything. The vision of Ophelia does not suggest to Hamlet passion, but purity. The mere presence of Ophelia makes Hamlet almost a saint. She has touched his bitter nature. He seems to say, not in anger or petulancy—

'Get thee to a nunnery, for God's sake! Why should you be a breeder of sinners? Why should you be contaminated by man, who is so often a beast? Oh, get thee to a nunnery! Save yourself from the contact and contamination of man while you can!'

But once Hamlet has seen the King and Polonius behind the arras, his whole nature changes, his philosophy is soured, his sacred ideas become a mad whirl of emotion. To put it vulgarly, this has been, as he thinks, on the part of Ophelia 'a put up job.' He can scarcely express himself for indignation and disgust. He is too well bred to rave and snort and swear, as most English Hamlets do. His disgust is expressed in a scornful sneer. I have never seen this passage more exquisitely played than by Sarah Bernhardt.

But what exquisite ideas she had! The crossing of herself before she follows the Ghost, the speaking of the speech to the players on the miniature stage, making Hamlet for the moment an actor addressing his audience; the feeling of his father's picture on the walls when the ghost has gone and materialism has come again; the effect of the poison in Hamlet's veins when his hand is scratched in the duel with Laertes; the kissing of his dead mother's hair,—all these are exquisite points never imagined before.

But the whole thing was imaginative, electrical, and poetical. I do not think I ever sat out the play of *Hamlet* with less fatigue. It all passed like a delightful dream. As a rule the play exhausts one. There was no exhaustion with Sarah Bernhardt—only exhilaration. I think I could have sat it out all over again the same evening—no bad compliment, was it?

The fact is, that with a new brain to interpret this master-piece, *Hamlet* is ever new. With the French version of the immortal text I was charmed. It conveyed Shakespeare's idea in a nutshell. Nothing was omitted that was absolutely essential; much was supplied that we often forget in our acting editions.

Clement Scott, *Some Notable Hamlets*

Othello

LIKE Hamlet, *Othello* enjoys a record of almost continuous performance since the earliest recorded performance in November, 1604. Again, as in *Hamlet*, the title role has been taken by every major tragic actor. Garrick acted it, but was generally felt to be inferior in this particular character to Spranger Barry. John Kemble succeeded him at the end of the 18th century, but Edmund Kean's portrayal of the noble

Moor has generally been recognised as one of the greatest pieces of Shakespearean acting ever seen. On March 25, 1833, Kean collapsed while playing Othello to his son's Iago. Earlier he had outshone his rival Junius Brutus Booth who played Iago to his Othello on February 20th, 1817 at Drury Lane. Many great actors, including Kean himself as well as Macready and Phelps have played the parts of Iago and Othello.

Elegy for Betterton

On the occasion of Thomas Betterton's funeral, Richard Steele recalls one of the great actor's celebrated portrayals.

I have hardly a notion, that any performer of antiquity could surpass the action of Mr. Betterton in any of the occasions in which he has appeared on our stage. The wonderful agony which he appeared in, when he examined the circumstance of the handkerchief in 'Othello'; the mixture of love that intruded upon his mind upon the innocent answers Desdemona makes, betrayed in his gesture such a variety and vicissitude of passions, as would admonish a man to be afraid of his own heart, and perfectly convince him, that it is to stab it to admit that worst of daggers, jealousy. Whoever reads in his closet this admirable scene, will find that he cannot, except he has as warm an imagination as Shakespeare himself, find any but dry, incoherent, and broken sentences: but a reader that has seen Betterton act it, observes there could not be a word added; that longer speeches had been unnatural, nay impossible, in Othello's circumstances. The charming passage in the same tragedy, where he tells the manner of winning the affection of his mistress, was urged with so moving and graceful an energy, that while I walked in the cloisters, I thought of him with the same concern as if I waited for the remains of a person who had in real life done all that I had seen him represent. The gloom of the place, and faint lights before the ceremony appeared, contributed to the melancholy disposition I was in; and I began to be extremely afflicted, that Brutus and Cassius had any difference; that Hotspur's gallantry was so unfortunate; and that the mirth and good humour of Falstaff could not exempt him from the grave.

The Tatler, No. 167, *May 4, 1710*

Barry and Quin[1]

If we may venture to say, that any performer ever was born for one part in particular, it must have been Mr. Barry for the Moor; his figure was a good apology for Desdemona's attachment, even if she had not seen a fair, instead of black visage in his mind, and the harmony of his voice to tell such a tale as he describes, must have raised favourable prejudice in any one who had an ear or heart to feel.

There is a length of periods and an extravagance of passion in this part, not to be found in any other, for so many successive scenes, to which Mr. Barry appeared peculiarly suitable, he happily exhibited the hero, the lover, and the distracted husband; he rose through all the passions to the utmost extent of critical imagination, yet still appeared to leave an unexhausted fund of expression behind; his rage and tenderness were equally interesting, but when he uttered these words, 'rude am I in my speech,' in tones, *as soft as feathered snow that melted as they fell,* we could by no means allow the sound an echo to the sense—though we are not at all fond of this gentleman's action in general, yet respecting both it and attitude, particularly when called by Æmilia after the murder, he was in this character extremely agreeable.

Mr. Quin—I am sorry to mention him so often disadvantageously—was—though Othello is in the vale of years, not a very probable external appearance to engage Desdemona, his declamation was as heavy as his person; his tones monotonous; his passions bellowing, his emphasis affected, and his under strokes growling—I remember once to see this esteemed performer play the Moor, in a large powdered major wig, which, with the black face, made such a magpye appearance of his head, as tended greatly to laughter; one stroke however, was not amiss, coming on in white gloves, by pulling off which the black hands became more realised.

Francis Gentleman, The Dramatic Censor

Colley Cibber Applauds

It has been said, that Colley Cibber preferred his Othello to the performances of Betterton and Booth in that part; and I

[1] Spranger Barry was the favourite Othello of the London stage for nearly 30 years from 1746. James Quin had played Othello earlier from 1722 to 1733.

should not wonder at it; for they, I believe, though most excellent actors, owed a great deal of their applause to art. Every word which Barry spoke in this the greatest character of the greatest poet, seemed to come from the heart; and I well remember, that I saw Colley Cibber in the boxes, on the first night of Barry's Othello[1], loudly applauding him by frequent clapping of his hands; a practice by no means usual to the old man, even when he was very well pleased with an actor. But indeed the same heart-rending feelings which charmed the audience in Othello, diffused themselves through all Barry's acting, when the softer passions predominate.

Thomas Davies, Dramatic Miscellanies

Kemble's Moor

SARAH SIDDONS as Desdemona, Drury Lane, 1785.

[1] October 4, 1746.

On the 8th of March 1785, the play of Othello was acted at Drury Lane Theatre: Othello by Mr. Kemble: Desdemona, Mrs. Siddons. The dress of the moor at that time, was a British general officer's uniform, equally improper with the moorish jacket and trowsers of modern times. The general of an Italian state would wear its uniform; he would never be indulged with a privilege of strutting about like 'a malignant and a turbaned turk' at the head of a christian army. Mr. Kemble always played parts of this character very finely. He was grand and awful and pathetic. But he was a European: there seemed to be philosophy in his bearing; there was reason in his rage: he acted as if Othello truly described himself, when he calls himself 'one not easily jealous.' He had never, I think, so completely worked himself into the character as to be identified with it, as was surely the case in his Hamlet, his Macbeth, and his King John. It was, at most, only a part very finely played. One of the sublimest things in language, the professional farewell of Othello, came rather coldly from him. But I can safely say, that Mr. Kemble's powers were in a state of gradual improvement for twenty years after this performance, until they attained their perfection, at Covent Garden Theatre, in the exhibition of Brutus, Coriolanus, and Cato.

James Boaden, *Life of Kemble*

Mr. Kean's Othello[1]

Drury Lane, May 6 [1814]

Othello was acted at Drury-Lane last night, the part of Othello by Mr. Kean. His success was fully equal to the arduousness of the undertaking. In general, we might observe that he displayed the same excellences and the same defects as in his former characters. His voice and person were not altogether in consonance with the character, nor was there throughout, that noble tide of deep and sustained passion, impetuous, but majestic, that 'flows on to the Propontic, and knows no ebb,' which raises our admiration and pity of the lofty-minded Moor. There were, however, repeated bursts of feeling and energy which we have never seen surpassed. The whole of the latter part of the third act was a master-piece of profound pathos and exquisite conception, and its effect on the house was electrical. The tone of voice in which he delivered

[1] Original title. Elsewhere Hazlitt called Kean's Othello 'the finest piece of acting in the world.'

the beautiful apostrophe, 'Oh farewell!' struck on the heart and the imagination like the swelling notes of some divine music. The look, the action, the expression of voice, with which he accompanied the exclamation, 'Not a jot, not a jot;' the reflection, 'I found not *Cassio's kisses* on her lips;' and his vow of revenge against Cassio, and abandonment of his love for Desdemona, laid open the very tumult and agony of the soul. In other parts, where we expected an equal interest to be excited, we were disappointed; and in the common scenes, we think Mr. Kean's manner, as we have remarked on other occasions, had more point and emphasis than the sense or character required.

The rest of the play was by no means judiciously cast; indeed, almost every individual appeared to be out of his proper place.

William Hazlitt, A View of the English Stage

Mr. Kean's Iago[1]

Drury Lane, May 9 [1814]

The part of Iago was played at Drury-Lane on Saturday by Mr. Kean, and played with admirable facility and effect. It was the most faultless of his performances, the most consistent and entire. Perhaps the accomplished hypocrite was never so finely, so adroitly portrayed—a gay, light-hearted monster, a careless, cordial, comfortable villain. The preservation of character was so complete, the air and manner were so much of a piece throughout, that the part seemed more like a detached scene or single *trait*, and of shorter duration than it usually does. The ease, familiarity, and tone of nature with which the text was delivered, were quite equal to any thing we have seen in the best comic acting. It was the least overdone of all his parts, though full of point, spirit, and brilliancy. The odiousness of the character was in fact, in some measure, glossed over by the extreme grace, alacrity and rapidity of the execution. Whether this effect were 'a consummation of the art devoutly to be wished,' is another question, on which we entertain some doubts. We have already stated it as our opinion, that Mr. Kean is not a literal transcriber of his author's text; he translates his characters with great freedom and ingenuity into a language of his own; but at the same time we cannot help preferring his

[1] Original title.

liberal and spirited dramatic versions, to the dull, literal, commonplace monotony of his competitors. Besides, after all, in the conception of the part, he may be right, and we may be wrong. We have before complained that Mr. Kean's Richard was not gay enough, and we should not be disposed to complain that his Iago is not grave enough.

Mr. Sowerby's Othello, we are sorry to add, was a complete failure, and the rest of the play was very ill got up.

William Hazlitt, *A View of the English Stage*

A Word from Lord Byron

Byron saw the play the same night as Hazlitt (Saturday May 7, 1814) 'was not Iago perfection?' he asks in a letter to Thomas Moore, 'particularly the last look. I was close to him (in the orchestra), and never saw an English countenance half so expressive.'

In my humble opinion Kean's acting in the third act of *Othello* is his best performance. The first night he acted it at Drury Lane, I sat in my seat in the orchestra, which was appropriated to me as Director of the Music, and next to me was Lord Byron, who said, 'Mr. Kelly, depend upon it, this is a man of genius.'

Michael Kelly, *Reminiscences*

Absence of Excellence

The tragedy of *Othello* was performed at this Theatre on Saturday night, for the purpose of showing how ready Variety is to engage in great undertakings, and how very apt it is to fail in the execution of them; at least such was the tendency of the performance. Mr. Kean, who, on Thursday, regardless of natural disqualifications, ventured on the character of *Othello*, in which he got most obstreperously applauded, with a view, no doubt, to display the versatility of his powers, in two nights afterwards appeared in the character of Iago, and was rewarded with a similar degree of clamorous approbation, and, indeed, had he thought proper to attempt Desdemona, (a thing by no means improbable with him), in the present state of public feeling, the same praise would in all likelihood have attended his exhibition. It is, however, our duty rather to lead

EDMUND KEAN as Othello, Drury Lane, 1814.

than to follow public opinion, and we shall therefore give our thoughts as freely as though we had never been stunned by the vociferous plaudits bestowed on this popular idol of the day.

The character of Iago is much more consonant to the capabilities of Mr. Kean than that of Othello; cold, and designing, and unvaried in its nature, it demands none of those powers which are absolutely necessary to depict those bursts of feeling or passion with which the latter abounds. In lieu of his natural qualifications, some acquired ones are necessary; a deep and comprehensive knowledge of human nature, acute

264

perceptions, and a discriminating judgment, are indispensable.
Iago should exhibit a rude and blunt honesty, which,
however, should be obtrusive, because it is not real; and a
candour which should sit uneasy, because merely affected. In
his intercourse with the other characters of the drama, he
should act the open soldier; in his soliloquies only should he
appear the villain; he should deceive everyone except himself;
and, above all, in the outset, a distinct feeling should be
assumed, and maintained throughout, with such a continuity
as to unite and give identity to the portrait. Of all this there was
almost nothing in the Iago of Mr. Kean: it is true, this
performance was not disfigured by those errors in detail which
attend most of his others, and distinct passages were given
with some effect; but there was one great and general error of
misconception, if a greater fault than this could be pointed out
it would be the total absence of anything that could be fairly
called excellence; the few conceptions were feeble and trifling,
and except the expression of triumphant revenge given at
Iago's final exit, there was nothing that might not be found in
any tolerable provincial theatre in the kingdom.

*　　*　　*

Morning Herald, May 9, 1814

A Kean Rival

*An account of a memorable night when Junius Brutus Booth (1796–
1852) challenged Kean in one of the latter's greatest roles. Booth, then
only 21, was attracting a good deal of appreciative attention at Covent
Garden and Kean invited him to play Othello to his Iago. Two days
after this, Booth did not turn up for the performance and went back to
Covent Garden.*

Drury Lane [1817]

Feb. 20. '*Othello.*' The novelty of this evening was the
appearance of Mr. Booth, from the other house, in the
character of Iago. The curiosity excited on this occasion
filled the house so fast, that many hundreds returned home,
after the most unavailing attempts to get admission into the
Pit; and the lobbies of the Boxes were filled with groups of
disappointed amateurs, who could only occasionally get a
glimpse through the small glasses in the doors. Mr. Booth

265

appeared at Covent Garden on the 12th of February, and the audience were so struck with the similarity in voice, in figure, and in feature, to Mr. Kean, that they unanimously called for its repetition on the following day. The character of the Crook-backed tyrant forms the pedestal on which popularity has erected the *colossal* edifice of Mr. Kean's theatrical fame. It was therefore presumption in any provincial actor to imagine he could *burst* into reputation by coming out in Gloster. The Managers no doubt, anticipated the result, and therefore offered this gentleman an engagement on terms they thought he deserved. Mistaking, however, the applause of his *imitation*, for approbation of his talents as an actor, he indignantly spurned the proposal; and the Managers of Drury Lane, according to the old adage,

'The value of a thing
Is what it will bring;'

immediately engaged him on terms equivalent to their expectations. If, however, it was presumption in Mr. Booth's attempt at Richard, in which Mr. Kean stands confessedly pre-eminent; how much more so was it to venture on the same boards with this gentleman in the character of Iago, in which Mr. Kean has no competitor! Mr. Booth was greeted on his *entree* with a most encouraging reception, and the applause of the audience was commensurate with that feeling with which John Bull always overwhelms himself. The performance was very passable throughout but where he tempts the unsuspicious Moor to jealousy, and works upon his ardent nature with the suspicion of Desdemona's honesty. It would, indeed, be strange, after the *display* we have witnessed in the Covent Garden bills, if this Gentleman did not possess some qualifications for an arduous profession—but we will not insult Mr. Kean, by comparing the *points* of the one with the *genius* of the other.— We have expressed our opinion so often of Mr. Kean's Othello, that we will not repeat it here; but we must candidly own, that his exertions on this occasion were superior to any we have yet witnessed and he was even more loudly applauded than in any character we have seen him in. The curtain fell amidst thunders of applause; and notwithstanding the defects of the performance, the piece was announced for repetition on Saturday without a dissentient voice.

European Magazine

A Consistent and Harmonious Whole[1]

May 30 [1822] Covent Garden. Mr. Macready performed *Othello* for his benefit; an undertaking of no small peril, while the excellence of Mr. Kean in the character is fresh in the public mind. Mr. Macready, however, without any imitation of Mr. Kean, and without disturbing the noble impressions which he has left on our memory, succeeded in giving a representation of the part, abounding with individual traits of grandeur and of beauty, and forming altogether a consistent and harmonious whole. In the oriental cast of his figure, and the richness and compass of his voice, he brought eminent physical advantages to his task, which his sense of the passion and poetry of the character enabled him excellently to improve. He did not electrify the audience with bursts of emotion so sudden or so terrific, or subdue them so often by unlooked-for pathos, as Mr. Kean, but he preserved throughout a loftier tone in his suffering and his revenge. His delivery of the speech to the Senate had less indiscriminate pomp of utterance than is usual; but it was a natural, varied, and affecting narration of the 'round unvarnished tale' of a soldier's wooing and success. Mr. Young made the villainy of Iago more palpable even than usual, so much so, as to occasionally almost destroy the decorum of the scene, and to raise a titter in the house. Miss Foote in Desdemona, acted as well as she looked. Abbot played Cassio very pleasantly, especially in the drunken scene. Mrs. Faucit would have been more effective in Emilia, if she had exerted herself less.

European Magazine

Kean and Macready[2]

Kean's range of expression, as already hinted, was very limited. His physical aptitudes were such as confined him to the strictly tragic passions; and for these he was magnificently endowed. Small and insignificant in figure, he could at times become impressively commanding by the lion-like power and grace of his bearing. I remember, the last time I saw him play

[1] Macready first played Othello on October 10, 1816, and Iago five nights later.
[2] Macready first played Iago to Kean's Othello in 1832.

Othello, how puny he appeared beside Macready, until in the third act, when roused by Iago's taunts and insinuations, he moved towards him with a gouty hobble, seized him by the throat, and, in a well-known explosion, 'Villain! be sure you prove,' &c., seemed to swell into a stature which made Macready appear small. On that very evening, when gout made it difficult for him to display his accustomed grace, when a drunken hoarseness had ruined the once matchless voice, such was the irresistible pathos — manly, not tearful — which vibrated in his tones and expressed itself in look and gestures, that old men leaned their heads upon their arms and fairly sobbed. It was, one must confess, a patchy performance considered as a whole; some parts were miserably tricky, others misconceived, others gabbled over in haste to reach the 'points'; but it was irradiated with such flashes that I would again risk broken ribs for the chance of a good place in the pit to see anything like it.

G. H. Lewes, *Actors and the Art of Acting*

Kean's Last Exit

On 25th of March in this year [1833] I had witnessed at Covent Garden the closing scene of another great genius. I was present at the last performance of Edmund Kean. He acted Othello to his son Charles's Iago. In the third act, having delivered the fine speech terminating with, 'Farewell, Othello's occupation's gone!' with undiminished expression, and seized, with his usual tiger-like spring, Iago by the throat, he had scarcely uttered the words, 'Villain! be sure—' when his voice died away in inarticulate murmurs, his head sank on his son's breast, and the curtain fell never again to rise upon that marvellous tragedian. He expired at Richmond, on the 15th of May following.

J. R. Planché, *Recollections and Reflections*

A Picturesque Iago

Dickens wrote his essay 'On Mr. Fechter's Acting' from which this is an extract, on the eve of Fechter's American tour. Fechter played Othello and Iago at the Princess Theatre during 1861–62.

That quality of picturesqueness, on which I have already

268

laid stress, is strikingly developed in his Iago, and yet it is so
judiciously governed that his Iago is not in the least picturesque
according to the conventional ways of frowning, sneering,
diabolically grinning, and elaborately doing everything else
that would induce Othello to run him through the body very
early in the play. Mr. Fechter's is the Iago who could, and did,
make friends; who could dissect his master's soul, without
flourishing his scalpel as if it were a walking-stick; who could
overpower Emilia by other arts than a sign-of-the Saracen's-
Head grimness; who could be a boon companion without
ipso facto warning all beholders off by the portentous pheno-
menon; who could sing a song and clink a can naturally enough,
and stab men really in the dark,—not in a transparent
notification of himself as going about seeking whom to stab.
Mr. Fechter's Iago is no more in the conventional psychological
mode than in the conventional hussar pantaloons and boots;
and you shall see the picturesqueness of his wearing borne out
in his bearing all through the tragedy down to the moment
when he becomes invincibly and consistently dumb.

Charles Dickens, Atlantic Monthly, August 1869

Timon of Athens

TILL late in the 19th century, only adaptations were
staged, with the exception of one performance in Dublin.
Samuel Phelps was praised for his production at Sadler's Wells
in 1851, which restored almost the whole of Shakespeare's
play. But the play has never been popular either among
readers or playgoers.

Kean as Timon

November 4, 1816, Drury-Lane

The tragedy of *Timon of Athens*, after a lapse of several years,
was revived at this theatre on Monday. The Managers, we
suppose, were led to their choice of it, not only by their general
desire to bring forward what is good, but by the great success

of Mr. Kean in characters of a certain caustic interest; yet although the selection is honourable to both parties, and the performance was received and given out for repetition with great applause, we doubted and still doubt whether it will have what is called a run. If it has, we shall save our self-love by attributing a part of it to the present times, which are certainly favourable ones for giving effect to representations of pecuniary difficulty, and of friendship put to the test. But the parts of this tragedy which contain the dramatic interest are comparatively few; the moral, though strong, is obvious, and in fact too easily anticipated; and when Timon has once fallen from his fortunes, there is little to excite further attention in the spectator. The *reader* is still delighted, but he would be still more so in his closet, where he could weigh every precious sentence at leisure, and lose none of the text either by the freaks of adapters or the failure of actors' voices.

*   *   *

The whole play indeed abounds in masterly delineation of character, and in passages equally poetical and profound; though the latter unfortunately reduced the adapter[1] of the piece to an awkward dilemma; for they constitute its main beauty, and yet he seems to have felt himself obliged to cut them short, either for fear of making it drag with the spectators, or in compliance with a sophisticated decorum. Thus many of the most striking pieces of satire are left out; and we see nothing of the two females who come in upon Timon's retreat with Alcibiades.

*   *   *

The play, upon the whole, was well performed. Mr. Kean, as usual, gave touches of natural excellence, such as no other living actor could produce. We suspect however that Timon will not rank as one of his first performances; it wants sufficient variety and flexibility of passion for him. Neither do we think that he succeeded in the first part of the play, where Timon is prosperous and indulges his credulous generosity. He was too stately and tragic. It is true this may appear reconcilable with the ostentation which is charged Timon; but as we have before observed, the charge appears to us to be unfounded, as far as the leading passion is concerned; and Timon is a man of ardent animal spirits, whose great enjoyment is the sense of a certain glorious fellowship, upon which he thinks he could

[1] George Lamb.

equally reckon in a time of adversity, and the disappointment of which drives him, in a manner, distracted.

*   *   *

We think Mr. Kean also had too great a tendency in some parts to be violent, or rather to carry the paroxysms of Timon to a pitch beyond true rage, and too often to mistake vehemence for intenseness. Timon's curses in general should have been 'not loud, but deep': and, where Mr. Kean's acting was of this description, it certainly had the greatest effect out of the pale of the galleries, though some of his passionate starts were deservedly admired also. The finest scene in the whole performance was the one with Alcibiades. We never remember the force of contrast to have been more truly pathetic. Timon, digging in the woods with his spade, hears the approach of military music; he starts, waits its approach sullenly, and at last in comes the gallant Alcibiades with a train of splendid soldiery. Never was scene more effectively managed. First, you heard a sprightly quick march playing in the distance; Kean started, listened, and leaned in a fixed and angry manner on his spade, with frowning eyes, and lips full of the truest feeling, compressed but not too much so; he seemed as if resolved not to be deceived, even by the charm of a thing inanimate; the audience were silent; the march threw forth its gallant note nearer and nearer; the Athenian standards appear, then the soldiers come treading on the scene with that air of confident progress which is produced by the accompaniment of music; and at last, while the squalid misanthrope still maintains his posture and keeps his back to the strangers, in steps the young and splendid Alcibiades, in the flush of victorious expectation. It is the encounter of hope with despair.

Alcibiades luckily had a representative in Mr. Wallack who, besides performing the rest of his part with good credit, dressed and looked it uncommonly well. He seemed to have been studying the bust of his hero, as well as the costume of the Greek soldier. Mr. Bengough, in Apemantus, made as good a Cynic philosopher as we wished to see; he did not look quite so shrewd or beggarly as Diogenes, but he was wise enough for the part. As to Mr. Holland in the kind and lamenting Steward, he seemed quite inspired. We do not know that we ever saw him in so much advantage: but Mr. Kean's acting, we suspect, has given a great fillip to all the minor performers now-a-days.

With respect to the scenery and other mechanical matters, the piece was excellently got up. One of the scenes was a striking view of Athens, composed perhaps, from the picture in

Hobhouse's *Travels*. Timon's solitude also was very leafy and to the purpose; and the splendour of the banquet-scene obtained great applause. We must protest however against the dance of young Amazons, clashing their swords and shields. Shakspeare, we allow, has specified Amazons for the occasion; but if Amazons there must be, they should at least have had lutes in their hands, which he has specified also, instead of weapons. We are at a loss to conjecture why Shakspeare introduced Amazons at all, which seem to be no more to his taste in general than they were to old Homer's; but did he find, anywhere, that an Amazon with a lute was Timon's device? We have not the commentators at hand to refer to; but Timon in thanking the dancers, tells them that they have entertained him with his 'own device'; and devices of this kind were common from time immemorial. A dramatic mask, it is true, was called a device; but the host in the present instance seems to have been taken unawares, and could hardly have spoken as he did, had he himself invented the subject of the dance. At all events, we should like to have as little of these unfeminine feminines as possible: lutes would make them more human, and might act as a sort of compliment to Alcibiades, who is one of the guests, or to the spirit of sociality in general, as much as to say—a spirit of harmony corrects what is barbarous. We doubt also the propriety of the diadem and fillet worn by Mr. Kean, as well as the want of another sort of wreath to the heads of him and his guests during the banquets. They should undoubtedly, as was the custom, wear roses, myrtles, or other flowers mentioned by Anacreon and Plutarch, which besides being proper, would also have a pleasing effect, and contribute to the luxury of the scene: not that all this is necessary to Shakspeare, or demanded by him, but that it is as well to complete the costume in all instances, where it is undertaken in most.

We thank the Managers for *Timon*, which for our part we could see over again, were it only for the fine scene before mentioned; though we are afraid they have miscalculated the chances of its long run. We hope their next reproduction will be equally creditable to their taste, and more likely to reward it.

Leigh Hunt, The Examiner (Nov. 4, 1816)

Samuel Phelps' Revival

This much admired production restored nearly all of Shakespeare's play and had no interpolations. It opened at Sadler's Wells in 1851 and Morley saw it on its revival in 1856.

It may be that one cause of its [*Timon's*] long neglect, as potent as the complaint that it excites no interest by female characters, is the large number of *dramatis personae*, to whom are assigned what many actors might consider parts of which they can make nothing, and who, being presented in a slovenly way, by a number of inferior performers, would leave only one part in the drama, and take all the power out of that. Such an objection has not, however, any weight at Sadler's Wells, where every member of the company is taught to regard the poetry he speaks according to its nature rather than its quantity. The personators of the poet and the painter in the first scene of the *Timon*, as now acted, manifestly say what Shakespeare has assigned to them to say with as much care, and as much certainty that it will be listened to with due respect, as if they were themselves Timons, Hamlets, or Macbeths. Nobody rants—it becomes his part that Alcibiades should be a little blustery—nothing is slurred; a servant who has anything to say says it in earnest, making his words heard and their meaning felt; and so it is that, although only in one or two cases we may have observed at Sadler's Wells originality of genius in the actor, we have nevertheless perceived something like the entire sense of one of Shakespeare's plays, and have been raised above ourselves by the perception.

It is not because of anything peculiar in the air of Islington, or because an audience at Pentonville is made of men differing in nature from those who would form an audience in the Strand, that Shakespeare is listened to at Sadler's Wells with reverence not shown elsewhere. What has been done at Islington could, if the same means were employed, be done at Drury Lane. But Shakespeare is not fairly heard when he is made to speak from behind masses of theatrical upholstery, or when it is assumed that there is but one character in any of his plays, and that the others may be acted as incompetent performers please. If *The Messiah* were performed at Exeter Hall, with special care to intrust some of the chief solos to a good bass or contralto, the rest being left to chance, and members of the chorus allowed liberty to sing together in all keys, we should enjoy Handel much as we are sometimes asked to enjoy

Shakespeare on the London stage. What Signor Costa will do for an orchestra, the manager must do for his company, if he would present a work of genius in such a way as to procure for it a full appreciation.

Such thoughts are suggested by the effect which *Timon of Athens* is producing on the audiences at Sadler's Wells. The play is a poem to them. The false friends, of whom one declares, 'The swallow follows not summer more willing than we your lordship', and upon whom Timon retorts, 'Nor more willingly leaves winter,' are as old as the institution of society. Since men had commerce first together to the present time the cry has been, 'Such summer birds are men'. The rush of a generous impulsive nature from one rash extreme into the other, the excesses of the man who never knew 'the middle of humanity', is but another common form of life; and when have men not hung—the poets, the philosophers, the lovers, the economists, men of all habits—over a contemplation of the contrast between that soft town-life represented by the luxury of Athens in its wealth and its effeminacy, and the life of a man who, like Timon before his cave's mouth, turns from gold because it is not eatable, and digs in the wood for roots? With a bold hand Shakespeare grasped the old fable of Timon, and moulded it into a form that expresses much of the perplexity and yearning of our nature. He takes up Timon, a free-handed and large-hearted lord, who, though 'to Lacedaemon did his lands extend', found them too little to content his restless wish to pour himself all out in kindness to his fellows. He leaves him dead by the shore of the mysterious eternal sea.

I do not dwell upon the play itself, for here the purpose only is to show in what way it can be made, when fitly represented—and is made at Sadler's Wells—to stir the spirit as a poem. Mr. Phelps in his own acting of Timon treats the character as an ideal, as the central figure in a mystery. As the liberal Athenian lord, his gestures are large, his movements free—out of himself everything pours, towards himself he will draw nothing. As the disappointed Timon, whose love of his kind is turned to hate, he sits on the ground self-contained, but miserable in the isolation, from first to last contrasting with Apemantus, whom 'fortune's tender arm never with favour clasped', who is a churl by the original sourness of his nature, hugs himself in his own ragged robe, and worships himself for his own ill manners. Mr. Marston's Apemantus is well acted, and helps much to secure a right understanding of the entire play.   Henry Morley, *Journal of a London Playgoer*

King Lear

FOR one hundred and fifty years, from 1681, Shakespeare's play was absent from the stage, its place being taken by Nahum Tate's version which improved on Shakespeare by making Edgar and Cordelia lovers, eliminating the Fool and giving the story a happy ending. Macready restored Shakespeare's play, albeit shortened and rearranged in 1838, with the Fool played by a girl. It was not till seven years later that Samuel Phelps presented the play with no rearrangement and virtually uncut.

Glimpses of Garrick

Garrick first played Lear in 1756, in a version substantially similar in plot to Nahum Tate's perversion (i.e., Edgar and Cordelia as lovers, no Fool and a happy ending with Cordelia restored to Lear), but with much of Shakespeare's poetry restored and most of Tate's left out.

Garrick rendered the curse so terribly affecting to the audience, that, during his utterance of it, they seemed to shrink from it as from a blast of lightning. His preparation for it was extremely affecting; his throwing away his crutch, kneeling on one knee, clasping his hands together, and lifting his eyes towards heaven, presented a picture worthy the pencil of a Raphael.

*　　*　　*

LEAR.

Do you but mark, how this becomes the house?
Dear daughter, I confess that I am old;

Age is unnecessary; on my knees I beg,
That you'll vouchsafe me raiment, bed, and food.

This presents to the spectator a most striking picture of an unhappy aged parent, who finds himself reduced to the necessity of representing, in his own person, by action, the absurdity, as well as wickedness, of his children's conduct to him. This was a dramatic situation utterly unknown to Booth, Boheme, and Quin, because this affecting passage was

275

DAVID GARRICK as King Lear, Drury Lane, 1760.

omitted in Tate's alteration of Lear. It was happily restored by Mr. Garrick, who knew its beauty. He threw himself on both knees, with his hands clasped, and, in a supplicating tone, repeated this touching, though ironical, petition.

* * *

When Lear awakes, Shakspeare, forgetting that Lear is a heathen, puts into his mouth the words of one in purgatory:

Thou art a soul in bliss; but I am bound
Upon a wheel of fire, that mine own tears
Do scald like molten lead.

On Cordelia's falling on her knees, and imploring his benediction, Lear kneels to his daughter, not knowing who she was or what he did.

The several breaks and interruptions, of imperfect reason and recovering sense, are superior to all commendation, and breathe the most affecting pathos:

——I am mightily abus'd!
I should die with pity to see another thus!—
I fear I am not in my perfect mind.

At last he recollects his dear Cordelia:

276

—— Do not laugh at me:
For, as I am a man, I think that lady
To be my child, Cordelia!

The audience, which had been sighing at the former part of the scene, could not sustain this affecting climax, but broke out into loud lamentations.

Be your tears wet?

says Lear, putting his hand upon the cheeks of Cordelia: as if he had said, Can you really feel grief for one who so cruelly treated you?

*　　*　　*

In the preceding scenes of Lear, Garrick had displayed all the force of quick transition from one passion to another: he had, from the most violent rage, descended to sedate calmness; had seized, with unutterable sensibility, the various impressions of terror, and faithfully represented all the turbid passions of the soul; he had pursued the progress of agonizing feelings to madness in its several stages. Yet, after he had done all this, he exhibited himself, in this fine scene, in such a superior taste, as to make it more interesting than any thing the audience had already enjoyed. But indeed the incident itself is very striking.— Every spectator feels for himself and common humanity, when he perceives man, while living, degraded to the deprivation of sense and loss of memory! Who does not rejoice, when the creative hand of the poet, in the great actor, restores him to the use of his faculties! Mrs. Cibber, the most pathetic of all actresses, was the only Cordelia of excellence. The discovery of Lear, in prison, sleeping with his head on her lap, his hand closed in her's, whose expressive look spoke more than the most eloquent language, raised the most sympathising emotions.—

Thomas Davies, *Dramatic Miscellanies*

Barry and Garrick Compared

Spranger Barry, the celebrated Irish actor appeared in King Lear *in 1750 at Covent Garden while Garrick played the same role at Drury Lane. The particular scene in which Barry is singled out for praise does not, of course, occur in Shakespeare's original play.*

277

I have seen both these gentlemen play King Lear within a few days of one another; I must confess I had pleasure from the performance of the lesser monarch in several passages. My expectations had indeed been greatly raised by the many encomiums lavished on him, but were not answered to my wish. There was a pettiness attended the performance which I thought not quite equal to the character; his behaviour often liable to censure, particularly I thought, at the end of those scenes where the unnatural behaviour of his daughters work him up almost to frenzy. Does not the preceding and following parts point out to us that Lear rushes wildly from beneath the roof where he has been so inhospitably treated? Why then is he to sink into the arms of his attendants? Thus helpless, as he there affects to appear, though his daughters turned him out of doors, surely his attendants would have conveyed him to some place of rest? Yet by the play we find he roams into the wood, exposing himself unto the storm. Besides the error of this fainting fit, let us examine how 'tis executed. His spirits being quite exhausted, he drops almost lifeless into the arms of his attendants. Do they carry him off? Why, no. Relaxed as we may suppose his whole machine (for his head and body are both thrown extravagantly behind, as if his neck and back were broke) yet his knees (which in nature would most likely falter first) are still so able to support him in that odd-bent condition that he walks off with the regular stiff-step of a soldier in his exercise on the parade. Is this consistent? Is this natural? Is this character? Does not this uncouth appearance, with his back-bent body and dropping head, rather resemble the uncomely distortion of a posture master when he walks the Sea Crab, as they call it?

* * *

I own I think Mr. Barry well deserved the uncommon applause he met with in this part; it may be a question whether, in this character, he has not shown more of the masterly actor than in all he has done before. . . . Though the whole was pleasing, there is a passage in the last act where his behaviour deserved particular notice, and wherein he merited that excess of applause, the roused admiration of an almost astonished audience most generously bestowed on him.

When the pious Cordelia, as the only means of escaping the anguish of a father's death, entreats the ruffians to despatch her first, which the villains seem ready to comply with—while Lear is withheld from the vain efforts of a fond father to preserve his darling—his action, look and voice most exquisitely expressed his distressful situation. His quick progression from surprise to terror, thence to rage, till all were absorbed in anguish and despair, were master strokes. At length his roused spirits catching the alarm, endeavouring to snatch her from her fate, his recollection of his unhappily being unarmed and unable to preserve her, when he throws himself on his knees, preserving majesty in distress, his whole figure and manner are finely expressive of the reduced monarch and heart-torn father.

Theophilus Cibber,
Dissertations on Theatrical Subjects

Art Without Nature

Charles Churchill, who admired Garrick, finds fault with Garrick's great rival Spranger Barry, in Lear *and* Hamlet.

What man, like B[A]R[R]Y, with such pains, can err
In elocution, action, character?
What man could give, if B[A]R[R]Y was not here,
Such well-applauded tenderness to Lear?
Who else can speak so very very fine,
That sense may kindly end with ev'ry line?

Some dozen lines before the ghost is there,
Behold him for the solemn scene prepare.
See how he frames his eyes, poises each limb,
Puts the whole body into proper trim,—
From whence we learn, with no great stretch of art,
Five lines hence comes a ghost, and, Ha! a start.

When he appears most perfect, still we find
Something which jars upon, and hurts the mind.
Whatever lights upon a part are thrown,
We see too plainly they are not his own.
No flame from Nature ever yet he caught,
Nor knew a feeling which he was not taught;
He rais'd his trophies on the base of art,
And conn'd his passions, as he conn'd his part.

Charles Churchill, *The Rosciad*

Kemble's Lear[1]

The first benefit of Mrs. Siddons was taken on the 21st of January [1788]; and Kemble acted, to her Cordelia, the prodigy of dramatic creation, King Lear. I have seen him since in the character, but he never again achieved the excellence of that night. Subsequently he was too elaborately aged, and quenched with infirmity the insane fire of the injured father. The curse, as he then uttered it, harrowed up the soul: the gathering himself together, with the hands convulsively clasped, the encreasing fervour and rapidity, and the suffocation of the conclusive words, all evinced consummate skill and original invention. The countenance too was finely made up, and in grandeur approached the *most* awful impersonation of Michael Angelo. It will not be suspected that I speak this profanely. The highest nature, from the pencil of man, must still be a modification of human form. The performance was hailed with delight by many of Mr. Garrick's friends. The truth seems to have been that, in a few points, there was no inferiority; as a whole, nothing ever approached the influence of Garrick in this, which, if I may venture upon a disputed question, I do from my heart and judgment pronounce to be greatly superior as dramatic character, to Hamlet, to Macbeth, to Othello. Mrs. Siddons acted the Cordelia of Tate. The passion for Edgar is an excrescence, but pardonable on the stage, which has endured the restoration of Lear.

On this occasion, £347 10s. was taken at the door, and this was the greatest sum that had ever been taken in that theatre, except at her first benefit, to Lady Macbeth, when £351 was the receipt at the doors.

James Boaden, *Life of Kemble*

Kean as King

Public expectation has seldom been raised to a greater height than by the announcement of Kean's appearance in *King Lear*, which, after numerous delays, took place yesterday evening. The admirers of this highly-gifted actor, confident in the extent and diversity of his talents, have long anticipated this trial as the last seal to his theatrical renown; while his enemies, on the other hand (for Kean, like other men of genius, has

[1] Except for very minor alterations, Kemble's version was the same as Tate's.

encountered the extremes of hostility as well as of admiration), have not scrupled to predict failure and loss of reputation. Such was the anxiety of all parties to witness the experiment, that a crowd was collected at the doors long before the period of admission; and the first rush filled the pit, with a great portion of those boxes where seats had not been secured. When the curtain rose, it was evident that a large majority of the spectators consisted of the friends of Kean, and he was received on his first appearance with a burst of applause truly enthusiastic. It soon ceased, however, and the play was listened to throughout, but especially in the scenes where Lear is present, with the most profound attention. The first scene contains nothing prominent; yet it was apparent, even then, that the actor, as if fully aware of the ordeal through which he had to pass, had tasked his powers to the utmost, and was resolved to let no occasion pass of making an impression. This was shown in his quick susceptibility to the reluctance of Cordelia to echo the professions of her sisters. The first symptoms of distrust of Goneril were beautifully developed, where he retains the disguised Kent in his service; and when distrust is changed into certainty by her behaviour; his manner denoted that the first inroads were already made on his reason. The passage containing the recollection of Cordelia, and remorse for his conduct—

'How small, Cordelia, was thy fault! O Lear,
Beat at this gate that let thy folly in,
And thy dear judgment out!'

was beautifully expressed. The curse on Goneril, which follows, can scarcely be contemplated without pain, but, aided by his action and manner, became truly terrific. On the arrival at Gloster's castle, as the interest increased, the actor rose in power. One of the finest passages in that scene was the appeal to Regan—

'Dear daughter, I confess that I am old;
Age is unnecessary; on my knees I beg
That you'll vouchsafe me raiment, bed, and food'

where to unite the tone of sarcasm with the dignified sorrow of the monarch forms so remarkable a difficulty. Kean, however, expressed it with truth and feeling. Nothing could evince greater judgment in this part of the play than the manner in which he represented the gradual aberration of reason under the repeated shocks to which it was exposed. Its last light seemed to be extinguished in this passage—

> No, you unnatural hags,
> I will have such revenges on you both,
> That all the world shall—I will do such things—
> What they are yet I know not; but they shall be
> The terrors of the earth.—You think I'll weep;
> No, I'll not weep;—
> I have full cause of weeping; but this heart
> Shall break into a hundred thousand flaws
> Or ere I'll weep.
> O gods, I shall go mad.

We cannot, without quoting more largely than our space will permit, follow the actor through the manifestations of genius he displayed in the character. The scene of the storm was less effective than many others, because the manager, by a strange error, had caused the tempest to be exhibited with so much accuracy that the performer could scarcely be heard amidst the confusion. He should have recollected that it is the bending of Lear's mind under his wrongs that is the object of interest, and not that of a forest beneath the hurricane. The machinery may be transferred to the next new pantomime. In the interview of Lear with Edgar, and the scene where he is carried off by the emissaries of Cordelia, the picture of mental alienation was completed, and we believe that a scene more perfect or pathetic has never been represented on the stage. The scene in the beginning of the 5th act, where the unhappy King is restored to reason, was the most masterly of the whole performance, there was scarcely a dry eye in the theatre. While it lasted, the silence would have rendered the fall of a pin audible; and it was followed by a burst of applause, unanimous, long, and enthusiastic. Whatever study Kean may have bestowed on the character of Lear, he has not been able to free it wholly from its prevailing faults; but they are as dust in the balance, in the consideration of a scene so highly wrought as that we have mentioned and, indeed, with his general conception and execution of this difficult part. It will be quoted as the *chef-d'oeuvre* of the English drama, and must be handed down to the emulation of future actors.

* * *

The Times, April 25, 1820

Re-enter the Fool

Charles Dickens praises Macready's production which opened at Covent Garden on January 25, 1838 and restored much of Shakespeare's play, including the Fool, for the first time in over one hundred and fifty years. A woman, Priscilla Horton, took the part of the Fool.

MACREADY as King Lear and HELEN FAUCIT as Cordelia, Covent Garden, 1838.

The Fool in the tragedy of *Lear* is one of the most wonderful creations of Shakespeare's genius. The picture of his quick and pregnant sarcasm, of his loving devotion, of his acute sensibility, of his despairing mirth, of his heartbroken silence — contrasted with the rigid sublimity of Lear's suffering, with the

283

huge desolation of Lear's sorrow, with the vast and outraged image of Lear's madness—is the noblest thought that ever entered into the heart and mind of man. Nor is it a noble thought alone. Three crowded houses in Covent Garden Theatre have now proved by something better than even the deepest attention that it is for action, for representation; that it is necessary to an audience as tears are to an overcharged heart; and necessary to Lear himself as the recollections of his kingdom, or as the worn and faded garments of his power. We predicted some years since that this would be felt, and we have the better right to repeat it now. We take leave again to say that Shakespeare would have as soon consented to the banishment of Lear from the tragedy as to the banishment of his Fool. We may fancy him, while planning his immortal work, feeling suddenly, with an instinct of divinest genius, that its gigantic sorrows could never be presented on the stage without a suffering too frightful, a sublimity too remote, a grandeur too terrible—unless relieved by quiet pathos, and in some way brought home to the apprehensions of the audience by homely and familiar illustration. At such a moment that Fool rose to his mind, and not till then could he have contemplated his marvellous work in the greatness and beauty of its final completion.

The Fool in *Lear* is the solitary instance of such a character, in all the writings of Shakespeare, being identified with the pathos and passion of the scene. He is interwoven with Lear, he is the link that still associates him with Cordelia's love, and the presence of the regal estate he has surrendered. The rage of the wolf Goneril is first stirred by a report that her favourite gentleman had been struck by her father 'for chiding of his fool,'—and the first impatient questions we hear from the dethroned old man are: 'Where's my knave—my fool? Go you and call my fool hither.'—'Where's my fool? Ho! I think the world's asleep.'—'But where's my fool? I have not seen him these two days.'—'Go you and call hither my fool,'—all which prepare us for that affecting answer stammered forth at last by the knight in attendance: 'Since my young lady's going into France, sir, the fool hath much pined away.' Mr. Macready's manner of turning off at this with an expression of half impatience, half ill-repressed emotion—'No more of that, *I have noted it well*'—was inexpressibly touching. We saw him, in the secret corner of his heart, still clinging to the memory of her who was used to be his best object, the argument of his praise, balm of his age, 'most best, most dearest.' And in the same noble and affecting spirit was his manner of fondling the Fool when he sees him first, and asks him with earnest care, 'How now, my pretty knave? *How dost thou?*' Can there be a doubt, after this, that his love for the Fool is associated with Cordelia, who had been kind to the poor boy, and for the loss of whom he pines away? And are we not even then prepared for the sublime pathos of the close, when Lear, bending over the dead body of all he had left to love upon the earth, connects with her the memory of that other gentle, faithful, and loving being who had passed from his side— unites, in that moment of final agony, the two hearts that had been broken in his service, and exclaims, 'And my poor fool is hanged!'

Mr. Macready's Lear, remarkable before for a masterly completeness of conception, is heightened by this introduction of the Fool to a surprising degree. It accords exactly with the view he seeks to present of Lear's character. The passages we have named, for instance, had even received illustration in the first scene, where something beyond the turbulent greatness or royal impatience of Lear had been presented—something to redeem him from his treatment of Cordelia. The bewildered pause after giving his 'father's heart' away—the hurry yet hesitation of his manner as he orders France to be called— 'Who stirs? Call Burgundy'—had told us at once how much consideration he needed, how much pity, of how little of himself he was indeed the master, how crushing and irrepressible was the strength of his sharp impatience. We saw no material change in his style of playing the first great scene with Goneril, which fills the stage with true and appalling touches of nature. In that scene he ascends indeed with the heights of Lear's passion; through all its changes of agony, of anger, of impatience, of turbulent assertion, of despair, and mighty grief, till on his knees, with arms upraised and head thrown back, the tremendous Curse bursts from him amid heaving and reluctant throes of suffering and anguish. The great scene of the second act had also its great passages of power and beauty: his self-persuading utterance of 'hysterica passio'—his anxious and fearful tenderness to Regan—the elevated grandeur of his appeal to the heavens—his terrible suppressed efforts, his pauses, his reluctant pangs of passion, in the speech 'I will not trouble thee, my child,'—and surpassing the whole, as we think, in deep simplicity as well as agony of pathos, that noble conception of shame as he *hides his face* on the arm of Goneril and says—

'I'll go with thee;
Thy fifty yet doth double five and twenty,
And thou art twice her love'

The Fool's presence then enabled him to give an effect,
unattempted before, to those little words which close the scene,
when, in the effort of bewildering passion with which he
strives to burst through the phalanx of amazed horrors that
have closed him round, he feels that his intellect is shaking, and
suddenly exclaims, 'O Fool! I shall go mad!' This is better than
hitting the forehead and ranting out a self-reproach.

But the presence of the Fool in the storm-scene! The reader
must witness this to judge its power and observe the deep
impression with which it affects the audience. Every resource
that the art of the painter and the mechanist can afford is called
in aid of this scene— every illustration is thrown on it of which
the great actor of Lear is capable, but these are nothing to
that simple presence of the Fool! He has changed his character
there. So long as hope existed he had sought by his hectic merriment and sarcasms to win Lear back to love and reason, but that
half of his work is now over, and all that remains for him is to
soothe and lessen the certainty of the worst. Kent asks who is
with Lear in the storm, and is answered—

'None but the Fool, who labours to outjest
His heart-struck injuries!'

When all his attempts have failed, either to soothe or to
outjest these injuries, he sings, in the shivering cold, about the
necessity of 'going to bed at noon.' He leaves the stage to die
in his youth, and we hear of him no more till we hear the
sublime touch of pathos over the dead body of the hanged
Cordelia.

The finest passage of Mr. Macready's scenes upon the heath
is his remembrance of the 'poor naked wretches,' wherein a
new world seems indeed to have broken upon his mind.
Other parts of these scenes wanted more of tumultuous
extravagance, more of a preternatural cast of wildness. We
should always be made to feel something beyond physical
distress predominant here. His colloquy with Mad Tom, however, was touching in the last degree, and so were the two last
scenes, the recognition of Cordelia and the death, which elicited
from the audience the truest and best of all tributes to their
beauty and pathos. Mr. Macready's representation of the father
at the end, broken down to his last despairing struggle, his heart

286

swelling gradually upwards till it bursts in its closing sigh, completed the only perfect picture that we have had of Lear since the age of Betterton.

Charles Dickens, The Examiner, February 4, 1838

A Many-Splendoured King

Charles Kean's revival was appropriately lavish and 'authentic' down to 8th century settings and costumes.

Princess.'—The revival of the 'Lear,' as we had previously announced, took place on Saturday evening at this theatre, and fully justified the expectations that had been formed: we may add, more than justified them, and in ways that had not been previously imagined. There is always danger in scenic illustration, pictorially carried out and archaeologically conducted, that the spectacular will overlay the dramatic, and thus the poetic and histrionic suffer from too violent a contrast with the stage appointments. In this case nothing of the kind happens. The subordination of the mechanist and the painter to the poet and actor is duly maintained throughout, and yet the widest scope has been accorded to their talents. The action of the drama being placed in the mythic period, there is, of course, no authority that can be appealed to; the manager is consequently left at liberty to select the epoch that may best answer the purpose of theatrical interpretation. The earliest that could be taken would of course be the most preferable, and therefore we think Mr. Kean has acted judiciously in choosing the Anglo-Saxon era of the eighth century 'for the regulation of the scenery and dresses, as affording a date sufficiently remote, while it is at the same time associated with the British soil.' His details are in all respects picturesque, and nothing finer in this way was ever done than the second scene of the first act, representative of the Room of State in the palace of the old Monarch. The Saxon adornments of spear, shield, shaft, and skin, antlers and body of the deer, with other trophies of the battle and the chase, the primitive hearthstone and the blazing yule-log, and similar accessories too numerous to record or to remember, gave to the long and slanting apartment a romantic appearance that could not be exceeded for its barbaric gorgeousness of state and ceremonial splendour. Then the grouping of the old King and his three daughters was admirable; and the motion of the scene, including the exits and entrances, was actualised in the most ingenious manner. The whole was full of invention, original, suggestive, and vitally pleasing. The next scene was the courtyard in the Duke of Albany's palace, rendered still more significant by the return of Lear from the boar-chase, attended by his knights and huntsmen. But this was far excelled by the scene that opened the second act, representing the exterior of the Earl of Gloster's castle by night, fortified, in the manner of the Anglo Saxons' camps, by pallisades. Nevertheless, greater excellence was attained, both in the mechanist's and scene-painter's department, in the second scene of the third act—that of the heath, with the storm of thunder and lightning. The clouds and electric fluid travelling rapidly across the sky in the distance, and with a lurid gloom investing the entire landscape, were grandly terrific; and, when associated by the mind with the animated figures in the foreground—the raving Lear, the exhausted Fool, and the provident Kent—composed a picture that was truly sublime. But art had yet something else in store; for in the scene of the hovel some Druidical remains are introduced, and the wind through the roofless columns blows its organ-notes, that sound like music. In act four there is also a fine picture—'the country near Dover, showing a Roman road and an ancient obelisk;' to which may be added the last scene of the fifth act, which is also near Dover, and exhibits the camp of the British forces, with the distant view of a Saxon castle. All these scenes were exquisitely painted; each had also some special merit of its own, but so judiciously introduced that the action was in no wise interfered with by its illustrative accessory.

The dominant excellence of the revival consisted in the histrionic *genius* by which it was supported. Mr. Walter Lacy as Edmund, Mr. Ryder as Edgar, Mr. Graham as the Earl of Gloster, Mr. Cooper as the Earl of Kent, and Miss Poole as the Fool, had each parts specially suited to their several aptitudes. More especial commendation still may be accorded to Miss Kate Terry, whose Cordelia was in all respects excellent— innocent and animated, intelligent and pathetic, modest and yet expressive. Miss Heath and Miss Buften were the Goneril and Regan, and both played with exemplary care these two most ungrateful parts. There was also a little part which, for its *vraisemblance*, should be mentioned: we mean Gloster's Old Tenant, impersonated by a Mr. Morris. In all these points we recognise the care of the manager equally present in the minute as in the large, in the least as well as the most demonstrative. Thus, there was a unity and a harmony between part and part, and a common relation between the different effects, conducting to a common origin, and answering one and the same intelligent purpose.

Mr. C. Kean had prepared us by his Louis XI. for a display of elaboration and finish in which the minutest points of character and dialogue should be profusely interpreted; but that part, thoroughly stage-eligible as it is, left yet the highest dramatic and poetic elements unvisited. In *Lear* these are the all-in-all. Every portion of it thoroughly demonstrates the most complete mastery over the wonderful language in which every conception and feeling of this magnificent tragedy is clothed.

Mr. Kean made good his impression right early in the play. No sooner does poor Cordelia falter in her utterance than the overloving King, feeling his heart rebuked by an unsatisfactory response, is constrained to give decided indications of the most grievous disappointment that he has undergone. The revulsion of feeling is as natural as it is powerful. When we next see him, Lear has recovered his serenity. He has returned cheerful and weary from the chase, his appetite awakened, and his desire for dinner urgent. But now come the signs of a change of mood; for neglect has usurped the place of observance, and the old King is purposely insulted by Goneril's menials; at last, by Goneril herself. This is too much. Astonishment seizes on the King; then for a while he collects himself, but at length he gives the full tide of passion way, and utters the wronged father's bitter malediction. Mr. Kean's delivery of the curse was perfect: the suppressed emotion, the irrepressible exclamatory impulse, and the passionate emphasis, were alike admirable.

At the end of the second act Lear is worked up to a similar state of mind in regard to Regan; and again the actor achieved an unparalleled triumph. At length nature, that always sympathises with the mind of man, represents by an external tempest the inward rage that consumes the outcast father and discrowned monarch; and the true actor is required to rise to the sublimity of the highest poetic conception, and the vigour of the boldest histrionic delineation. Mr. Kean's success was complete. With Lear's madness began a series of new triumphs. 'Reason in madness': that was the poet's problem, that is the actor's test. In the blending of these opposites the highest skill was exhibited. In the fourth and fifth acts Shakespeare, as his manner is, has diverted his subject into the calmer regions of fancy and feeling; and there revelling, mitigated the pain that the mere circumstantial horror of his story would else have inflicted. Fantastic frenzy succeeds to fierce madness; and restoration to sanity, preceding a catastrophe that crushes the heart, demonstrates that the world is no place for the pure affections, but one of probation only, where compromises of all sorts are needed—

> Vex not his ghost. O, let him pass! He hates him
> That would upon the rack of this tough world
> Stretch him out longer.

The triumphant development of genius displayed by Mr. Kean in his embodiment of Shakspeare's sublime creation places beyond doubt his supremacy as a histrionic artist. We have only to add that the audience testified their sense of its excellence by repeated plaudits and frequent summons before the curtain.

Illustrated London News, April 24, 1858

Too Infirm a King?

Phelps' production, which had very few cuts and followed the order of Shakespeare's scenes, also had the Fool played by a man. It opened on November 5, 1845; Morley saw the revival of 1861, the year before Phelps retired.

June 1 [1861] The *King Lear* of Mr. Phelps draws full houses to the Princess's. In the opening of the play the actor represents the Lear of the old legend. Infirm with age, he is led to his seat. His hands tremble, and everything indicates the weakness of body in which a weak mind is working. The curse upon Goneril is spoken, as the whole character is conceived, with a sense rather of the pathetic than the terrible. But I miss the majesty of absolute dominion in the royal Lear whom Shakespeare brought into grand contrast with the Lear in the storm, slave of the elements, 'a poor, infirm, weak, and despised old man', who goes shivering to the straw of the hovel. Mr. Phelps does not make full use of all the hints given by Shakespeare to the actor for expressing the imperious habit of King Lear, who had grown old in despotic rule. Even in his entry from the hunt, when at Albany's castle, with the 'Let me not wait a jot for dinner', which Mr. Charles Kean interpreted as the words of a jovially hungry man (generally treating

Lear at this stage of his tragedy as a comic character), Mr. Phelps misses the true dramatic meaning of the words. In all the first scene the impatient majesty upon which Shakespeare dwelt is sacrificed to representation of the age and infirmity of which alone the legend teaches us. But the infirmity has in a great measure to be laid aside. The shaking head and trembling hands cannot be carried through the play. Thus there is double loss rather than gain in laying at the outset too much stress upon infirmity. There is another shortcoming in the early part of Mr. Phelps's Lear. With unusual literalness, Shakespeare indicates to the actor of Lear the exact course of the change to madness. It is preceded by a pang of terror in the close of the first act:—

'O let me not be mad, not mad, sweet heaven!
Keep me in temper; I would not be mad!'

There are well-marked struggles with the rising pang at his heart indicated throughout the scenes in the second act; where the character formed by long habit of rule overlies even the natural agony of the father. Of Kent set in the stocks by his son and daughter, the first exclamation is 'They *durst* not do't'; and in the scene which opens with their denial to speak with him, it is the wounded majesty that rages first, and the wrung heart that appears through it. The first act ended for Lear with terror lest he should go mad. In the second his last words are, 'O fool, I shall go mad'. In the third act the first scene on the heath is a sane frenzy; and towards the close of it, as majesty creeps to the hovel, Lear simply defines his state: 'My wits begin to turn.' He is not mad when, in the next scene, he reads one of the grand lessons of the play, praying in the storm outside the hovel, mindful of the world's 'looped and windowed raggedness'.

'Take physic, pomp;
Expose thyself to feel what wretches feel.'

Just before, when thinking of his daughters, he had shuddered and recoiled at the thought, 'that way madness lies; let me shun that'. But the night of exposure to the storm completes the ruin. 'This cold night,' says the Fool, 'will turn us all to fools and madmen'; and the wild talk of Edgar, in his assumed madness, precipitates the real madness of Lear. When he is talking with this philosopher, Kent urges Gloster to importune him to go, because 'his wits begin to unsettle'; and when he is brought by Gloster into the farmhouse, we are, at last, warned by Kent's first words that 'all the power of his wits have given way to his impatience'. Now, although Mr. Phelps gives a fine reading of the part, I do not think that he contrasts sufficiently the royal state with the abject misery; the imperious way, strong in weak characters, with the lowest humility of the infirm, weak, and despised old man. Neither in the accession of Lear's madness do we get from Mr. Phelps, what, indeed, no actor in our time has altogether given, a satisfactory embodiment of Shakespeare's conception. But from the time that Lear enters with his robes washed almost colourless by the rain, a feeble old man, weary and witless after his night's wandering under the storm, everything is exquisitely done, the story being read wholly with regard to its pathos, not to its terror. The king is utterly lost in the father. The wound to the heart has struck, as no hurt to the dignity of royal robes can strike a man. Majesty has been contemned in its rags. Humanity lives to assert itself. The quiet broken spirit, the strayed wits, the tender nursing and rocking of the body of Cordelia in the closing scene; the faint interest in all but her by whose love Lear's broken heart was held together; the tenderness with which he lays her down, as for an instant, while he lifts his hands to the throat in which the last convulsive throe of death is rising; his quiet death, with his eyes, his pointing hands, and his last words directed to her lips, are exquisitely touching.

Henry Morley—*Journal of a London Playgoer*

Macbeth

SIMON Forman saw the play in 1611 and Pepys some fifty years later, when he particularly admired the music and dancing. When Garrick proclaimed in 1744 that he was reviving the play as Shakespeare wrote it, the reigning Macbeth, James Quin, was surprised to learn that the play he himself had been acting in was not Shakespeare's, being largely Davenant's handiwork. When John Kemble played the role in 1809, he could not be heard because of the noise made by a section of the audience protesting over increased seat prices. Sarah Siddons, Kemble's sister made the part of Lady Macbeth uniquely her own and Kean and Macready were outstanding as Macbeth in their time. While green-room tradition considers Macbeth unlucky, it has been one of the most often performed Shakespearean plays.

Rogues in Black Periwigs

It is not improbable, but that from Sandford's[1] so masterly personating characters of guilt, the inferior actors might think his success chiefly owing to the defects of his person; and from thence might take occasion, whenever they appear'd as bravo[e]s, or murtherers, to make themselves as frightful and as inhuman figures as possible. In King Charles's time, this low skill was carry'd to such an extravagance, that the king himself, who was black-brow'd, and of a swarthy complexion, pass'd a pleasant remark upon his observing the grim looks of the murtherers in *Macbeth*; when, turning to his people, in the box about him, 'Pray, what is the meaning,' said he, 'that we never see a rogue in a play, but, godsfish, they always clap him on a black perriwig? when, it is well known, one of the greatest rogues in England always wears a fair one?' Now, whether or no Dr. Oates[2], at that time, wore his own hair, I cannot be positive; or, if his majesty pointed at some greater man, then out of power, I leave those to guess at him, who may yet remember the changing complexion of his ministers. This story I had from Betterton, who was a man of veracity; and, I confess, I should have thought the king's observation a very just one, though he himself had been fair as Adonis. Nor can I, in this question, help voting with the Court; for were it not too gross a weakness to employ, in wicked purposes, men whose very suspected looks might be enough to betray them? Or are we to suppose it unnatural, that a murther should be thoroughly committed out of an old red coat and a black perriwig?

Colley Cibber, Apology

---

[1] Samuel Sandford (?1640–1699) a Restoration actor whom Charles II once called 'the best villain in the world.'

[2] Titus Oates (1648–1705) whose false allegation of a popish plot to murder the king in 1678 led to the execution of many Catholics.

Mr. Spectator Changes his Seat

Some years ago, I was at the tragedy of *Macbeth*, and unfortunately placed my self under a woman of quality that is since dead; who, as I found by the noise she made, was newly returned from France. A little before the rising of the curtain, she broke out into a loud soliloquy, *When will the dear Witches enter*; and immediately upon their first appearance, asked a lady that sat three boxes from her, on her right hand, if those witches were not charming creatures. A little after, as Betterton was in one of the finest speeches of the play, she shook her fan at another lady, who sat as far on the left hand, and told her with a whisper, that might be heard all over the pit, We must not expect to see Balloon[1] to night. Not long after, calling out to a young baronet by his name, who sat three seats before me, she asked him whether Macbeth's wife was still alive; and (before he could give an answer) fell a talking of the Ghost of Banquo. She had by this time formed a little audience to her self, and fixed the attention of all about her. But as I had a mind to hear the play, I got out of the sphere of her impertinence, and planted my self in one of the remotest corners of the pit.

Joseph Addison, *The Spectator (45) 1711*

A Climax of Terror

Garrick revived Shakespeare's play, without most of Davenant's additions but with singing and dancing witches on January 7, 1744.

Conscious of his full design, Macbeth, with terror and dismay says, *'Is this a dagger that I see before me?'* Garrick's attitude, his consternation, and his pause, while his soul appeared in his countenance, and the accents that followed, astonished the spectators. The sequel was a climax of terror, till at last he finds it to be the effect of a disordered imagination, and his conscience forces him to say,

It is the bloody business, which informs
Thus to my eyes.

If anything can deter the mind of man from embarking in projects of guilt, the horrors, here represented in such glaring colours, would, upon due reflection, be sufficient to alarm his

[1] Balon, a French dancer.

heart, and call him back to the paths of virtue. But Macbeth, incited by his wife, pursues his evil purpose, and executes the murder. When Garrick re-entered the scene, with the bloody dagger in his hand, he was absolutely scared out of his senses; he looked like a ghastly spectacle, and his complexion grew whiter every moment, till at length, his conscience stung and pierced to the quick, he said in a tone of wild despair,

> Will all great Neptune's ocean wash this blood
> Clean from my hand? No, this my hand will rather
> The multitudinous sea incarnadine,
> Making the *Green*—ONE RED.

It is true, that he was for some time in the habit of saying, the *green-one red*; but upon consideration, he adopted the alteration, which was first proposed by this writer in the Gray's Inn Journal.

Arthur Murphy, Life of Garrick

More Last Words for Macbeth

He composed, indeed, a pretty long speech for Macbeth, when dying, which, though suitable perhaps to the character, was unlike Shakespeare's manner, who was not prodigal of bestowing abundance of matter on characters in that situation. But Garrick excelled in the expression of convulsive throes and dying agonies, and would not lose any opportunity that offered to shew his skill in that part of his profession.

Thomas Davies, Dramatic Miscellanies

Garrick and Mrs. Pritchard[1]

The representation of this terrible part of the play [the murder], by Garrick and Mrs. Pritchard, can no more be described than I believe it can be equalled. I will not separate these performers, for the merits of both were transcendent. His distraction of mind and agonising horrors were finely contrasted by her seeming apathy, tranquillity, and confidence. The beginning of the scene after the murder was conducted in

[1] Hannah Pritchard, Garrick's second Lady Macbeth (the first was Anna Giffard) took over the role in 1748 and was undisputed mistress of it till the arrival of Mrs. Siddons.

DAVID GARRICK and HANNAH PRITCHARD in *Macbeth*, Drury Lane, 1768.

terrifying whispers. Their looks and action supplied the place of words. You heard what they spoke, but you learned more from the agitation of mind displayed in their action and deportment. The poet here gives only an outline to the consummate actor.—*I have done the deed!—Didst thou not hear a noise?—When?—Did you not speak?*—The dark colouring, given by the actor to these abrupt speeches, makes the scene awful and tremendous to the auditors! The wonderful expression of heartful horror, which Garrick felt when he shewed his bloody hands, can only be conceived and described by those who saw him!

* * *

This admirable scene [the banquet] was greatly supported by the speaking terrors of Garrick's look and action. Mrs. Pritchard shewed admirable art in endeavouring to hide Macbeth's frenzy from the observation of the guests, by drawing their attention to conviviality. She smiled on one, whispered to another, and distantly saluted a third; in short, she practised every possible artifice to hide the transaction that passed between her husband and the vision his disturbed imagination had raised. Her reproving and angry looks, which glanced towards Macbeth, at the same time were mixed with marks of inward vexation and uneasiness. When, at last, as if unable to support her feelings any longer, she rose from her seat, and seized his arm, and, with a half-whisper of terror, said, '*Are you a man!'* she assumed a look of such anger, indignation, and contempt, as cannot be surpassed.

Thomas Davies, *Dramatic Miscellanies*

The Greatest Lady Macbeth

Kemble's biographer describes Mrs. Siddons' first portrayal of her greatest role before a London audience. She had already played Lady Macbeth in Liverpool, Bath and Bristol and is said to have first played the role when she was only twenty.

SARAH SIDDONS as Lady Macbeth, Dury Lane, 1785.

Her benefit, [therefore,] on the 2nd of February, [1785] exhibited this great actress in the crown of all her achievements, Lady Macbeth. And, certainly, if ever the slanderer of excellence was put to shame, as well as flight, it must have been at this noble exhibition. Language seemed really to sink under her eulogists. It was the triumph of the art; it was at once, simple, grand, and striking; it was such an impersonation as Raffaele might have conceived, had Shakspeare been his contemporary, and which Reynolds had painted, being so fortunate as to be hers. Sir Joshua on that night occupied his privileged seat in the orchestra, and never availed himself of his other privilege, until the tragic queen had quitted the last scene of *sleeping horrour*. Then,—

'He shifted his trumpet, and only took snuff.'

Part of the pit, on this occasion, was laid into the boxes; a practice which can hardly be defended, because an usurpation upon the territory of a most respectable class of admirers. But on such nights, the additional splendour gained by the jewels and feathers of the ladies, made up a *coup d'oeil* of the most fascinating description. When I have returned from such exhibitions, it seemed the dispelling of a dream of eastern magnificence. I take the liberty to remark, that there appeared more *soul* in the applause given to these triumphs of Mrs. Siddons, than I have ever felt in the audiences, who were attracted by any succeeding magnet of the drama.

James Boaden, *Life of Kemble*

Toil and Trouble

In spite of the elaborate safety measures taken at the New Theatre, including tanks of water on the roof and a reservoir on stage across which the first night audience saw a boatman row, the building was burnt down fifteen years after its opening. Mrs. Siddons played Lady Macbeth on the first night.

On April 21, 1793, the theatre opened for the performance of dramatic pieces, to the great terror of the performers of the other house, who had not yet taken their benefits. The first dramatic exhibition was Macbeth, which, though one of Shakspeare's well known plays, was now attended with much novelty, owing to some very material alterations: the scenes were all new, and the Witches no longer wore mittens, plaited

298

ELIZABETH FARREN, speaking the Epilogue at the opening of the New
Theatre, April 21, 1794. The play was *Macbeth*.

caps, laced aprons, red stomachers, ruffs, &c. (which was the
dress of those *weird sisters*, when Messrs. Beard, Champness,
&c. represented them with Garrick's Macbeth), or any human
garb, but appeared as preternatural beings, distinguishable
only by the fellness of their purposes and the fatality of their
delusions. Hecate's accompanying spirit descended on the
cloud, and rose again with her. In the cauldron scene, new
groups were introduced to personify the black spirits and
white, blue spirits and grey. The evil spirits had serpents
writhing round them, which had a striking effect. A prologue
for opening of the house was written by the Right Hon.
Major-General Fitzpatrick, and spoken by Mr. Kemble. The
present Mr. Colman wrote an epilogue, which was spoken by
Miss Farren, in the character of Housekeeper to the new edifice.
She assured the audience that they need be in no fear of fire,
for they had water enough to drown them; and the curtain
drawing, displayed a very fine river on the stage, on which a
waterman in his boat passed to and fro; in addition to this she
told them they had an iron curtain, so that the *scenes* only and
the *actors* could be *burnt*. It concluded with a view of
Shakspeare's monument, under his mulberry tree, surrounded
by a group of his own characters, with the Tragic and Comic
Muses. The scene finished with the song of 'The Mulberry
Tree,' and the glee of 'Where The Bee Sucks.'

Charles Gildon, *The Dramatic Mirror*

299

The O.P. Riots

The 'Old Prices' riots began when Kemble decided to increase admission prices because of the heavy expenditure involved in rebuilding Covent Garden Theatre after the fire on September 20, 1808. The riots lasted for sixty-one nights and ended only when Kemble gave way and made a formal apology, whereupon a placard saying 'We are satisfied' was displayed in the pit.

KEMBLE as Macbeth during the O.P. Riots, Covent Garden, 1809 (caricature by Cruickshank).

On the 18th of September, [1809] the new theatre, which had been completely finished within nine months, opened with Macbeth, the most attractive tragedy of Shakspeare, and the musical farce of The Quaker.

A slight advance in the price of admission had been announced in the play-bills, and adequately justified by the proprietors. To obviate a clamour, which assigned the engagement of Madame Catalani as the cause of this advance, it was distinctly affirmed that, had that lady been unknown to the public, the proprietors would have felt themselves compelled to solicit their indulgence as to the rate of admission.

The theatre was soon filled, and the audience took their seats without any striking demonstration of the hostile intentions among them. The orchestra commenced with the national anthem, and God save the King was sung by the whole vocal strength of the theatre. It was attended by the usual tokens of respect from the audience.

Mr. Kemble then made his appearance with the intention of speaking a poetical *address*, upon the opening of the new theatre. As he was, almost immediately after, to re-enter as Macbeth, he appeared in the dress of that character. The sight of him was the *assigned* moment for displaying hostility; and he was saluted by a yell of clamour and execration, which did not allow one line of his *address* to be heard in the body of the house. It spoke, however, of the origin and progress of the drama, and when it arrived at its brightest period, it took credit for the improvements of scenic representation in the following couplet—

'Thus Shakspeare's fire burns brighter than of yore;
And may the stage that boasts him *burn no more*.'

It ended with no very poetical allusion to the *solidity* of the building, and the *burthen* of its cost; and expressed a hope, that the ardour to raise a nation's *taste* would be repaid by its *liberality*.

The tumult was kept up, whatever performers were upon the stage; but the faction distinguished itself by a peculiar clamour on the appearance of any member of Mr. Kemble's family. They demonstrated their taste, as well as contempt, by standing with their backs turned to the stage, and keeping their hats on during the whole of the performance.

On the termination of these entertainments, two gentlemen appeared upon the stage, who were supposed to be magistrates from the Bow-street office. One of them attempted to speak, but, not being able to obtain the slightest attention, took a paper from his pocket, which was presumed to be the Riot Act. The hisses with which they were saluted induced them, after a short time, to withdraw—but several riotous persons were, by the police, take[n] into custody, and held to bail for their appearance at the ensuing sessions.

James Boaden, *Life of Kemble*

Two Electric Moments

I may briefly state that I saw Mrs. Jordan act in 'The Country Girl,' and George Frederick Cooke play Iago to Pope's Othello, at Drury Lane; John Kemble, in Macbeth, Brutus, and King Lear; and Mrs. Siddons, in Lady Macbeth, at Covent Garden; but it would be impertinence in me to express my opinion of performances I was much too young to appreciate. I can remember, however, being greatly impressed by two effects; one, the wonderful expression of Kemble's face in his interview with Lady Macbeth after the murder of Duncan, act iii. scene 2. I can see him now, standing in the door-way in the centre of the scene. The kingly crown appeared a burthen and a torture to him. How terribly clear it was, before he uttered a word, that his mind was 'full of scorpions',—that he acutely felt—

——'Better be with the dead,
Whom we, to gain our peace, have sent to peace,
Than on the torture of the mind to lie
In restless ecstacy.'

The other was the exulting exclamation of Mrs. Siddons, when, as Lady Macbeth, having read the letter, she greets her husband on his entrance with—

'Great Glamis! worthy Cawdor!
Greater than both, by the "all-hail" *hereafter!*'

The effect was electrical. Her whole performance, indeed, impressed me with an awe that, when I met her in society, several years afterwards, I could not entirely divest myself of on being presented to her.

J. R. Planché, *Recollections and Reflections*

Lady Macbeth Observed

In 1809 G. J. Bell, Professor of Scottish Law in the University of Edinburgh saw Mrs. Siddons as Lady Mabeth and made detailed notes on her performance which were printed seventy years later by Fleeming Jenkin. The original copy of the play which Professor Bell annotated appears to have been lost since.

Act II. Scene 2.

Enter LADY MACBETH.

Lady.[1] That which hath made them drunk hath made me
    bold;
What hath quenched them hath given me fire. *Hark! Peace!*[2]
It was the owl that shrieked, the fatal bellman,
Which gives the stern'st good-night. *He is about it.*[3]
The doors are open, and the surfeited grooms
Do mock their charge with snores: I have drugg'd their possets,
That death and nature do contend about them,
Whether they live or die.
    Macbeth. [*Within.*] Who's there? what, ho!
    Lady.[4] Alack, I am afraid they have awaked,
And 'tis not done. The attempt and not the deed
Confounds us. Hark! I laid their daggers ready:
He could not miss them. Had he not resembled
My father as he slept, I had done't.[5] — *My husband!*

Enter MACBETH.

    Macbeth. [6]I have done the deed. Didst thou not hear a
    noise?
    Lady. I heard the owl scream and the crickets cry.
Did not you speak?[5]
    Macbeth.   When?[6]
    Lady.   Now.
    Macbeth.   As I descended?[7]
    Lady. Ay.
    Macbeth. Hark!
Who lies i' the second chamber?
    Lady.   Donalbain.
    Macbeth. This is a sorry sight.   [*Looking on his hands.*]
    Lady. A foolish thought, to say a sorry sight.
    Macbeth.[8] There's one did laugh in his sleep, and one
    cried 'Murder!'
That they did wake each other: I stood and heard them:
But they did say their prayers, and address'd them

Again to sleep.

    Lady.   There are two lodged together.

    Macbeth.   One cried 'God bless us!' and 'Amen' the other;
As they had seen me with these hangman's hands:
Listening their fear, I could not say 'Amen,'
When they did say 'God bless us!'

    Lady.   Consider it not so deeply.

    Macbeth.   But wherefore could not I pronounce 'Amen'?
I had most need of blessing, and 'Amen'
Stuck in my throat.

    Lady.   These deeds must not be thought
After these ways; *so, it will make us mad.*[8]

    Macbeth.   Methought I heard a voice cry 'Sleep no more!'
         .... to all the house:
'Glamis hath murder'd sleep, and therefore Cawdor
Shall sleep no more; Macbeth shall sleep no more.'[9]

    Lady.   *Who* was it that thus cried? Why, worthy thane,
[10] You do unbend your noble strength, to think
So brainsickly of things. Go get some water,
And wash this filthy witness from your hand.[10]
[11] *Why did you bring these daggers from the place?*
They must lie there: go carry them, and smear
The sleepy grooms with blood.

    Macbeth.   I'll go no more:
I am afraid to think what I have done;
Look on't again I dare not.

    Lady.   Infirm of purpose!
[12] Give me the daggers: the sleeping and the dead
Are but as pictures: 'tis the eye of childhood
That fears a painted devil.[12] *If he do bleed,*[13]
I'll gild the faces of the grooms withal;
For it must seem their guilt.   [*Exit. Knocking within.*

    Macbeth.   Whence is that knocking?
How is't with me, when every noise appals me?
What hands are here? ha! they pluck out mine eyes.
Will all great Neptune's ocean wash this blood
Clean from my hand? No; this my hand will rather
The multitudinous seas incarnadine,
Making the green one red.

Re-enter LADY MACBETH.

    Lady.   [14] My *hands* are of your colour; but I shame
To wear a *heart* so white. [*Knocking within.*] I hear a knocking

At the south entry: retire we to our chamber:
A little water clears us of this deed:
How easy is it, then! Your constancy
Hath left you unattended. [*Knocking within.*] Hark, more
    knocking,
Get on your nightgown, lest occasion call us
And show us to be watchers. Be not lost
So poorly in your thoughts.
    Macbeth.   To know my deed, 'twere best not know myself.
                                     [*Knocking within.*
Wake Duncan with this knocking! Oh would thou couldst![14]
                                           [*Exeunt.*

The Nineteenth Century, February 1878

[1] With a ghastly horrid smile.

[2] Hsh! hsh! Whisper.

[3] Breathes with difficulty, hearkens towards the door. Whisper horrible.

[4] The finest agony; tossing of the arms.

[5] Agonised suspense, as if speechless with uncertainty whether discovered.

[6] Macbeth speaks all this like some horrid secret—a whisper in the dark.

[7] Very well spoken; horrid whisper.

[8] Mrs. Siddons here displays her wonderful power and knowledge of nature. As if her inhuman strength of spirit overcome by the contagion of his remorse and terror. Her arms about her neck and bosom, shuddering.

[9] Her horror changes to agony and alarm at his derangement, uncertain what to do; calling up the resources of her spirit.

[10] She comes near him, attempts to call back his wandering thoughts to ideas of common life. Strong emphasis on *who*. Speaks forcibly into his ear, looks at him steadfastly. 'Why, worthy thane,' &c.: fine remonstrance, tone fit to work on his mind.

[11] Now only at leisure to observe the daggers.

[12] Seizing the daggers very contemptuously.

[13] As stealing out she turns towards him stooping, and with the finger pointed to him with malignant energy says, 'If he do bleed,' &c.

[14] Contempt. Kemble plays well here; stands motionless; his bloody hands near his face; his eye fixed; agony in his brow; quite rooted to the spot. She at first directs him with an assured and confident air. Then alarm steals on her, increasing to agony lest his reason be quite gone and discovery be inevitable. Strikes him on the shoulder, pulls him from his fixed posture, forces him away, he talking as he goes.

Mr. Kean's Macbeth[1]

Measured praise from Hazlitt who saw Kean's first performance as
Macbeth at Drury Lane on November 5, 1814.

His Richard comes nearer to the original than his Macbeth.
He was deficient in the poetry of the character. He did not look
like a man who had encountered the Weird Sisters. There
should be nothing tight or compact in Macbeth, no tenseness
of fibre, nor pointed decision of manner. He has, indeed, energy
and manliness of soul, but subject 'to all the skyey influences.'
He is sure of nothing. All is left at issue. He runs a-tilt with
fortune, and is baffled with preternatural riddles. The agitation
of his mind resembles the rolling of the sea in a storm; or, he
is like a lion in the toils—fierce, impetuous, and ungovernable.
In the fifth act in particular, which is in itself as busy and
turbulent as possible, there was not that giddy whirl of the
imagination—the character did not burnish out on all sides
with those flashes of genius, of which Mr. Kean had given so
fine an earnest in the conclusion of his Richard. The scene
stood still—the parts might be perfect in themselves, but they
were not joined together; they wanted vitality. The pauses in
the speeches were too long—the actor seemed to be studying
the part, rather than performing it—striving to make every
word more emphatic than the last, and 'lost too poorly in himself,' instead of being carried away with the grandeur of his
subject. The text was not given accurately. Macbeth is represented in the play, arming before the castle, which adds to the
interest of the scene.

In the delivery of the beautiful soliloquy, 'My way of life
is fallen into the sear, the yellow leaf,' Mr. Kean was unsuccessful. That fine thoughtful melancholy did not seem to come over
his mind, which characterises Mr. Kemble's recitation of
these lines. The very tone of Mr. Kemble's voice has something
retrospective in it—it is an echo of the past. Mr. Kean in his
dress was occasionally too much docked and curtailed for the
gravity of the character. His movements were too agile and
mercurial, and he fought more like a modern fencing-master
than a Scottish chieftain of the eleventh century. He fell at
last finely, with his face downwards, as if to cover the shame
of his defeat. We recollect that Mr. Cooke discovered the great
actor both in the death-scene in Macbeth, and in that of
Richard. He fell like the ruin of a state, like a king with his

[1] Original title.

regalia about him.

The two finest things that Mr. Kean has ever done, are his recitation of the passage in Othello, 'Then, oh, farewell the tranquil mind,' and the scene in Macbeth after the murder. The former was the highest and most perfect effort of his art. To inquire whether his manner in the latter scene was that of a king who commits a murder, or of a man who commits a murder to become a king, would be 'to consider too curiously.' But, as a lesson of common humanity, it was heart-rending. The hesitation, the bewildered look, the coming to himself when he sees his hands bloody; the manner in which his voice clung to his throat, and choked his utterance; his agony and tears, the force of nature overcome by passion—beggared description. It was a scene, which no one who saw it can ever efface from his recollection.

William Hazlitt, *A View of the English Stage*

Macready's First Macbeth

Covent Garden.—The tragedy of 'Macbeth' was acted at this theatre last night for the benefit of Mr. Macready. It was his first performance of that admirable character, and he has reason to be doubly gratified with his selection of its performance for his benefit. It attracted a crowded and remarkably brilliant audience, and in this new essay he met with signal success. His air of bewildered agitation upon coming on the stage after the interview with the weird sisters was a most judicious and effective innovation upon the style of his predecessors. In the banquet scene, too, he made an original and admirable effect. Instead of intimidating the Ghost into a retreat, he fell back, sank into a chair, covered his face with his hands, then looked again, perceived the Ghost had disappeared, and upon being relieved from the fearful vision recovered once more the spring of his soul and body. The effect was powerful. His expression of terror after the murder produced a long-continued stillness. The pathos which he infused into Macbeth was a principal merit in his delineation. At the fall of the curtain, upon Mr. Connor's appearing to announce the performance of the next evening, there was a universal clamour for Mr. Macready. After some delay he did appear, but was quite exhausted by the exertions of the last act. He was so overpowered by fatigue and perhaps by the enthusiasm which the audience manifested towards him, that

Mr. Fawcett came out and said that, in consequence of the estimation which the audience had expressed of Mr. Macready's performance, the play should be repeated on Thursday.

Morning Herald, June 10, 1820

French Dressing

A moment during Macready's Paris tour. The performance was at the Salle Favart.

The witches in 'Macbeth' excited laughter. In the scene of the cauldron an auditor exclaimed at the enumeration of the ingredients thrown into it: 'Oh, mon Dieu! quel mélange!'

Macready's *Diary (April 1828)*

Helen Faucit[1]

December 3. [1864] It is to be wished that, by way of special favour to a portion of the public for which it already shows a wise respect, the management of Drury Lane would announce that their *Macbeth* would be acted, for a few nights at least, *without* Locke's music, and the corps of witches jigging to Davenant's misfitted rhymes. The very substantial Hecate, who looks like a cross between a beef-eater from the Tower and a ghost from the Styx, talks of anointing herself, and sings of the pleasure it is 'to sing, to toy, to dance, and kiss', belongs to the stage of a very different sort of Restoration than that which the Drury Lane management has now in hand. To those shadowy weird sisters who lie at the heart of the tragedy, this singing and jigging corps de ballet is—so far as their poetry is concerned—a ruinous accompaniment. By untuning the key-note they spoil the harmonies of the whole play.

Mr. Phelps's Macbeth is a half-barbarous warrior chief, around whom the powers of evil weave their fatal spell. The strife of the elements that rolls over the acting of his crime suggests the co-operation of the fiendish spirits who have him in thrall. By nature he is a rude, impulsive soldier, 'valour's minion', 'Bellona's bridegroom', turbulent of mind, restless, imaginative, quick of ambition', but with a religion strong in leaf, although fruitless and weak of root. As his wife says, in

---

[1] Helen Faucit (1817–98) whose real name was Helena Savile played many Shakespearean roles and wrote a book *On Some of Shakespeare's Female Characters* (1885).

words to which Miss Faucit rightly gives clear, unmistakable emphasis,

> 'not without ambition, but without
> The illness should attend it. What thou wouldst highly
> That wouldst thou holily: wouldst not play false
> And yet wouldst wrongly win.'

The last words of the witches before Macbeth's entry are of a 'pilot's thumb, wrecked as homeward he did come'; at the words, Macbeth, who has been piloting through storm the vessel of the State, is heard approaching, and on his homeward way they wait to wreck him. An evil influence that fastens on his soul comes with the foreboding of royalty. His heart has been stirred by a breath from hell, that has warmed into life damnable thoughts of the swift way to the promised height of sovereignty. In the subsequent scene with Duncan, Macbeth, still preoccupied, starts from his reverie at the naming of Malcolm as Prince of Cumberland. But though under the fatal spell of the weird sisters, unless a power of earth, in the urging force of his wife's will, join itself to the powers of hell, Duncan yet will sleep unharmed in Macbeth's castle.

And here, in the acted play, appears the chief defect of Miss Faucit's Lady Macbeth, which is weakest in the scenes before the murder of Duncan. Miss Faucit is too essentially feminine, too exclusively gifted with the art of expressing all that is most graceful and beautiful in womanhood, to succeed in inspiring anything like awe or terror. The lines beginning,

> 'Come all you spirits
> That tend on mortal thoughts, unsex me here,'

are simply spouted: at the closing passage—

> 'Nor Heaven peep through the blanket of the dark
> To cry "Hold, hold!"'—

Miss Faucit shouts 'Hold! hold!' in a most unheavenly manner, and throughout the early stage of the character it may be said that her Lady Macbeth is too demonstrative and noisy.

Of Macbeth's 'letting I dare not wait upon I would', her censure is vixenish in manner. The famous passage in delivering which Mrs. Siddons is said to have transformed herself into a terrible she-fiend, 'I have given suck,' etc., is poured out by Miss Faucit in a way that, by tones and gestures, vividly recalls a common spectacle of passion in our London streets— the scold at the door of a gin-shop. The comparison is by no means so degrading as it sounds, for the gin-shop scold pours out a true passion; and in passion, whatever the cause of it, high and low display alike the common nature. But such tones belong to an outpouring of emotion inconsistent with the self-possessed determination that makes Lady Macbeth terrible in this part of the play. In the latter part of the scene Miss Faucit is still too noisy[1], and when she suggests how upon Duncan's death they will make their 'griefs and clamour roar', she ends her part in the scene with voice pitched to its highest key and outspread fingers all abroad. There is the same excess of displayed emotion when she chides Macbeth as 'Infirm of purpose', and tells him ' 'tis the eye of childhood that fears a painted devil', spitting out at him the word 'painted'.

This defect in the representation disappears, of course, when the second phase of the character, that which is far more congenial to the actress, has to be represented. Miss Faucit's voice fails physically to express high tragic passion, and it possibly is part of a softer, though, we think, erroneous view taken by her of Lady Macbeth's character, to make her at the outset of the play passionately womanish, and herself impulsive.

The reaction of disappointment and hidden suffering after the crime is delicately shown by Miss Faucit. From the words opening that new phase of the character—

'Nought's had, all's spent,
When our desire is got without content:
'Tis safer to be that which we destroy,
Than, by destruction, dwell in doubtful joy'—

Miss Faucit's Lady Macbeth becomes a performance that no other English actress can approach. When Macbeth hints to her of a new deed, a new crime, admirable in various expression is his wife's tone of weariness of wonder and of dread in the question 'What's to be done?' And when Macbeth replies—

'Be innocent of the knowledge, dearest chuck,
Till thou applaud the deed'—

she stands averted as he crosses, and mechanically follows as he leads. In the murder of Banquo, Lady Macbeth is no accomplice. We have seen Miss Faucit praised for representation of smooth treachery in the tender playing of her fingers about the head of the child Fleance while Macbeth is sending father and child into the toils set for them. Miss Faucit knows

[1] A fortnight later, Morley reported that the noise level had been reduced.

her Shakespeare better than that. The fingers of the woman who has been a mother, and has murder on her soul, wander sadly and tenderly over the type of her lost innocence. In the banquet scene, where it should be remembered that she, ignorant of Banquo's fate, believes it to be the murdered Duncan of whom Macbeth speaks (save only a weakly scolding note or two in the private warning to Macbeth, 'O, these flaws, and starts', etc.), Miss Faucit is admirably good. Her by-play during Macbeth's speech, 'What man dare I dare', is perfect, and her collapse into weariness of life-long torture after the departure of the guests, with all that follows to the close of that scene, shows our best actress at her best. The sleep-walking scene is very carefully delivered, but has too much the air of a well-studied dramatic recitation. It is Miss Faucit's Lady Macbeth, not Lady Macbeth, whose nature sinks under the weight of her fatal secret, even in the sleep that has brought no rest to her guilty soul.

Henry Morley, Journal of a London Playgoer

Antony and Cleopatra

F OR over 80 years, from 1678, Dryden's *All for Love* ousted Shakespeare's play. When Garrick revived the original, with cuts and alterations, the production was a failure. So were most of the revivals, more or less approximating to the original play, up to the end of the 19th century, mostly because the spectacle seems to have smothered the dramatic poetry.

Eros Remembers[1]

Thomas Davies was apparently an indifferent Eros.

Mr. Garrick, from his passionate desire to give the public as much of their admired poet as possible, reviv'd it [*Antony and Cleopatra*], as altered by Mr. Capel, with all the advantages

[1] Thomas Davies played Eros in Garrick's lavish but unsuccessful production which ran for six nights, opening on January 3, 1759.

of new scenes, habits, and other decorations proper to the play. However, it did not answer his own and the public expectation. It must be confessed, that, in Antony, he wanted one necessary accomplishment: his person was not sufficiently important and commanding to represent the part. There is more dignity of action than variety of passion in the character, though it is not deficient in the latter. The actor, who is obliged continually to traverse the stage, should from person attract respect, as well as from the power of speech. Mrs. Yates was then a young actress and had not manifested such proofs of genius, and such admirable elocution, as she has since displayed; but her fine figure and pleasing manner of speaking were well adapted to the enchanting Cleopatra. Mossop wanted the essential part of Enobarbus, humour.

Thomas Davies, *Dramatic Miscellanies*

The Return of Shakespeare[1]

Sadler's Wells Theatre

On Monday the tragedy of 'Antony and Cleopatra' was revived. This magnificent play is a masterpiece of dramatic construction with the most difficult of subjects. Our admiration of it will increase if we compare it with Dryden's 'All for Love', confessedly written in emulation (and a noble emulation it was) of the diviner Shakespeare's. Dryden found it necessary to make *Antony* a weak man, so weak that, as Mr. Campbell has rightly observed, 'any wanton might have seduced him'. Shakespeare's Roman required the Egyptian Queen. The *Cleopatra* of Dryden, also, is even such a woman as his hero needed—no more; but the heroine of Shakespeare is a splendid creature, such as history has suggested to the imagination, such as was suitable to the lofty spirit, whose sense of beauty and taste for luxury had been cultivated into heroism. The persons of this wonderful drama are ideas—of voluptuous sublimity and gorgeous pleasure—gifted with almost divine capacities for enjoyment, having, as it were, the patent of heaven itself for the privilege; clothed gloriously in 'barbaric pearl and gold';

[1] Samuel Phelps' 1849 production was the first of Shakespeare's play for 100 years. Isabella Glyn (1823–1889) was Phelps' leading lady.

Antony and Cleopatra, at Sadlers' Wells Theatre, 1849.

and revelling in their own proper Elysium, like spirits delivered
from legal restraints, and free to indulge the bent of their genius
and the disposition of their nature, without hindrance either
from gods or men. To maintain the action of this elevation, and
yet to enable it to touch our human sympathies at innumerable
points, required the Poet whose myriad-mindedness has been
the wonder of philosophers and critics in exact proportion to
the competency of their judgment for the due appreciation
of the highest creative efforts. We are not surprised that such
a work should have proved *caviare* to the general public, and
that there was a period when, as Campbell records, Dryden's
play was infinitely preferred, having been 'acted ten times
oftener than Shakespeare's', though so decidedly inferior.

The management of this theatre have certainly endeavoured
to put this 'wonderful tragedy' of 'Antony and Cleopatra' on
the stage in the spirit in which it was composed. They have
done their best to realise the past, and to bring the historic into
actual presence. The Egyptian scenes are exceedingly *vrais-
emblable*; that on board of Pompey's galley, with the banqueting
sovereigns of the world as drunk as cobblers, is exceedingly
life-like. As it is managed, too, on the boards, it is rendered

313

one of the most picturesque and exciting incidents in the representation. Mr. Phelps, in particular, aided the pictorial, by his well-studied bacchanalian attitudes, some of which were exceedingly fine. We may here mention that Mr. Phelps' make-up of the character of Antony was capital. The illusion was almost perfect; the actor could scarcely be recognised through the disguise. He played the character also with great spirit; neither was it lacking in the higher qualifications of histrionic art. Antony's passion, his infatuation, his absorption of being for and in that of Cleopatra was interpreted 'excellent well'. It was, indeed, a remarkable triumph over difficulties, and will go far to raise his reputation as an actor, which must increase just in proportion as he succeeds in delivering himself from mere individualities. Such characters as these break up a performer's mannerisms, and do him accordingly infinite good.

A similar effect was produced on Miss Glyn. In this almost impossible character of Cleopatra she put forth new energies, and exhibited a versatility of power which surprised those most acquainted with her style and the scope of her genius. She dared at once at the 'infinite variety' of Cleopatra's character which 'custom could not stale'; and realised the conception to an almost miraculous extent. She combined grace and dignity—all the fascination of a Vestris with the majesty of a Pasta; she was, as it were, the impersonation at once of the sublime and the beautiful. Critics who before doubted her capacity, were now astonished at the extent of her resources, and the grandeur of the results. Gorgeous in person, in costume, and in her style of action, she moved, the Egyptian Venus, Minerva, Juno—now pleased, now angry—now eloquent, now silent—capricious, and resolved, according to the situation and sentiment to be rendered. Withal she was classical, and her *poses* severely statuesque. Her death was sublime. With a magnificent smile of triumph, she is, as it were, translated to the shades, there to meet her imperial lover. Altogether, Miss Glyn's performance of Cleopatra is the most superb thing ever witnessed on the modern stage. At the end of the play she was called before the curtain; and, led on by Mr. Phelps, received the well-merited ovation of an over-crowded house.

Illustrated London News,
October 27, 1849

A Pair of Spectacles[1]

LILLIE LANGTRY as Cleopatra, Princess's, 1890.

The first spectacle classic and Shakespearian: t'other burles-
quian, and PETTIT-cum-SIMS. The one at the Princess's, the
other at the Gaiety. *Place au* 'DIVINE WILLIAMS'! *Antony and
Cleopatra* is magnificently put on the stage. The costumes are
probably O.K.—'all correct'—seeing Mr. LEWIS WINGFIELD
pledges his honourable name for the fact. We might have done
with a few less, perhaps, but, as in the celebrated case of the
war-song of the Jingoes, if we've got the men, and the money
too, then there was every reason why the redoubtable LEWIS
(whose name, as brotherly Masons will call to mind, means
'Strength') should have put a whole army of Romans on the

[1] In 1890 Lillie Langtry (1853–1929), society beauty turned actress, went
into stage management and put on *Antony and Cleopatra* at the Princess's.
Though lavish, the production was apparently as tasteless and heavy-handed
as *Punch*'s review of it. I have retained the original title.

stage, if it so pleased him.

For its *mise-en-scene* alone the revival should attract all London. But there is more than this—there is the clever and careful impersonation of *Enobarbus* by His Gracious Heaviness, Mr. ARTHUR STIRLING; then there is a lighter-comedy touch in the courteous and gentlemanly rendering of *Octavius Caesar* by Mr. F. KEMBLE COOPER—one of the best things in the piece, but from the inheritor of two such good old theatrical names, much is expected. And then there is the *Mark Antony* of Mr. CHARLES COGHLAN, a rantin', roarin' boy, this *Antony*, whom no one, I believe, could ever have made really effective; and finally, Her Graceful Majesty, Mrs. LANGTRY, Queen of Egyptian Witchery. Now honestly I do not consider *Cleopatra* a good part, nor is the play a good play for the matter of that. I believe it never has been a success, but if, apart from the really great attraction of gorgeous spectacular effects, there is any one scene above another which might well draw all London, it is the death of *Cleopatra*, which to my mind is— after the fall of WOLSEY, and a long way after, too—one of the most pathetic pictures ever presented on the stage. So lonely in her grandeur, so grand, and yet so pitiable in her loneliness is this poor Queen of Beauty, this Empress-Butterfly, who can conquer conquerors, and for whose sake not only her noble lovers, but her poor humble serving-maids, are willing to die.

Her last scene is beyond all compare her best, and to those who are inclined to be disappointed with the play after the First Act is over, I say, 'Wait for the end,' and don't leave until the Curtain has descended on that gracious figure of the Queen of Egypt, attired in her regal robes crowned with her diadem, holding her sceptre, but dead in her chair of state. *Ça donne à penser.*

Punch, December 6, 1890

'Antony and Cleopatra' in Manchester[1]

20 March, 1897

Mr Calvert's Antony is rugged, forcible, and effective. It lacks elevation, and is not very strong in diction; but it has

---

[1] Original title. The production was by Louis Calvert (Anthony) whose father Charles had presented a mangled version of the play in London 30 years earlier.

plenty of impetuosity and vitality. Cleopatra is perhaps the most overwhelming character in all drama—not, indeed, the most difficult to *act*, but the most impossible to *be*. The imagination of ages has dwelt upon this woman until it has not so much idealised as deified her. Not Helen herself has assumed in our thoughts such superhuman proportions. In defiance of reason and even of history, we endue her with the greatness of her great lovers.

> 'Did I, Charmian,
> Ever love Caesar so?'

is a terrible phrase to live up to; and yet the greatest of her lovers was not Caesar, not Pompey, not Antony, but the man who said of her:

> 'Age cannot wither her, nor custom stale
> Her infinite variety,'

and who put on her dying lips such incomparable words as:

> 'Show me, my women, like a queen:—go fetch
> My best attires;—*I am again for Cydnus*,
> *To meet Mark Antony.*'

How simple they are—how obvious, one might almost say—and yet how utterly beyond the reach of any other poet than Shakespeare! As the actress spoke them on Saturday night, they took me by the throat, as it were, with a sense of absolute beauty and miraculous fitness that comes only with the greatest things in literature. To say, then, that Miss Achurch is not the Cleopatra of the imagination is only to say that she is human. But I think she might, in the earlier acts, come nearer the ideal, if she would seize upon the poetry of the part, and let the comedy take care of itself. It is true that there is warrant, and more than warrant, in the text for all her comedy, except one or two touches of by-play which seem to me founded on verbal misconceptions. It is true that the actor who 'boy'd her greatness' in Shakespeare's own day probably went much further than Miss Achurch in the direction of the ludicrous. But just because this side of the part is so plainly marked, I think a modern actress would do well to lay no unnecessary stress upon it, and to concentrate her thoughts on the dignity, the fascination—in a word, the poetry of the character. Miss Achurch seemed to me quite at her best in the last act, where she gave a haggard nobility to the figure of the dying Queen that was original and memorable. Some of her emphases she should either study more or not so much; they are either unconsidered or paradoxical. Why, for instance, should Cleopatra say

'I am fire and air; my other elements
I *give* to baser life'

—as though it were likely that she should sell or lease them? And finally I implore Miss Achurch not to be led astray by a mere misprint in the ordinary editions, but to follow the Folio and the metre and say

'Rather make
My country's high pyrámidës my gibbet.'

'Pyramids' is impossible. The effect of this scene, by the way, would be heightened if the Clown who brings the asps were made a frankly comic personage. Shakespeare knew what he was about in introducing this grim jester. Among the subordinate characters, those which struck me most were the Octavius Caesar of Mr. G. F. Black, a very able performance, and the curiously devoted and almost dog-like Iras of Miss Maria Fauvet.

William Archer, Theatrical World of 1897

Coriolanus

NAHUM Tate and John Dennis both made adaptations of the play, but the version most often performed until well into the 19th century was an amalgam of Shakespeare's play and one by James Thomson. Kean, Macready and Phelps played the title role, the two latter with distinction, but Coriolanus is indelibly associated with John Kemble's interpretation, with his sister Mrs. Siddons playing Volumnia.

An Apple of Discord

By the time his friend and biographer saw this performance, Kemble's first at Covent Garden as Coriolanus, Kemble had already achieved fame in the role, in which he first appeared in February 7, 1789 at Drury Lane.

The winter season of 1806–7 had one proud distinction, great beyond all modern rivalry, the revival, by Mr. Kemble, of Coriolanus. It has given a *cognomen* to Kemble; and remains at the head of his performances, and of the art itself, as one of those felicitous things where the actor is absolutely identified with the part, and it becomes impossible to think of either the character or the man, without reference to each other.

He felt now assured of confirmed influence upon the public; 'Hope brightened his crest,' and expanded his frame, and perhaps neither memory nor picture has, at any time, presented a more heroic figure than Mr. Kemble displayed, when he rushed upon the stage as Caius Marcius, on the 3rd of November 1806.

I certainly, however pleasing it would be to me, shall not go through the character to mark the passages most applauded, and best given. The great Roman lives in the wisest censure, and the tablet of the general memory is inscribed with his perfections. Mr. Kemble fully shares in Coriolanus with Shakspeare himself. But he gave one passage with sublime effect in this play to which Shakspeare can lay no claim—the author of it was the poet of the Seasons. It is addressed by Coriolanus to Aufidius, and is in the last scene:—

> ' 'Tis not for such as thou—so often spared
> By her victorious sword, to speak of ROME
> But with respect, and awful veneration.
> Whate'er her blots, whate'er her giddy factions,
> There is more VIRTUE in one single year
> Of Roman story, than your Volscian annals
> Can boast through ALL your *creeping dark duration*.'[1]

This is indeed the true tone of tragedy; could he have held it, the fame of Rowe would have melted into *thin air* before him.

Nor will I omit one occasion of mentioning the noble woman, who, with sister excellence, performed the mother of Coriolanus. She indeed towered above her sex, and seemed worthy to bear about her the destinies of imperial Rome. From the first line to the last, all was coloured from one abstract principle; that, if Rome was the queen of nations, her sway was only commensurate with her courage. This it was that taught her to glory in the wounds of victory, and to mock the feeble shrinking from the sight of blood.

[1] I have retained the capitals and italics as they may suggest Kemble's distinctive delivery. G. S.

> '*Vol.*—   His bloody brow
> With his mail'd hand then wiping, forth he goes.
> *Vir.*—His bloody brow! O Jupiter, no blood!
> *Vol.*—Away, you fool! it more *becomes* a man,
> Than *gilt* his trophy.'

It really hurts one to remember that persons accomplished like the two great performers just mentioned, should ever have been subjected to insult, particularly at the proudest display of their beautiful and ennobling powers. But on the 18th of the month, at a repetition of this tragedy, and at the very moment when Mrs. Siddons was supplicating as Volumnia, the conqueror, her son, to spare his country; when every eye should have been rivetted to the scene, every ear burning with the pure flame of patriot vehemence— at such a moment an *apple* was thrown upon the stage, and fell between Mrs. Siddons and Mr. Kemble. He did not, nor would I have had him, quite dismiss the *character* he played for the *manager*, but, taking up the apple, he advanced indignantly to the front of the stage, and thus addressed the audience:—

'LADIES AND GENTLEMEN,
'I have been many years acquainted with the benevolence and liberality of a London audience; but we cannot proceed this evening with the performance unless we are protected, especially when *ladies* are thus exposed to insult.'
A person in the gallery called out—'We can't hear.'
'Mr. Kemble, (*with increased spirit*,) I will *raise* my voice, and the GALLERIES shall *hear* me.' (*Great tumult.*)
'This protection is what the AUDIENCE owe it to themselves to *grant*—what the PERFORMERS, for the credit of their profession, have a right to *demand*—and WHAT I will venture so far to *assert*, that, on the part of the PROPRIETORS, I here offer a hundred guineas to any man, who will disclose the *ruffian* who has been guilty of this act.' (A murmur, only in the gallery.)
'I throw myself, Ladies and Gentlemen, upon the high sense of breeding, that distinguishes a London audience; and I hope I shall never be wanting in my duty to the public; but nothing shall induce me to suffer insult.'
The gallery told him that this apple of discord was thrown at some of the disorderly females in the boxes, and only by accident fell upon the stage. Our moral friends, too, sent down a request, that those riotous ladies might be suppressed, and

Mr. Kemble good naturedly promised 'that all possible methods should be taken to keep them in order.' And then the play was finished.

James Boaden, *Life of J. P. Kemble*

A Cooler View of Kemble

JOHN PHILIP KEMBLE as Coriolanus, Covent Garden, 1806.

On the 3rd of November [1806] was acted the Tragedy of *Coriolanus*, altered from Shakspeare. In this play Mr. Kemble appeared in all his glory; the Roman manliness of his face and figure, the haughty dignity of his carriage, and the fire of his eye, conspired to render his Coriolanus one of the most striking performances that was ever exhibited upon the stage. It is thought by many, that this is Mr. Kemble's *chef d'oeuvre*: where several masterpieces are exhibited, it is difficult to

321

select one that shall be considered as best; but we cannot, for ourselves, prefer his Coriolanus, to his Pierre, to his Penruddock, to his Octavian, or to his Hotspur. We will not speak of his performance on the first night; because we thought that, whether through some physical cause, or through the idea that much was expected from him, or wherefore we know not, he rather over-acted the part on that evening. We will rather speak of his performance on the 18th of the month; because a review of that night's entertainment will give us an opportunity of mentioning the unwarrantable insult that was then offered to the theatrical profession.[1] Throughout the character of Coriolanus Mr. Kemble was uniformly great—there was no husbanding of the breath and strength, to produce a great effect at last, and leave the early portion of the play flat and insipid: no tameness on the one hand, nor unnecessary rant upon the other. Perhaps the excellences most prominent were displayed in the canvassing of the people, the remonstrance with Volumnia, and the quarrel with Tullus Aufidius. In that quarrel Mr. Kemble used at first to give Tullus an insulting tap with his finger, which we are happy to state that he has now discontinued: for such an action would be neither suitable to the dignity of Coriolanus, nor tolerable to the spirit of Tullus. There is one piece of pomp and pride which we think Mr. Kemble might dispense with—namely, the throwing away his shield, after the battle, to be carried by one of the leaders: would a Roman commanding officer have carried the shield of another general? Coriolanus could hardly have ventured on so arrogant a proceeding.

*   *   *

Mrs. Siddons, in Volumnia, was all that could be wished, and more than could be expected—from any other actress. But when is it otherwise? Munden's Menenius deserves our panegyric, though he now begins to be a little too broad in his humour. At first he preserved a happier course between patrician dignity and low comedy. Pope, in Tullus Aufidius, has not answered our hopes: he employs, as usual, rather too much whining.

The dresses and spectacle, particularly the ovation in the second act, are classical and beautiful beyond description; and the performance still continues to attract crowded houses, and excite the most rapturous applauses.

Fashionable Magazine, Nov. 1806

[1] See previous extract.

The Last of Kemble

Ludwig Tieck (1773–1853), the German Romantic critic, dramatist and translator of Shakespeare, describes Kemble's farewell performance, at the age of sixty.

On the 23 of June [1817] Kemble appeared upon the stage for the last time, and took leave for ever of the public, which held him in the highest honour, in his most celebrated part, the Coriolanus of Shakespeare. The house was fuller than ever, for no friend of the artist would have missed this evening. Again I must express my regret, that the piece was so unmercifully mangled, and its finest passages cut out; a proceeding the more childish, seeing that they had interpolated a superfluous pageant for the hero's triumphal entry, in the shape of a procession with trophies and eagles, which, entering at the back of the stage, and extending over its whole expanse, consumed a great deal of time.[1] If I cannot agree in regarding the performance as the artist's masterpiece, as his admirers here do, his Wolsey in my opinion being quite as fine, still it is past all question, that Kemble proved himself once more a great actor in many of the scenes. Nobler or more marked expression could not be given to the proud nature of Coriolanus, and figure, look, and voice here stood the artist in excellent stead. His heroic wrath, indeed, seemed too feeble, and his fury failed altogether, because his organ was too weak for these supreme efforts, and the actor had to economise it for the most important passages. Greatest and most exciting of all was the close; without exaggeration it might be pronounced sublime.

*   *   *

When Coriolanus exclaims, 'Hear'st thou, Mars?' and Aufidius says, 'Name not the God, thou boy of tears!' the exclamation 'Ha!' to which Coriolanus gives vent in the height of his rage was terrible. The power and the tones of the following speech, as well as the look and bearing, were indescribable:—

> Measureless liar, thou hast made my heart
> Too great for what contains it. Boy! oh slave!

*   *   *

> Cut me to pieces, Volsces! Men and lads,
> Stain all your edges on me! Boy! False hound!

[1] At the end of Act II, after the victory at Corioli. For a description of Mrs. Siddons in this added scene, see the next extract.

If you have writ your annals true, 'tis there,
That, like an eagle in a dove-cot, I
Fluttered your Volsces in Corioli.
Alone I did it! Boy!

This is the grand feature in the art of the stage, that it can bring out, nay, can create effects so vast, that for the moment our remembrance of every other pleasure that art can give seems feeble, and but a shadow of what the stage can do. True it is, that its manifestations also fleet away like a shadow, leaving no trace behind; and an unsatisfying remembrance of the great moments of delight and rapture fills us with sadness, for no memorial can restore these fleeting phenomena for those who have hung upon them with transport, because all that language or the painter's skill can do are inadequate to portray what the rapt spectator has seen and heard. Therefore it is only fair that the artist should in any case be requited, however poorly, by the loudest applause directly face to face, for he is powerless to preserve even for an instant the product of his genius to tell to a future generation of what quality it was.

Such were the plaudits, the cheers, the shouts of rapture and tears of emotion given to the noble veteran, the honoured favourite, whom the public were never to see again. The loudest outburst of applause I had ever heard, even in Italy, was but feeble, compared to the indescribable din, which, after the curtain fell, arose on every side. There were thousands present, packed closely together, and the huge area of the house was changed as if into one vast machine, which produced a supernatural clangour and jubilation, men and women shouting, clapping, smiting the sides of the boxes might and main, with fans and with sticks, while, to add to the tumult, everybody was making what noise he could with his feet.

After this unheard-of din had lasted for some time Kemble deeply moved and in tears, again came forward. What seemed impossible nevertheless took place, the clamour grew louder and louder, until the tumult of sound aroused the feeling of something awful and sublime. Kemble bowed, and attempted more than once to give utterance to a few words of parting; at length he regained his composure, but was frequently interrupted by his emotion. Not a sound was heard, save from many points a suppressed low sob. And, when he finished, the storm broke forth again with all its force.

Ludwig Tieck, *The Nineteenth Century, February 1880*
(Theodore Martin)

Mrs. Siddons Walks On

In the celebrated triumphal procession at the end of the second act of Coriolanus, *Sarah Siddons shows her dramatic power. Charles Mayne Young (1777–1856) the author's father acted with Kemble and played many Shakespearean roles, being occasionally accused of imitating Kemble.*

'In this procession, and as one of the central figures in it, Mrs. Siddons had to walk. Had she been content to follow in the beaten track of her predecessors in the part, she would have marched across the stage, from right to left, with the solemn, stately, almost funeral, step conventional. But at the time, as she often did, she forgot her own identity. She was no longer Sarah Siddons, tied down to the directions of the prompter's book, or trammelled by old traditions. She was Volumnia, the proud mother of a proud son and conquering hero. So that, when it was time for her to come on, instead of dropping each foot at equi-distance in its place, with mechanical exactitude, and in cadence subservient to the orchestra, deaf to the guidance of her woman's ear, but sensitive to the throbbings of her haughty mother's heart, with flashing eye, and proudest smile, and head erect, and hands pressed firmly on her bosom, as if to repress by manual force its triumphant swellings, she towered above all around, and rolled, and almost reeled across the stage, her very soul, as it were, dilating and rioting in its exultation, until her action lost all grace, and yet became so true to nature, so picturesque, and so descriptive, that pit and gallery sprang to their feet electrified by the transcendent execution of an original conception.'

Rev. J. C. Young,
Memoirs of Charles Mayne Young, 1840

Enter Macready

Macready was the next great Coriolanus after Kemble. This extract describes the first night's performance.

'Mr. Macready by his performance of Coriolanus last night has again won the first honours of the stage. The previous development of this great performer's genius in Richard stripped his last night's enterprise of all its peril and much of its aspiring . . . We have merely room to state that in the scenes where he consents, at the entreaty of his mother, to go back and conciliate the incensed people, and where he gives vent to his scorn and defiance of the tribunes, he gave proofs of variety, flexibility, and power rarely equalled and absolutely un-excelled . . . The quarrel with Aufidius, particularly that passage in which Kemble was so fine—the retort of 'Boy'—produced acclamation . . . There is one grand point in which no other living actor but Mr. Macready can approach Kemble,—we mean the magic power of imposing an illusive image of physical grandeur upon the very sense of the beholder, merely by some slight change of attitude or action. From the death of Coriolanus to the fall of the curtain the house resounded with applause, and in the pit the waving of hats was universal. Mr. Egerton came on to announce the next performance, but was obliged to give way for a general cry of Macready. He did accordingly make his appearance, was received with the liveliest expressions of kindness by the audience, and an-nounced the repetition of "Coriolanus" on Wednesday.'

from the *Morning Herald*, *November 30 1819*
(reprinted in Macready's *Reminiscences*)

In Kemble's Shadow

Edmund Kean's praiseworthy restoration of Shakespeare's text with a few omissions ran for four nights only, at Drury Lane.

Jan. 25, 1820. Mr. Kean made his first appearance in the character of Coriolanus tonight, at this Theatre. The just discrimination—the exquisite knowledge of the human pas-sions, above all the grand and imposing dignity which Mr. Kemble exhibited, almost rendered any attempt at originality in the performance of this character presumptuous and unsuccessful. To have seen him play Coriolanus was an event in every man's life, and no wonder that neither time nor circumstances could efface the precious balm of its recollection. It was here that his measured mode of acting, correct declama-tion, and noble deportment, found a firm basis, and procured for him an exalted reputation: and even those who were quite willing to applaud Mr. Kean's natural and unpremeditated energy, could not be prevailed upon to admit that his Coriolanus would prove successful. They had identified the character with Mr. Kemble; there was but one conception, and one way of executing it, and yet Mr. Kean played it off in his own natural way to the satisfaction of an admiring audience. He portrayed the towering hero, in whose soul the detestation of the 'rabble curs' of Rome had, at one moment, almost extinguished every generous emotion, who in the pursuit of his darling vengeance advanced, in hostile array, even to the walls of his native city, with a spirit and dignity that excited the warmest applause, yet, fastidious as it may appear, we were not entirely pleased. Mr. Kean was a Plebeian, not a Patrician Coriolanus; and he appeared much more like a mob-orator, than a noble Roman. It has, however, been since repeated to crowded audiences with increased effect; and its career of popularity only interrupted by the mournful bereavements which the nation so sincerely deplores.[1] We have only to add, that the other characters were mostly well-sustained, the scenery and appointments were extremely splendid, and that in the play itself the text of Shakespeare is restored, and all interpolations omitted, which latter arrangement is by George Soane, Esq.

European Magazine

Truth and Harmony

Mr. Phelps has opened the campaign with two plays of Shakespeare—*As You Like It* and *Coriolanus*. *Coriolanus* I have been to see,[2] and here as ever the first mention is due to the whole truth and harmony of the representation. The actors are all in accord together; and although the company includes few bright particular stars, yet each does justice to the dignity of his profession. Mr. Barrett is a genial and genuine Menenius Agrippa; Mr. Herman Vezin, a new member of the company, who, I believe, has earned honours as first tragedian in a transpontine house, is a discreet and serious Aufidius, who mars nothing by errors of commission, and errs only on the hopeful side by under-acting his part. The Roman mob, admirably grouped and disciplined, cannot easily be represented by a better first citizen than Mr. Lewis Ball.

The little part of the domestic friend and gossip of the women in the hero's household is spoken delightfully by Mrs. Marston. Miss Kate Saxon, an intelligent actress, who

[1] The death of George III.

[2] On September 22, 1860 at Sadler's Wells. Phelps produced the play on four occasions, the first time in 1848.

supplies one of the losses of the company, delivers with all due simplicity the few sentences that fall to her lot as the wife of Coriolanus, and expresses quietly by her stage-bearing the modest, faithful gentleness that follows, strong in love, the warrior's career. As the proud mother of the prouder son, Miss Atkinson also labours her best, but she does not achieve her best. When she desires with face and gesture to express scorn, it not seldom happens that she fails to suggest more than intensity of spite. For this reason her Volumnia is wanting in some of the dignity with which the character has been invested by the poet. It is a hard trial, no doubt, to measure the expression of a Roman mother's pride with the show of pride that a man can put into the part of Coriolanus. Pride, after all, is not a woman's passion, for what passes by the name is often vanity.

The pride of Coriolanus is heroic, and is a man's pride, from which vanity is altogether absent. His own praises are irksome in his ears. That which he is, he is; and it is little in his simple estimation of himself, for he esteems himself by what he feels the power of becoming. Upon comparisons between himself and the base multitude he never wastes a thought. It matters not at what level other men are content to dwell; his mind abides on its own heights. Thus when Caius Marcius in the camp, beset with irksome praises that he is compelled to hear, is named Coriolanus, and there is added to this honour the exhortation 'Bear the addition nobly ever', Mr. Phelps represents him stirred by the warning into a large sense of what is in his soul, and lifted upon tiptoe by his soaring thought. The same action gives grandeur to the words,

'I'd rather be their servant in my way
Than sway with them in theirs,'

and is afterwards more than once used, not ostentatiously, and never without giving the emphasis intended.

As in the action of the piece, that pomp of processions with the constant noise of drum and trumpet, which in the good old days of the drama formed a prominent part of the play, is subdued, and made to follow instead of leading the march of the poem, so in the action of Coriolanus himself it is remembered that heroic pride is self-contained.

* * *

The expulsion of Coriolanus from Rome is presented in a capital stage-picture by the grouping of the mob, and here the actor's reading of his part is marked very distinctly. He had been wrung by the urgency of his friends and the commands of his mother to attempt to flatter into quiet the excited mob. The attempt to do this is presented with all signs of suppressed passion, and impatient, yet in itself almost heroic, endurance of what is really intense torture. When the tribune calls Coriolanus traitor, he recoils as from a blow, and lets his wrath have way. But when the mob raising their staves expel him from the city, he mounts proudly the steps from which as from his mental height he looks down on them, and he is lord of himself, lord as he feels of Rome. With a sublimity of disdain he retorts on them that 'I banish you', which Edmund Kean erred in delivering with an ungovernable passion.

The scenic effect of the view of Antium by the light of the rising moon, when the banished Coriolanus haunts the door of Aufidius, his deadly enemy, is contrived to give colour to the poetry. But there is no scene in the play more impressive to the eye than the succeeding picture of the muffled figure of Coriolanus, seated by the glowing embers of the brazier that represents his enemy's hearth.

* * *

I must not dwell much longer upon this performance. Let me add only that the meaning of the heroic close furnished by Shakespeare to the play is well brought out at Sadler's Wells. The lofty pride that when defied by Rome had defied Rome herself, and was to set a foot upon the neck of the world's ruler, had, after painful struggle, knelt at the voice of a mother, yielding nobly when to yield was dangerous, if not mortal. When Coriolanus has attained his greatest height, Aufidius, fallen to his lowest, has sunk into a dastardly chief of assassins. All hearts are thus secured for sympathy with the pride with which, as Mr. Phelps shows us, the hero resents the taunt of an enemy basely triumphant. His whole frame enlarges, and his hands press on the expanding breast, as he cries,

'Measureless liar, thou hast made my heart
Too great for what contains it!'

And so at last the loftiness of his disdain carries all sympathies with it when he whets the swords of the conspirators by telling them

'How, like an eagle in a dovecote, I
Fluttered your Volsces in Corioli:
Alone I did it.—Boy!'

Henry Morley, *Journal of a London Playgoer*

329

Pericles

T HERE is a good deal of evidence for the popularity of this play when it was first produced, and it was the first Shakespeare play to be presented when the theatre reopened at the Restoration. Since then, performances of the original play have been few, but Samuel Phelps was responsible for a notably spectacular production at Sadler's Wells in October, 1854.

Splendour Governed by Taste

Samuel Phelps' revival, which apparently eliminated Gower, was otherwise fairly faithful to Shakespeare. It opened at Sadler's Wells in October 1854.

In telling such a story as this, Shakespeare felt—and young as he may have been, his judgment decided rightly—that it should be shown distinctly as a tale such as

'Hath been sung at festivals,
On Ember eves and holy ales';

and he therefore brought forward Gower himself very much in the character of an Eastern story-teller to begin the narrative and to carry it on to the end, subject to the large interruption of five acts of dramatic illustration. A tale was being told; every person was to feel that, although much of it would be told to the eye. But in the revival of the play, Mr. Phelps was left to choose between two difficulties. The omission of Gower would be a loss to the play, in an artistic sense, yet the introduction of Gower before every act would very probably endanger its effect in a theatrical sense, unless the part were spoken by an actor of unusual power. The former plan was taken; and in adding to certain scenes in the drama passages of his own writing, strictly confined to the explanation of those parts of the story which Shakespeare represents Gower as narrating

330

between the acts, Mr. Phelps may have used his best judgment as a manager. Certainly, unless he could have been himself the Gower as well as the Pericles of the piece, the frequent introduction of a story-telling gentleman in a long coat and long curls would have been an extremely hazardous experiment, even before such an earnest audience as that at Sadler's Wells.

The change did inevitably, to a certain extent, disturb the poetical effect of the story; but assuming its necessity, it was effected modestly and well. The other changes also were in no case superfluous, and were made with considerable judgment. The two scenes at Mitylene, which present Marina pure as an ermine that no filth can touch, were compressed into one; and although the plot of the drama was not compromised by a false delicacy, there remained not a syllable at which true delicacy could have conceived offence. The calling of Blount and his Mistress was covered in the pure language of Marina with so hearty a contempt, that the scene was really one in which the purest minds might be those which would take the most especial pleasure.

The conception of the character of Pericles by Mr. Phelps seemed to accord exactly with the view just taken of the play. He was the Prince pursued by evil fate. A melancholy that could not be shaken off oppressed him even in the midst of the gay court of King Simonides, and the hand of Thaisa was received with only the rapture of a love that dared not feel assured of its good fortune. Mr. Phelps represented the Prince sinking gradually under the successive blows of fate, with an unostentatious truthfulness; but in that one scene which calls forth all the strength of the artist, the recognition of Marina and the sudden lifting of the Prince's bruised and fallen spirit to an ecstasy of joy, there was an opportunity for one of the most effective displays of the power of an actor that the stage, as it now is, affords. With immense energy, yet with a true feeling for the pathos of the situation that had the most genuine effect, Mr. Phelps achieved in this passage a triumph marked by plaudit after plaudit. They do not applaud rant at Sadler's Wells. The scene was presented truly by the actor and felt fully by his audience.

The youthful voice and person, and the quiet acting of Miss Edith Heraud, who made her *début* as Marina, greatly helped to set forth the beauty of that scene. The other parts had also been judiciously allotted, so that each actor did what he or she was best able to do, and did it up to the full measure of the ability of each. Miss Cooper gave much effect to the scene of

331

the recovery of Thaisa, which was not less well felt by those who provided the appointments of the stage, and who marked that portion of the drama by many delicacies of detail.

Of the scenery indeed it is to be said that so much splendour of decoration is rarely governed by so pure a taste. The play, of which the text is instability of fortune, has its characteristic place of action on the sea. Pericles is perpetually shown (literally as well as metaphorically) tempest-tost, or in the immediate vicinity of the treacherous water; and this idea is most happily enforced at Sadler's Wells by scene-painter and machinist. They reproduce the rolling of the billows and the whistling of the winds when Pericles lies senseless, a wrecked man on a shore. When he is shown on board ship in the storm during the birth of Marina, the ship tosses vigorously. When he sails at last to the temple of Diana of the Ephesians, rowers take their places on their banks, the vessel seems to glide along the coast, an admirably-painted panorama slides before the eye, and the whole theatre seems to be in the course of actual transportation to the temple at Ephesus, which is the crowning scenic glory of the play. The dresses, too, are brilliant. As beseems an Eastern story, the events all pass among princes. Now the spectator has a scene presented to him occupied by characters who appear to have stepped out of a Greek vase; and presently he looks into an Assyrian palace and sees figures that have come to life and colour from the stones of Nineveh. There are noble banquets and glittering processions, and in the banquet-hall of King Simonides there is a dance which is a marvel of glitter, combinations of colour, and quaint picturesque effect. There are splendid trains of courtiers, there are shining rows of vestal virgins, and there is Diana herself in the sky.

We are told that the play of *Pericles* enjoyed, for its own sake, when it first appeared, a run of popularity that excited the surprise and envy of some playwrights, and became almost proverbial. It ceased to be acted in the days of Queen Anne; and whether it would attract now as a mere acted play, in spite of the slight put upon it by our fathers and grandfathers, it is impossible to say, since the *Pericles* of Sadler's Wells may be said to succeed only because it is a spectacle.

Henry Morley, Journal of a London Playgoer

Cymbeline

S I M O N Forman saw the play some time before September 1611 and it was performed before Charles I and Queen Henrietta Maria in 1634. At the Restoration, D'Urfey's adaptation, *The Injured Princess* supplanted the original more or less completely till 1746. Posthumus was a favourite role of Garrick, and in 1785 Sarah Siddons made a memorable Imogen to John Kemble's Posthumus. Macready is said to have made a fine Iachimo in 1820.

Kemble and Mrs. Siddons

The benefits of Mrs. Siddons usually presented some interesting novelty to the public; her first night, the 29th January, 1787, she acted Imogen in the really *romantic* drama of Cymbeline. A taste which I will neither censure nor examine on the present occasion calls upon females, who assume the male habit, for a more complete display of the figure, than suits the decorum of a delicate mind. Mrs. Siddons assumed as little of the man as possible; so that her most powerful scenes were those in the dress of her sex. I have said what was wanting in the Imogen of Mrs. Jordan. In Mrs. Siddons it was all to be seen in the utmost perfection. Her scene with Iachimo, I am satisfied, was never approached. The variety of her manner and expression was quite astonishing: the reluctant reception of the imputations as to her lord's fidelity, the detection of the villainy, the scorn of her virtuous indignation, and the dignity with which she called upon Pisanio, to relieve her from the wretch who had too long 'abused her credulous ears,' were triumphs even for Mrs. Siddons. I freely admit, that in the scenes of disguise, a form less majestic, while it indicated more fragility, bespoke more sympathy; and that a figure nearer to that of a boy, would, by increasing the visible probability, have heightened her effect with her brothers in the cave. But I have balanced fairly the *pour et contre*, and preserve a very lively sense of so exquisite a performance. Mr. Kemble was, by a thousand degrees, the best Posthumus of my time. It was a learned, judicious, and in the fine burst upon Iachimo at the close, a most powerful effort; and such it continued through his theatric life. Among the many excellencies of my departed friend, one, which strongly impresses me at the present moment, was that admirable skill which kept the utmost vehemence from the remotest appearance of rant. His voice, though not what could be considered powerful, was exquisitely modulated through its whole compass; it was never for a moment harsh or out of scale: and this may beget a reasonable surprise at the general applause which has attended *certain* efforts in this difficult art; where the most discordant noises have at times rendered the ear doubtful, whether such sounds could proceed from a human organ.

James Boaden, *Life of Kemble*

Mrs. Worthington on Stage

March 1797

Mrs. Worthington appeared the first time on any Stage at Drury Lane, in the character of Imogen, in *Cymbeline*. Her person is elegant, her face pleasing, and not without expression, and her manner interesting. She was however, so much affected on her entrance, that, notwithstanding the cheering plaudits of the audience, she was for a considerable time unable to proceed. Her great defect appeared to be want of sufficient powers of voice. On a smaller Theatre she may perhaps be more successful.

European Magazine

Kemble in Decline[1]

On his first entrance John Kemble reminded me by his noble presence, his stature, and speaking expressive face of our excellent Heinrich Jacobi. . . . The English themselves admit that, even when he was young, the part of Posthumus was one of his weakest; how much more now! His voice is weak and tremulous, but full of expression, and there is a ring of feeling and intelligence in every word, only much too strongly marked, and between every second and third word there comes a pause, and most of the verses or speeches end in a high key. . . . In consequence of this tedious style of delivery the piece, even though probably one half of it was cut out, lasted an unusual time. This, so to speak, musical declamation was incompatible

[1] Tieck saw Kemble at Covent Garden on May 30, 1817.

with all real acting, nay, in a certain degree made it impossible; for when everything is made to depend on little *nuances* of speaking, and every monologue and every single passage is sought to be rounded off into an artistic whole, any delineation of character, of the ebb and flow of passion and feeling, is out of the question. Here and there one saw the great master; for example, in the second Act, when Iachimo after his return tells how he has succeeded; the despair, mingled with rage, the kindling of fresh hope, and the falling back into comfortless anguish, were admirably given, and one could see clearly that if Kemble had not succumbed to mannerism, and a one-sided school, he would have been a truly great actor.

Ludwig Tieck, *The Nineteenth Century, February 1880*
(Theodore Martin)

Italian Subtlety and Roman Strength[1]

Oct. 18. [1820]. Shakespeare's *'Cymbeline'* was revived to-night with considerable novelty in its *cast*. Iachimo was Macready, Posthumus C. Kemble, and Imogen Miss Foote. The performance was of course well sustained, and received with all the applause which a London audience is in the habit of giving to its favourites. As a drama, *'Cymbeline'* is inferior to the majority of its author's plays, though containing passages of beauty fully equal to the highest successes of Shakspeare's poetry. The character of Imogen is among the most graceful of human imaginations; and the love-sick complainings, the gentle joys, and tender troubles of 'that most rare boy,' fill the spirit with exquisite pictures of melancholy and passion. The character was well looked by Miss Foote, and well played where she was audible. But her voice was inferior to her conception, and an important portion of the dialogue was lost. The fault is formidable, but it is only the more necessary to be corrected. Macready's Iachimo was a fine performance, full of Italian subtlety and Roman strength, and was greatly applauded. This is probably the chief character of the play, and he went through it with a due sense of its importance. Kemble's Posthumus had the grace, the purity, and the interest of his habitual style, but Posthumus palters too doubtfully between affection and revenge, is too

[1] Macready's Iachimo (to Charles Kemble's Posthumus) at Covent Garden was much applauded.

lightly deceived, and too severe in vindication of his honour to be a favourite but through the ability of his representative. Connor was Pisanio, and he made more of the part than is usual. Abbott, Duruset, and Chapman, bore the parts of the old hunter and the royal youths. Farley was a bustling Cloten, and Egerton sustained the Majesty of Britain with becoming gravity. The allusions to Imogen's culpability and Italian deceit, were, of course, caught up in reference to present proceedings[1], and excited much applause, mingled, however, with much hissing, where the division of opinion appeared nearly equal. Some of the lines thus lauded in the recital were certainly appropriate enough, though the characters thereby intended to be placed in comparison are not, we conceive, throughout entirely similar: Imogen is young, and gentle, and beautiful, and pious—she is represented pure as 'dreams of angels are,' and unsuspicious of others, because she knows herself to be above all suspicion. '*She is punished for her truth,*' though but one earthly object has a place in her innocent heart, and reverence for the Gods alone divides it with affection for her husband. Now this immaculate simplicity of Imogen certainly, in our opinion, appears rather as a contrast than a parallel to ———; but, we beg pardon: we are writing a theatrical critique, not a political disquisition; and we conclude with stating, that the house was crowded to an overflow, and that the play was re-announced amidst the loudest applause.

Unidentified newspaper cutting
(Birmingham Shakespeare Library)

Eloquent To Our Eyes[2]

November 5 [1864].—At Drury Lane the reappearance of Miss Helen Faucit brought us *Cymbeline*; for Imogen, the most beautiful of Shakespeare's female characters, is that in which this lady seems most to delight and to excel, and with this she desired, in returning to the London stage of which she was some years since a chief ornament, to make her first impression. The play had been formerly acted at Drury Lane with very good scenery of its own, so that on its recent revival it was found to

[1] A reference to the trial of Queen Caroline, who was accused, among other things, of an intrigue with an Italian coachman.

[2] Helen Faucit first played Imogen in 1837 and was acclaimed as Mrs. Siddons' natural successor in the role.

be in all respects well mounted, and the acting did not greatly impede the sense in following the exquisite freedom of the poet's fancy through the swiftly changing scene of British court and Roman camp and royalty of man in savage mountain-life. No mortal actors, perhaps, can fitly speak the lament of Guiderius and Arviragus over the body of Fidele. There was inevitably much that jarred in the representation. But Miss Faucit was on the whole well supported, and she had Mr. Phelps for Posthumus and Mr. Creswick for Iachimo, parts that no living actors could have better filled. In its tenderness and grace of womanhood, in the simple piety that looks to the gods when Imogen commits herself to rest or is about to read a letter from her husband, in the wife's absolute love and perfect innocence, void of false shame, slow to believe ill, strong to resist it, Miss Faucit's Imogen is eloquent to our eyes, even when she fails, now and then, to satisfy our ears. She is an actress trained in the school of the Kembles, careful to make every gesture an embodiment of thought, too careful sometimes, as when, after the cry, 'What ho, Pisanio!' she remains with upraised arm throughout half the speech of Iachimo that begins 'O happy Leonatus!' There is a graver fault of excess in the first part of the representation of womanly fear when, as Fidele, she calls at the mouth of the unoccupied cavern, and runs from the sound herself had made. The warning of her error might be found in the fact that her pantomime here excites rather general laughter, where surely Shakespeare never meant that even the dullest boor should grin. But that short sin of excess is followed by the entry into the cavern, which is made most charmingly.

Miss Faucit's voice is more often at fault; it fails her whenever she has a violent emotion to express, and passion sounds often like petulance. The voice may not obey the prompting of the will, or there may be defect of that higher dramatic genius which can make words sound as 'thoughts that breathe'. Whatever be the cause, she fails to express by voice such phases of the character of Imogen as we have in the scene with Pisanio near Milford Haven. Yet where the mere emotion to be expressed is more tender than violent she attains often—though even then, perhaps, with a too visible art—to the utmost delicacy of expression. An example of this is in her picture to Pisanio of how she would have strained her eye to look on her departing lord,

'till he had melted from

337

The smallness of a gnat *to air; and then*
Have turned mine eye and wept.'

The sense of the final vanishing, and of the tears that
follow it, is here exquisitely rendered by the actress.

Henry Morley, *Journal of a London Playgoer*

Ellen Terry's Imogen

Henry James, not generally one of her admirers, praises Ellen Terry.

Those lovers of the theatre with whom it is a complaint that
they are not more often treated to Shakespeare encounter in
Cymbeline one of those stumbling-blocks with which the path of
this particular regret is not unplentifully strewn: it brings them
face to face with so many of the questions that flutter up in the
presence of all attempts to put the plays to the proof of the contemporary stage. None of them practically takes so little
account as *Cymbeline* of the general effort of the theatre of our
day to hug closer and closer the scenic illusion. The thing is a
florid fairytale, of a construction so loose and unpropped that
it can scarce be said to stand upright at all, and of a psychological sketchiness that never touches firm ground, but plays,
at its better times, with an indifferent shake of golden locks, in
the high, sunny air of delightful poetry. Here it disports itself
beyond the reach of all challenge. Meanwhile the mere action
swings, like a painted cloth in the wind, between England and
Italy, flapping merrily back and forth and in and out,
alternately crumpling up the picture and waving it in the blue.
It is these latter charming moments, of so happy a fairy-tale
quality, that tempt the producer. This is so much the case with
all the moments allotted to Imogen, that it was inevitable the
play should sooner or later be attempted by a manager so
fortunate as to command the services of Miss Ellen Terry. As
Mr. Irving gives it, he gives it frankly for Miss Terry's sake,
contenting himself with a very moderate personal chance.

So far as she is concerned he gives it with great success; no
part that she has played of late years is so much of the exact fit
of her particular gifts. Her performance is naturally poetic, has
delightful breadth and tenderness, delightful grace and youth.
Youth above all—Miss Terry has never, without effort, been so
young and so fresh. Short-skirted and free, crowned with roses by
Mr. Alma-Tadema's hand, and dressed in the unmistakable

'note' of one of that painter's learned visions, she is exactly the heroine demanded by an old-time story for a circle—not too critical—round the fire. That is the formula of *Cymbeline,* and Mr. Irving has accepted it without making difficulties. The spirit in which he has accommodated himself to the question of mounting shows the happy tact of not taking any part of the business too seriously. He has had the co-operation of Mr. Alma-Tadema, and Mr. Tadema, it is true, is nothing if not archaeological; but by avoiding an aggressive solidity the documentary stamp, the 'reconstruction' as it were, has been kept in the right key—the key of the amusing. The Britons are figures on a tapestry, the Romans are figures on a mock triumphal arch, and as the play never leaves us for many minutes in one place, the place is indulgently impressionistic. When Romans and Britons meet, at the end, in the shock of battle, the carnage is as merry a game as all the rest. When Iachimo, at dead of night, emerges from the trunk in Imogen's room, hovers about her bed; takes off her bracelet, and catalogues at his leisure the items of proof by which he shall win his wager, we are in an order of things as delightfully idle as the verse in which he subsequently retails his observations:

> '*The chimney*
> *Is south the chamber; and the chimney-piece*
> *Chaste Dian, bathing.'*

Imogen, in a soft lamp-light that seems to confound itself with the radiance of her purity, sleeps under the protection of this goddess, and that of a cloud canopy, which, like the curtain in an old-fashioned portrait, is vaguely caught up to where

> '*The roof o' the chamber*
> *With golden cherubim is fretted;'*

and when her gentlewoman has retired, and the lid of the big gruesome box has begun slowly to rise, we feel the thrill of early years, a shudder almost pantomimic. There is not much to be done with Iachimo but to make him picturesque, and Mr. Irving wisely lets him abound in the sense of his villany, qualified as it is by the quaintness of a masquerade, of which the 'happy ending' is 'pardon's the word for all.' He gives the character the benefit of his great art of visible composition—a duskiness of romance, an eccentricity of distinction—and is content to let it, so far as it *is* a character, profit by the half-reluctant good humour into which we settle when the story, at once so disagreeable and so pretty, brings us at last to Milford Haven and the delightful cave in Wales. Why should the reprobate Roman be more 'natural' than the lamentable Briton? The Kembles and Keans and Macreadys used, I believe, to amuse themselves in their lighter hours with Posthumus, but he can scarcely be said to be first-rate sport— there is still less to be done with him than with Iachimo. The wicked queen is a fine scarlet patch, which Miss Geneviève Ward keeps full in the light; she is like some vivified portrait-bust of the Vatican or the Capitol, some hard, high-frizzled Agrippina or Faustina. But there is no great sport for any one save Imogen till we reach the fourth act, which fairly hums, like a bee among flowers, with the spirit of poetry. Belarius in his cave, the hidden young princes—with the Briton's love of sport—in their goat-skins, the frightened Fidele, the decapitated Cloten, the clothes of Posthumus, the invading Romans, the enchanting verse, make a sweet jumble, from which even the footlights can scarcely brush the bloom. Italy crops up in a sense still different from that of 'the legions garrisoned in Gallia' —even those who come under the conduct of 'bold Iachimo, Sienna's brother.' The whole scene becomes a carnival procession, a fantasy of the Renaissance. Miss Terry, as Fidele, grows younger and younger, and in her beautiful melancholy boy's dress shows admirably that the more chance she has for freedom of motion the more easily she surmounts its dangers. Her immense naturalness throughout the character is of the highest value, through its enabling her to throw all her weight, without any of the arts usually employed to that end, into the positive innocence of it—that of the young wife youthfully in love with her absent husband. The impulsiveness of this innocence, breaking out in confident high spirits, draws, by its vivid opposition to the evil that is believed of her, the one happy effect that *can* be drawn from the foolish story of the husband's instantaneous surrender. But everything in *Cymbeline* is instantaneous—doubt and faith, love and hate, recognition and despair, damnation and forgiveness, victory and defeat— everything, down to the lively congruity of the figures with old, vague, but remembered, pictorial types—a sort of success that is stamped with the *coup de pouce* of Mr. Tadema and the great scenic art of Mr. Irving.

Henry James, *Harper's Weekly, November 21, 1896*

The Winter's Tale

THERE were seven performances of the play at court before the theatres were closed in 1642. But for the next 100 years there is no record of a performance. In 1756, Garrick reduced the play to the story of Florizel and Perdita, which apparently was good enough for audiences for the next 50 years. Kemble was acclaimed as Leontes and Sarah Siddons' Hermione was her last new Shakespearean role. In 1856 Charles Kean presented a spectacular version of the play, historically and architecturally accurate to the last detail, assuming that when Shakespeare wrote of an imaginary Bohemia he was thinking of a real Bithynia.

A Muse in Profile

It was on the 24th of the month that Mr. Kemble presented his revival of the *Winter's Tale*, in all the splendor of decoration and power of acting, that he could impress upon it. I have already remarked the studies of Mrs. Siddons after the antique; in Paulina's chapel, she now stood one of the noblest statues, that even Grecian taste ever invented. The figure composed something like one of the muses in profile. The drapery was ample in its folds, and seemingly stony in its texture. Upon the magical words, pronounced by Paulina, 'Music; awake her: strike;' the sudden action of the head absolutely *startled*, as though such a miracle had really vivified the marble; and the descent from the pedestal was equally graceful and affecting. In Leontes Mr. Kemble was every thing that either feeling or taste could require; and the affection of Paulina never had a representative equal to Mrs. Powell. The Perdita was a very delicate and pretty young lady of the name of Hickes, thus much I remember of her; but whether she had more or fewer requisites than other candidates for this lovely character, I am now unable to decide.

James Boaden, *Life of Kemble*

Grandeur of Effect

The Winter's Tale is one of the best-acting of our author's plays. We remember seeing it with great pleasure many years ago. It was on the night that King[1] took leave of the stage, when he and Mrs. Jordan played together in the after-piece of the Wedding-day. Nothing could go off with more *éclat*, with more spirit, and grandeur of effect. Mrs. Siddons played Hermione, and in the last scene acted the painted statue to the life—with true monumental dignity and noble passion; Mr. Kemble, in Leontes, worked himself up into a very fine classical phrensy; and Bannister, as Autolycus, roared as loud for pity as a sturdy beggar could do who felt none of the pain he counterfeited, and was sound of wind and limb. We shall never see these parts so acted again; or if we did, it would be in vain. Actors grow old, or no longer surprise us by their novelty. But true poetry, like nature, is always young; and we still read the courtship of Florizel and Perdita, as we welcome the return of spring, with the same feelings as ever.

William Hazlitt, *Characters of Shakespeare's Plays, 1817*

A Tale of Bithynia

Charles Kean's lavish production carried the passion for historical and geographical exactitude to the length of identifying Bohemia with Bithynia. A contemporary witness tells us that the bear chased Antigonus 'with peculiar zest' while the programme note solemnly informed the audience that 'the existence of bears in the East, is exemplified in the second chapter of the Second Book of Kings'.

Princess'.—The production of Shakspeare's 'Winter's Tale,' with proper scenic accessories and illustrations, took place as announced on Monday evening, and was most enthusiastically received by a fashionable and distinguished audience—her Majesty being present. The house was excessively crowded, but the utmost attention prevailed. Mr. Kean's taste has produced results which must be highly satisfactory to every judicious mind. The play was well selected for spectacular interpretation, for not only does it overflow with the most exquisite poetry, but as a drama it is full of interest and character—touching, various, and picturesque; and was evidently designed by the author himself for the introduction

[1] Tom King (1730–1804) made his last appearance in 1802.

THE STATUE SCENE, from Charles Kean's production of *The Winter's Tale*, Princess's, 1856 (*Illustrated London News*).

of pageantry. The hints for this are extant on the poet's page. Thus in the pastoral scenes he has the circumstances for introducing a Dionysian revel, and has carried it out most admirably, painting the Bacchant enthusiasm and madness to the life, and stimulating the spectator with the inspiration of orgies the classicality of which preserves their 'beauty as a joy for ever,' and gives even to animal appetite the consecration of genius. Another opportunity has been taken in regard to the Chorus, under the name of 'Time,' with which Shakspeare directs the fourth act to commence, in order to account for the lapse of sixteen years. Mr. Kean has chosen the classical figure of Chronos, surmounting the ascending globe, and associated with kindred pictorial conceptions, allegorical in their nature, personifying Luna and the stars, as sinking before the chariot of Phoebus, which rises in all its glory—the figures being supplied by the antique and the works of Flaxman. Great use is made throughout the performance, of *tableaux vivants*, which serve to inaugurate the sustained scenes, and present the manner of life among the Greeks and in Asia Minor, as we have already stated, adopting the suggestion of Sir Thomas Hanmer. Mr. Kean, instead of Bohemia, has accepted Bithynia as the place intended by the poet and the novelist—a good suggestion on many accounts, and enabling

343

the manager to present the pastoral peculiarities and social condition of that primitive state. Here the costumes are very skilfully chosen, and the introduction of camels, sheep, and goats, add a picturesque beauty to the scenic panorama, much to be commended. Nor are the manners of Sicilia and Syracuse left without copious illustration. Witness the pyrrhic dance, as introduced at the feast solemnised prior to the departure of Polixenes, with its accompanying music, all appropriately in keeping. The 'Hymn to Apollo' is played during the progress of the banquet; and the authority of Dr. Burney and others is accepted for the style and character of the music in general. We have especially to commend the arrangement of the trial scene, which is made to take place in the theatre of Syracuse before the assembled people, and is accompanied with the solemnities of religion, and consecrated by the presence of an altar and the Ark of the Oracle. Instead of breaking up this scene at the termination of the trial, as is commonly done, the set is properly continued to the re-entrance of Paulina, and its sacred accessories are called into play for aiding the histrionic business of the situation. This scene is indeed very beautiful, perfect, and complete. Information on the subject of the music is very sparse, but the utmost has been made of it by Mr. J. L. Hatton, to whom the public are indebted for the overture, *entr'actes*, and incidental airs, that add to the graces of the present performance. While mentioning the names of persons whose talents or learning have conduced to the various beauties of this dramatic diorama, we may add that Mr. Kean acknowledges the aid received by him from Geo. Godwin, Esq., F.R.S., who has superintended the architectural portions, and from Geo. Scharf, Esq., Jun., F.S.A., who has contributed many of the most important general details throughout, and in particular his private drawings, taken on the spot, of the vegetation peculiar to Bithynia; thus devoting them to the grateful and genial purpose of illustrating this great Shakspearian revival. We might have said 'the greatest,' without exaggeration, for not only has Mr. Kean surpassed his former efforts in the accuracy and splendour of the *mise en scène*, but the acting of the drama throughout is worthy of the occasion.

Mr. Charles Kean's representation of Leontes is one of those minute studies in which, as in his great Shakspearean characters and his Louis XI., he stands unrivalled. Shakspeare has been careful, by altering many of the details in Robert Greene's novel, to lend a dignity to the part which is not to be found in

CHARLES KEAN as Leontes and ELLEN TERRY (1847–1928) as Mamillius
in *The Winter's Tale*, Princess's, 1856.

the 'Docastus and Fawnia,' and thus to preserve for him a
title to our respect, notwithstanding his groundless jealousy.
Mr. Kean has been mindful of this, and was rightfully solicitous
to display at full the sentiment of justice with which the most

345

harsh of his actions was attended. The moral greatness of the
King, however, comes out, in his repentance, in which we see
the truly loving man, who had been so sorely tried for the
habitual want of discipline in regulating the passions to which
he was liable. We know of nothing finer on the modern stage
than Mr. Kean's interpretation of the banquet-scene in the
first act. His fondness for his boy Mamillius, expressed in tones
of the most exquisite pathos, went to the heart of the audience.
Perhaps there is no scene superior to this in all the range of the
great characters which Mr. Kean has made his own; the hero
has to perform a double part—to amuse his child, while watching with jealous eagerness his wife's behaviour to Polixenes.
His sudden exclamation, intended alike as a relief to his own
feelings and a rebuke to Hermione, 'Are you my boy,
Mamillius?' was startling from its cruel meaning and terrible
accent. In the subsequent conversation with Camillo, and the
concluding soliloquy, Mr. Kean attained a climax of eloquent
declamation, and retired amidst prolonged and well merited
plaudits.

Mrs. Kean's Hermione was always a great performance. It
has lost nothing of its remarkable pathos, and has gained much
by the beauties that are now added. The new arrangements
of the stage give rise to new developments of action, and in all
these Mrs. Kean manifested a delightful originality, and a
truth of feeling that at once penetrates the heart. Her intuitions
are ever in fine harmony with the grace and sentiment of
nature; and her expression of them is set off by an elocution
the music of which is inimitable. There are tones in this which
entrance and take captive the soul that is at all capable of
sensibility. Her wooing of Polixenes to prolong his visit was
irresistible; her various appeals to her husband were full of
sweetness and dignity; her defence on her trial was as feminine
as it was powerful. But we must pass on to her statue scene.
The *pose* was wonderful. The stage had vanished; substituted
for it was indeed a gallery of the highest art, with its one
image, and that one divine. We might here close our criticism;
but it would be doing injustice to Miss Heath not to record that
her Florizel was the best we ever witnessed; and to Miss
Carlotta Leclercq, not to express our unqualified approbation
of her Perdita. Nor must Mr. Harley's Autolycus be forgotten—
the same we saw it twenty years ago, yet still fresh, vigorous,
and effective. Mr. Ryder, as Polixenes, was still himself, and
acted with force and majesty. Mr. Meadows, in the Old
Shepherd, was as usual rich and racy. Nor was Mrs. Ternan

without special merit in Paulina—a part well adapted for her natural powers. This magnificent revival must become extensively popular, and maintain its position on the stage for a long period. The scenery, painted under the direction of Mr. Grieve, is throughout in the highest style of pictorial art.

Illustrated London News, May 3, 1856

The Tempest

OF all Shakespeare's plays, *The Tempest* probably suffered most at the hands of the adapters, notably in the Dryden-Davenant version called *The Enchanted Island*, which includes a sister for Miranda and for Caliban. Till late in the 18th century this was the nearest you could get to Shakespeare's play. It was not till 1757 that Shakespeare returned in Garrick's production, though various *Tempest*-born operettas and other perversions kept rearing their heads till well into the 19th century.

Shakespeare Unalloyed

I am tempted here to notice, to the credit of the old stage, that on the 28th of April, [1785] the Tempest of Shakspeare was acted at Drury Lane, pure and unmixed. They had not yet embraced the additions of Davenant and Dryden; it will, therefore, be a fit opportunity to take leave of that simple enchanting production. The exquisite beauty of Miss Philips was not more characteristic of Miranda, than her manner of speaking the language. Bensley was the Prospero of the night, and in truth the *only* Prospero. Old Bannister's Caliban contrasted finely with the Ariel of Miss Field. Some prejudice existed against the *masque* introduced by the immortal author, and it was, therefore, here omitted. To prove that it is *beautiful*, and that it can be *done* upon the stage, my friend Reynolds has introduced it in Twelfth Night, where it is greatly attractive, but has no business whatever: besides, that there, having no *magic* for the means, it becomes an interlude *pour passer le temps*, and all imagination is forcibly extinguished.

James Boaden, *Life of Kemble*

347

Caliban as Poet

Mr. Emery[1], notwithstanding the coarseness of style necessary to the parts he performs, is a truly poetical actor, and in
all the varieties of his poet's flight keeps by his side with the
quickest observation. In this character he again approaches
to terrific tragedy, when he describes the various tortures
inflicted on him by the magician and the surrounding snakes
that 'stare and hiss him into madness.' This idea, which is truly
the 'fine frenzy' of the poet and hovers on that verge of fancy
beyond which it is a pain even for poetry to venture, is brought
before the spectators with all the loathing and violence of
desperate wretchedness: the monster hugs and shrinks into
himself, grows louder and more shuddering as he proceeds,
and when he pictures the torment that almost turns his brain,
glares with his eyes and gnashes his teeth with an impatient
impotence of revenge.

Leigh Hunt,
Critical Essays on Performers in the London Theatres

A Prospero Without Magic

*Hazlitt has some harsh words for Charles Mayne Young's Prospero in
the Covent Garden production of 1815. He saw it on July 23 that year.*

As long as he contents himself to play indifferent characters,
we shall say nothing: but whenever he plays Shakespeare, we
must be excused if we take unequal revenge for the martyrdom
which our feelings suffer. His Prospero was good for nothing;
and consequently, was indescribably bad. It was grave without solemnity, stately without dignity, pompous without being
impressive, and totally destitute of the wild, mysterious,
preternatural character of the original. Prospero, as depicted
by Mr. Young, did not appear the potent wizard brooding in
gloomy abstraction over the secrets of his art, and around whom
spirits and airy shapes throng numberless 'at his bidding;'
but seemed himself an automaton, stupidly prompted by
others: his lips moved up and down as if pulled by wires, not
governed by the deep and varied impulses of passion; and his
painted face, and snowy hair and beard, reminded us of the
masks for the representation of Pantaloon. In a word, Mr.

[1] In John Kemble's 1806 production at Covent Garden.

Young did not personate Prospero, but a pedagogue teaching his scholars how to recite the part, and not teaching them well.

William Hazlitt, *A View of the English Stage*

Ariel as Sea-Nymph

The Tempest, William Telbin's seascape design for Charles Kean's production, Princess's Theatre.

July 3. [1857] In the evening we visited the Princess's: the pieces were *A Game of Romps* [one-act farce by J. M. Morton] and *The Tempest*. The scenic effects in *The Tempest* certainly surpass anything I ever saw there or elsewhere. The most marvellous was the shipwreck in the first scene, where, (to all appearance), a real ship is heaving about on huge waves, and is finally wrecked under a cliff that reaches up to the roof. The machinery that works this must be something wonderful: the scene quite brought back to my mind the storm I saw at Whitby last year, and the vessels plunging through the harbour-mouth. Kean was good [as Prospero] Caliban a very well-conceived monster, almost grotesquely hideous; Trinculo and Stephano (Harley and Mathews) were very amusing: but the gem of the piece was the exquisitely graceful and beautiful Ariel, acted by Miss Kate Terry. Her appearance as a sea-nymph was one of the most beautiful living pictures I ever saw, but this, and every other one in my recollection (except Queen Katherine's dream) were all outdone by the concluding scene, where Ariel is left alone, hovering over the wide ocean, watching the retreating ship. It is an innovation on Shakespeare, but a worthy one, and the conception of a true poet.

Miss Carlotta Leclerque made a charming Miranda.

The Diaries of Lewis Carroll, ed. R. L. Green

Modern Elizabethans

Bernard Shaw praised this production by the Elizabethan Stage Society, but his colleague William Archer was less sympathetic.

In the performance of *The Tempest* by the Elizabethan Stage Society at the Mansion House[1], there was diligence, enthusiasm, even talent—everything, in fact, except common sense. This quality one has long ceased to hope for in the otherwise meritorious efforts of Mr. Poel and his comrades. Whatever the ancient Elizabethans obviously did *not* do—whatever contradicts the text and flies in the face of reason—that the modern Elizabethans conscientiously set themselves to achieve. Their choice of a play is this time beyond criticism. Nothing could have been more curious than an endeavour to realise the original presentment of *The Tempest*. But what is the first thing our Elizabethans do? They choose a side gallery or balcony, cut in the very cornice of the lofty hall, to represent the ship at sea, and they make Miranda watch the wreck from the stage, some thirty or forty feet below! Now if Shakespeare intended Miranda to be visible during the shipwreck, he would clearly place her on the raised platform at the back of the scene, looking down, as though from some headland, upon the main stage, which would represent the deck of the ship. It seems to me more probable, however, that Shakespeare intended both the lower and the upper stage to be used as parts of the ship, representing the main deck and some poop or fo'c's'le. The boatswain and mariners would appear aloft, the passengers below, and they would hail each other at some distance through the howling of the storm. This is simply my own conjecture, which must be taken for what it is worth. All we can say with absolute assurance is that Shakespeare did not picture Miranda gazing skywards, as though at Tennyson's vision of 'navies grappling in the central blue.' He depicts a

[1] 5 November, 1897.

shipwreck, not a balloon catastrophe. Then Prospero and Miranda appear, both speaking with a slow and plaintive drawl which is precisely the reverse of what must have been the method of elocution on the Shakespearian stage: crisp in attack, rapid, sonorous, and compelling attention. Prospero breaks his long speech some half-dozen times by saying to Miranda, 'Dost thou hear?' or 'Thou attend'st not,' evidently implying that Miranda is so placed that she can turn away her head from him. Therefore, in the E.S.S. arrangement, she is made to stand directly opposite him, her eyes riveted upon him, and obviously intent on every syllable he utters. At the end of the narration Shakespeare makes Prospero say 'Now I arise'; but Mr. Poel, disdaining the old superstition about suiting the action to the word, has had him on his feet for several minutes, and pacing about the stage. It was in the first apparition of Ariel, however, that the Society achieved its triumph of wrongheadedness. The dress (from a contemporary print) was plausible enough; but imagine a curate-Ariel mechanically intoning his rote-learnt lines, with his eyes fixed on the ceiling, motionless, expressionless, like one in a dream! Was ever perversity more elaborately destructive! The other incarnations of Ariel, the Sea-Nymph and the Harpy, were played by different performers—a most unsatisfactory device. It is not quite clear, of course, how the character was treated in Shakespeare's day, but the probable, or at any rate the safe, thing would be to assign it to a clever and well-grown boy, and let him simply change his costumes. It would be tedious to go through the play and enumerate the absurdities of grouping, stage-arrangement, and 'business.' The upper stage was never brought into use at all, though it stood there ready, and though the stage-direction in the folio (Act III., Sc. 3) says expressly: *Prospero on the top (invisible)*. The 'shapes' were well habited, but their action was slow and spiritless; the music, under the direction of Mr. Dolmetsch, and with Miss Louise Macpherson as vocalist, was delightfully rendered, but no attempt was made to suggest its supernatural origin. The actors spoke the text with tolerable accuracy, but with no feeling for the metrical quality of the elusively exquisite verse. Of individual performers the best were Mr. A. Broughton as Stephano, and Mr. Hodges as Caliban, effectively got-up after the fashion of the Bayreuth Alberich or Mime. Mr. E. Playford was good as the Boatswain, and Miss Hilda Swan made a very graceful Miranda.

William Archer, *Theatrical World of 1897*

Henry VIII

THIS play got off to a spectacular start when the Globe Theatre caught fire during the first performance as a result of a cannon being fired to signal the entrance of the King towards the end of Act I. This tradition of dramatic pageantry has been continued, if less drastically, in subsequent productions. It is possible, but unlikely that Betterton, who played the title role at the Restoration was coached in the part by an old actor who was himself instructed by Shakespeare. The Kemble family appeared together in this play and Queen Katharine was one of Sarah Siddons' great roles. Charles Kean's performance in 1855 ran for 100 nights and featured an elaborate pageant of London as it was supposed to be in the time of Henry VIII.

Carroll in Wonderland[1]

June 22 [*1855*]. The evening began with a capital farce *Away with Melancholy*. And then came the great play *Henry VIII*, the greatest theatrical treat I ever had or ever expect to have—I had no idea that anything so superb as the scenery and dresses was ever to be seen on the stage. Kean was magnificent as Cardinal Wolsey, Mrs. Kean a worthy successor to Mrs. Siddons in Queen Catherine, and all the accessories without exception were good—But oh, that exquisite vision of Queen Catherine! I almost held my breath to watch; the illusion is perfect, and I felt as if in a dream all the time it lasted. It was like a delicious reverie, or the most beautiful poetry. This is the true end and object of acting—to raise the mind above itself, and out of its petty everyday cares—never shall I forget that wonderful evening, that exquisite vision—sunbeams broke in through the roof and gradually revealed two angel forms,

---

[1] The famous Charles Kean production, with moving barge and panoramic view of London.

Henry VIII, York Palace, Princess's, 1855. CHARLES KEAN played Wolsey and MRS. KEAN, Queen Katherine (from a watercolour by F. Lloyds, one of the scenic artists at the theatre).

floating in front of the carved work on the ceiling: the column of sunbeams shone down upon the sleeping queen, and gradually down it floated a troop of angelic forms, transparent, and carrying palm branches in their hands: they waved these over the sleeping queen, with oh! such a sad and solemn grace. —So could I fancy (if the thought be not profane) would real angels seem to our mortal vision, though doubtless our conception is poor and mean to the reality. She in an ecstasy raises her arms towards them, and to sweet slow music they vanish as marvellously as they came. Then the profound silence of the audience burst at once into a rapture of applause; but even that scarcely marred the effect of the beautiful sad waking words of the Queen, 'Spirits of peace, where are ye?' I never enjoyed anything so much in my life before—and never felt so inclined to shed tears at anything fictitious, save perhaps at that poetical gem of Dickens, the death of Little Paul.

The Diaries of Lewis Carroll ed. R. L. Green

353

Epilogue—A Backward Glance

A last look, from the vantage point of the mid nineteen-fifties.

Towards the end of the last century Shakespearean acting was dominated by Henry Irving at the Lyceum, and I must begin with him although he was not the first actor I saw in Shakespeare.

My first sight of him was as King Lear. And it is a thrilling experience to recall, even after sixty years. Kent and the others have spoken their opening dialogue ending with 'the king is coming.' And here he comes down the steps, a striking figure with masses of white hair. He is leaning on a huge scabbarded sword which he raises with a wild cry in answer to the shouted greetings of his guards. His gait, his looks, his geatures, all reveal the noble, imperious mind already degenerating into senile irritability and ready to fall into utter ruin under the coming shocks of grief and rage.

Gordon Crosse, Shakespearean Playgoing 1890–1952

INDEX OF CONTRIBUTORS

(Anonymous contributions listed under subject or title of work)

360